Electric w

Manchester University Press

Electric wind

An energy history of modern Britain

Marianna Dudley

MANCHESTER UNIVERSITY PRESS

Published by Manchester University Press
Oxford Road, Manchester, M13 9PL

www.manchesteruniversitypress.co.uk

British Library Cataloguing-in-Publication Data
A catalogue record for this book is available from the British Library

ISBN   978 1 5261 8294 4   hardback
ISBN   978 1 5261 8296 8   paperback

First published 2025

EU authorised representative for GPSR:
Easy Access System Europe, Mustamäe tee 50, 10621 Tallinn, Estonia
gpsr.requests@easproject.com

Typeset
by New Best-set Typesetters Ltd
Printed in Great Britain
by CPI Group (UK) Ltd, Croydon CR0 4YY

Dedicated to Walter George Dudley (1950–2021)

Contents

Figures

List of figures

Abbreviations

AC – Alternating current
AIOC – Anglo-Iranian Oil Company
BEA – British Electrical Authority
CAT – Centre for Alternative Technology
CBAB – *Coimhearsnachd Bharraidh Agus Bhatersaigh* (Barra and Vatersay Community Ltd.)
CCGT – Combined-cycle gas turbine
CEB – Central Electricity Board
CEGB – Central Electricity Generating Board
CO_2 – Carbon dioxide
CPRW – Council for the Protection of Rural Wales
DC – Direct current
EEZ – Exclusive Economic Zones
ERA – British Electrical and Allied Industries Research Association
GEEC – Glasgow Electrical Engineering Company
MA – Mills Archive
NFFO – Non-Fossil Fuel Obligation
NIMBY – Not in my back yard
NLW – National Library of Wales
NMOA – National Meteorological Office Archive
NSHEB – The North of Scotland Hydro-Electricity Board
OA – Orkney Archive
OEEC – Organisation for European Economic Co-operation
OPEC – Organisation of Petroleum Exporting Countries
REE – Rare earth element
RP – Received pronunciation
SO_2 – Sulphur dioxide

List of abbreviations

SWEB – South West Electricity Board

TNA – The National Archives

TNES – *Tasglann nan Eilean Siar* (Hebridean Archives)

UGA – University of Glasgow Archive

UNCLOS – United Nations Convention on the Law of the Sea

Introduction

In recent decades, a quiet but tremendous transformation has taken place in the British landscape. Tall white turbines have appeared, etched on horizons, blades turning with metronomic rhythm. At the turn of the twenty-first century, 839 wind turbines stood in the British landscape.[1] Nearly a quarter of a century later we share our islands with well over 11,000 of the machines. About 2,500 of these are offshore, the remainder on land across the length and breadth of the country.[2] A new energy sector has grown, gradually but significantly, generating electricity from the wind to power public supply grids.

When the first commercial wind farm in the UK was opened in 1991 it made headlines because of its novelty. Today, renewable energy records are broken on a regular basis. As more (and more efficient) turbines are built, the proportion of the UK's electricity that is generated by the wind climbs higher and higher. In 2023, wind powered 29.4 per cent of the UK's total electricity generation. December of that year was the fifteenth month in a row that renewable energy sources (wind, solar, hydro, and biomass) produced more electricity than fossil fuels.[3] On a blustery 4 January 2023, for a brief half hour, 90.1 per cent of British energy demand was met by 'clean' power – renewable and nuclear power combined – the highest percentage yet, a record that doubtless won't stand for long.[4]

Not all energy headlines belong to wind. The closure of the UK's last coal-burning power station at Ratcliffe-on-Soar on 30 September 2024 was reported across national and international news media. The power plant manager Phil O'Grady said that when he started his career 36 years ago, 'none of us imagined a future without coal generation within our lifetimes'.[5] The closure was widely described as 'the end of an era'.[6]

Energy in Britain is changing. How and where we source energy shapes lifetimes and landscapes. It filters into our sense of what makes a nation: like education and healthcare, it affects us all. Energy has long been a topic for state policy, economic planning, and labour organisation. The major shifts underway affect the nation in ways that transcend these categories. Indeed, by following the trail of wind energy into time and place, we move away from traditional centres of power (broadly defined) and into regions, places, and communities that have often been overlooked by established narratives and national politics. The history of wind energy is a new history of Britain.

Is this an energy transition in action? It is rare for one energy system to replace another, and wind has not really 'replaced' coal – it is superb at driving turbines but is no good for domestic hearths, for example. New fuels become available and change how energy is used, adding to the available fuels rather than replacing the old. The history of energy has been a history, so far, of accumulation.[7] Transitions, when they occur, are messy, and long, and often incomplete.

There is a big shift to electrification underway, so that the lines separating the three major components of total energy use – electricity generation, transport, and heating – are becoming less distinct. Coal for the fire, gas for the oven, and oil for the car is becoming electricity for all three (and more besides). Wind is uniquely well-placed to power an electrified future, with functional, increasingly cheap and efficient technology, and being an infinite resource from which to draw. But it remains entwined with old and existing energy systems. Fossil fuel use is dwindling, but the UK continues to burn large amounts of gas to produce electricity – in 2024 it remained just ahead of wind as the largest single source of electricity.[8] Britain also imports electricity from other nations (and exports, too), notably France, Norway, Belgium, the Netherlands, and Denmark.[9] And some of these still use coal and gas to produce electricity. Wind is in the ascendant, but the door is not yet shut on fossil fuels. This is even more evident when we consider the global picture, where coal remains the largest source of electricity. In 2023, 35.5 per cent of world electricity production was from coal, followed by 22.5 per cent from gas; together these fossil fuels produced almost 58 per cent of global electricity.[10] Can we untangle a clean energy future from a past built on coal, oil, and gas? What happens next with electric wind affects us all.

Energy, climate, history

We humans have released vast amounts of carbon dioxide (CO_2) into the atmosphere by burning fossil fuels. CO_2 sits high in the atmosphere, acting as an insulating chemical layer that prevents heat from escaping into the solar system. A series of biophysical cycles are altered in turn: ice melts, algae blooms, sea levels rise, weather patterns shift. The Intergovernmental Panel on Climate Change states that 'it is unequivocal that human influence has warmed the atmosphere, ocean, and land'.[11] January 2024 was an unprecedented twelfth consecutive month with a mean global average temperature more than 1.5 degrees Celsius higher than pre-industrial times.[12] All modelled pathways to limit global warming to this 1.5 °C level require rapid reduction of 60 per cent of greenhouse gases and 65 per cent of CO_2, from 2019 levels, by 2035.[13]

The global warming we experience today is, in part, the delayed effect of coal burning on a grand scale from the industrial revolution onwards.[14] As historian John McNeill identified, cheap and abundant energy has probably done more to shape the human–environment relationship than anything else in the past 150 years.[15] Coal-fired steam-powered processes of mechanisation, urbanisation, and imperialist expansion and oppression created 'ecological teleconnections' whereby places far apart became decisively linked in processes of production and consumption – the example McNeill provides is that forest lands in the southwestern United States were replaced by cotton plantations in the mid-nineteenth century, driven by demand for cotton in Britain. British industry relied on these outsourced 'ghost acres'.[16] Historian Corinne Fowler has drawn out the colonial connections hidden in plain sight in the British countryside, finding traces in the stately homes of the rich and in the working landscapes of the rural and urban poor.[17] The engines of empire ran on cheap energy and on outsourced enslaved and cheap labour.

The industrial revolution set a path to global warming by unlocking the energy potential of fossilised carbon. The twentieth century accelerated it dramatically.[18] Since 1950 global fossil fuel use has increased eightfold.[19] Coal use was overtaken by oil use, and steep rises in resource extraction, pollution, land use change, population rise, and consumerism dialled up the global indicators of the Anthropocene – a new geological epoch, in which humans have permanently altered the functioning of the Earth system.[20] If we think again of delayed effects, we can begin to appreciate the concern that Earth scientists like Will Steffen have expressed over the future impacts of these late-twentieth century CO_2 levels: put bluntly, they push the planet far beyond its natural state of self-regulation and stability, and become impossible to predict. Steffen named this a 'hothouse' Earth scenario, where climate change wreaks unpredictable havoc, which is also beyond the ability of the most advanced computers to model – and so it creates a future *more uncertain* than one that any other humans have faced in the past. We continue to build a slow-burning carbon bomb.[21] Wind energy is one of the tools for diffusing it: already available, cheap, and functional.

Identifying climate breakdown has been a matter of science. Now we have the data the response should be straightforward. We know what we need to do and, when it comes to energy, we have the technology needed to switch from carbon-intensive systems. But knowing the science and enacting the necessary political, social, and cultural, change relies on much more than finding the right technology. We are human, and we are messy, inconsistent, and changeable. This history is interested in the pitfalls and pauses in wind energy's past as well as its successes and leaps forward. How energy has shaped modern life, and how modernity has shaped energy, is much more interesting to me than a straightforward industry or business history. Those accounts tend to centre technology and understand change to be top-down in nature, directed from the boardroom and the government office. If the story was that simple, we'd have solved climate change by now. Energy is a lens for understanding how complex a society's relationship with power, and place, and politics is. And so this history is about material changes in where we get our energy from, and how it reaches us; broad social and political shifts that have shaped the contexts in which decisions about energy are made; and cultures of energy in Britain. It draws on state papers; industry publications; correspondences between workers and managers; meteorological data; songs, poems and folklore; glossaries, dictionaries and biographies; paintings and sculptures; maps; machines; museums. I travelled to national and local archives, spoke with people who shared their experiences and knowledge, and undertook fieldwork in the sites where the wind is made electric. This book is the result. It shows that energy is a lens through which we can better understand the nation. The nation, as a political and geophysical entity, offers a scale through which we can better grasp energy as planetary agent, and wind as a force of nature. It is history blown in from the bottom up, the top down, and sideways too. Rich and surprising, this history offers examples, models, and ideas with which to revive our hopes and plans for a clean-energy future and rethink our relationship with the world around us.

Wind, weather, technology

Who has seen the wind?
Neither I nor you:

4

Introduction

But when the leaves hang trembling,
The wind is passing through.

Who has seen the wind?
Neither you nor I:
But when the trees bow down their heads,
The wind is passing by.[22]

Who has seen the wind? All of us and none of us. We see its effects and feel its force, but wind itself remains uncontainable and hard to see and quantify. The Beaufort scale gives us a measure for wind strength by gauging its effects on the surrounding environment, using all the senses: 'wind felt on face' (light breeze) ... 'whistling heard in telephone wires' (strong breeze) ... 'whole trees in motion' (near gale). The wind writes itself visible, whipping surface water, billowing through grasses, grazing cheeks, mussing hair to a brush's despair. It writes itself into diagrams and clean lines, too, through instruments developed to measure it. In the first national wind survey, conducted from 1947–1951, anemometers captured the wind as data, translating its presence and character at sites across Britain and Ireland into formats useful to engineers and meteorologists. Wind speed, direction, and location were rendered in pen and ink by machines. There are many of these charts in the Met Office archives in Exeter, documents I found strangely moving to encounter some seventy years after they were produced. Winds move fleetingly through space and time even in the present; unlike many historical subjects, they leave no material trace to encounter and ponder. But here were texts authored by the wind itself – charts that showed wind's, not a heart's, pulses. I could read these and almost feel the gusts hitting Carn Brea, Holy Island, and Bell Rock in the mid-twentieth century.

Wind energy redraws the power map of Britain, taking us to its outer edges and windiest outcrops. Here, in landscapes more often thought of as 'peripheral' than productive, wind energy took shape. While a traditional energy history may start with the political centres of decision-making and industrial power, wind calls for attention to be paid to landscapes and communities that are often rural and considered remote by those who live in urban centres. These qualities are not coincidence but context for what happens through the twentieth century. By upending the traditional geographies of power, wind energy offers a lens into rethinking the role of the countryside in modern Britain. It resists a narrative of the rural as a passive, pleasant canvas onto which cultural projections of stasis, leisure, and nostalgia can be projected – a narrative described by Raymond Williams in his 1973 work *The country and the city* that endures still. Instead, wind energy has put rural communities at the forefront of development, a factor that has created opportunities – and conflicts.

Some communities have welcomed the arrival of wind energy. Others have fought it bitterly. These fights were not simple rejections of 'modern' technology. Dismissal of concerns over visual (and other) impacts of turbines on landscapes as NIMBYism overlooks a strategic exaggeration by politicians and attendant media eager to shore up a nascent neoliberalism from the late 1980s into the 1990s. The debates were often as much about landownership, class, and different conceptions of what the countryside is 'for', as they were about energy and landscape. As Chapter 6 shows, when farmers and engineers worked together to build wind farms in mid-Wales in the 1990s, the loudest protests came from those who had moved to rural Wales from elsewhere (often England) in search of an idealised rural way of life. When communities in the Outer Hebrides organised to resist a new, large wind farm in the 2000s, they placed it within a longer history of forced 'improvement' of land and indigenous culture, and challenged the assumption that a local resource (the wind) should be exploited for profits channelled away from the local community and into shareholder's pockets.

Contestations of wind farms were and continue to be complex, and form one aspect of the response to the arrival of new forms of infrastructure to lived landscapes. In this, wind energy is not unique. Bill Luckin's work on electrification in the interwar years highlighted how some places – the South Downs, the Lake District, the New Forest, and the Scottish Highlands – became battlegrounds for opposing visions of how modernity would manifest in the countryside.[23] He framed the contestation over electricity pylons as one of 'rural preservation' versus electricity 'triumphalism'. It's a theme Katrina Navickas develops in her study of the siting of high-voltage 'super grid' pylons in the Pennines in the 1950s.[24] The conflict between the need for pylons and amenity in the national park speak to how matters of landscape, and technology within them, in Britain are always riven with class and often with economic disparity between centres of administrative power and the regions, too.

These themes help to show why a focus on place, and people, is vital for an energy history of Britain. Not only, but especially in a densely populated nation, technology can never operate without interacting both with the contemporary setting and the layered histories of power, identity, and belonging that underpin it. Add to this a relationship with the future – how we imagine it, plan it, and how we fuel its unfolding – and we see that a conversation between the past, the present, and the future is ongoing. This energy history shows how wind technologies and technological knowledge were developed in relation to, and as a result of, interactions between locals and outsiders, experts and enthusiasts, traditions and innovations. It shows wind technology to be a product of social, cultural, and environmental interactions, and argues that consideration of these factors in the inevitable and necessary future expansion of wind energy will create fairer, cleaner, better energy for all.

Interactions between wind and technology run through this book. Technology has been a tool by which wind has been rendered tangible and productive for human use, from flags to sails to mills to weather balloons. A litany of machines and materials connect wind-as-electricity – the electric wind – to people: the turbine that turns wind's kinetic energy into electrical power; the cable that carries that power from turbine base to electricity substation; wires that are organised as supply lines and grids, to bear electricity over telegraph poles and under earth to homes; metals that conduct the power, and plastics to protect us from it; flick a switch, and finally we see the brightness of the wind (firing filaments and radiating from bulbs), and feel its warmth (flowing through our radiators), and know its efficacy (cooking our food and charging our devices).[25] But through that technologised flow, a sense of the wind *as wind* is lost. Electricity, no matter how it is produced, all mixes in to the National Grid and is apportioned where needed. We cannot distinguish between wind electricity and coal electricity and nuclear electricity; nor, I imagine, do most people care to. It comes to us through the supply lines of the grid, safely packaged and ready to charge phones and cars, light our homes, and power our televisions. It arrives already transcribed into daily life. As Vaclav Smil notes, in this sense there are no electric cars, only battery vehicles which reflect the electricity's origins. So, 'in North China it is a 90 percent coal car, in France it is a 70 percent nuclear car, in Russia mostly a natural gas car and in Denmark a 50 percent wind car'.[26] How that electricity is produced, who gets to use it, and with what consequences for the planet, are the key considerations.

Historians have shown how electrical systems grew and were organised at national and regional levels.[27] They have explored the cultural impacts of electricity, and the creation of new spheres of consumerism that drew on ideas of modernity, nationality, gender, and class.[28] But the historical relationship between wind and electricity has been largely unexplored until now. The roles of engineers, inventors, and technological enthusiasts are important to the story, as are the devices, instruments, and tools that they made. All of

7

these things are taken seriously and find their place in this narrative, but I hope to also give room to a more expansive sense of wind in the world than a focus on the machines alone can achieve. The wind, it seems to me, demands due recognition of its own hand in this history. No fossilised relic, buried deep and inert in the strata for eons, wind is constantly in motion and has always been so. The moment it stops, it dissolves to mere atmosphere. This motion is intimately linked to that of the whole Earth, whose axial spin sends air into curving streams from the equator to the poles thanks to the Coriolis effect; to the climate, whose cool and warm air masses sink and rise respectively, creating atmospheric movement; and how the air reacts to different topographies of land and sea. As the following pages show, grappling with the unpredictability of wind, the *vitality* of the resource, has been central to the development of successful technology. This is not a tale of ecological submission.

While electricity becomes part of one big energy mix, wind as the origin source has some distinct qualities and characteristics. Specific environments produce timber, peat, and coal, but ultimately the material can be extracted and removed from the origin; oil and gas also tend to need to be pumped and piped to the surface, where they can be stored and moved – though in the case of tar sands, the oil is already at surface level and needs processing to separate it from the earth. The energy of wind has to be harnessed where it happens to blow, and so while the electricity can be transmitted over distance, and comes from a movable source, the production of wind energy (like solar energy) is situated in place. Wind energy at the point of generation produces no other material than the electricity generated by the turbines on site, and so all emphasis lies on the reliable production, and successful supply, of that energy from the turbine to the grid.

Wind energy is no longer solely a localised supply, as it was in its early years; undersea cables connect wind-rich islands like Orkney to the national grid. But neither can it be wholly severed from its place of origin. Place runs through this book, not just as a setting upon which technology was placed and energy extracted, but as a component in the generative process of turning wind electric. It mattered where wind was measured, where early turbines were erected, where communities encountered wind energy infrastructure and discourse – and it matters still.

We experience wind in place every day, as weather. It is also how wind's vitality can be intuited most directly. Weather has been well documented across time and cultures. Great storms that destroyed crops, felled trees, or flattened buildings are exactly the kind of notable occasions that make their way into diaries and folklore, official records and survivor testimonies. Recent work to collect memories of extreme weather in the UK has emphasised what a rich cultural archive weather-lore and weather memory is, with events such as winter storms punctuating seasonal cycles with force and testing community resilience. The TEMPEST database holds around 18,000 records of weather events in the UK made over 500 years, drawn from archives.[29] Research by its authors shows how, in memories of weather, national, local, and individual narratives intersect, and a tendency towards nostalgia can inflect how events such as extreme winds or snow are remembered.[30] Weather records can also reveal social vulnerabilities. Simon Naylor, Neil McDonald, James Bowen, and Georgina Endfield found nineteenth-century school logbooks from the Hebrides to contain valuable historical climate data. Weather affected children's school attendance. At Tigharry, North Uist in 1883, 'a wet day brings out the children much better'; on fine days, in crofting communities, children helped with herding livestock. There was a close relationship between weather, crofting, and school absenteeism because families often relied on children to help with seasonal work. In extreme cold, the logbooks recorded children suffering from no shoes or inadequate clothing, and poor health and exposure made islanders more susceptible to disease.[31] These were expressions of wider vulnerabilities, exacerbated by a history of attempted/forced 'improvement' of Hebridean environment, culture, and society. It reminds us that weather is 'not always a universal experience, but rather affected certain communities more than others, materially and culturally'. As climate change brings more extreme weather events to bear, a look to the past stands as a clear warning that the reduction of social inequality must be prioritised.

It is often winds that bring climate impacts to our doors. Hurricanes and typhoons inflict direct and well-documented damage.[32] Forest fires are fanned by winds, spreading flames quickly through fire-friendly trees like eucalypts, which cultivate the flames by growing loose tinder-dry strips of bark to catch them, and re-sprout following the burn. Other species, such as redwoods, have evolved as fire-resistant and contain protective tannic acids in their thick bark. However, recent 'mega fires' afflicting California and elsewhere are capable of destroying such habitats, whose evolutionary fire adaptations are being outstripped by the startling speed and intensity of fire in a time of human-induced climate change.[33] Winds convey the sensory news of fire to surrounding communities. Drifting smoke has become the medium through which people experience forest fire, building on other, older relationships with smoke as a signifier of pollution and forest management.[34] Wind is both a direct bearer, and cultural signifier, of climate change.

We are all likely to experience more severe winds in years to come. Geographers Martin Mahony and Samuel Randalls remind us that 'as global temperatures rise under the forcing hand of humanity's greenhouse gas emissions, new questions are being asked of how societies make sense of their weather, of the cultural values afforded to climate, and of how environmental futures are imagined, feared, predicted and remade'.[35] The history of wind energy shows that understandings of weather, and of climate, were vital for the development of technological capability. A wind industry developed in response to localised needs, national political priorities, and growing international understandings of climate change and the impact of fossil fuels.

Some winds are consistently present, and notably characteristic enough, to be named. We can see this as humans conferring language on wind, or as the winds writing themselves into language through their presence. The Mistral (from the Occitane for 'master') is a strong and cold northwesterly that blows across southern France into the Mediterranean, a feature of winter and spring. A *foehn* wind can occur anywhere in the lee of a mountain range, where warm air falls down to lower plains following rainfall to create a strong, hot wind. But *foehn* wind is particularly associated with Southern Germany, Austria, and Switzerland and Northern Italy, where *foehn* is also a colloquial term for 'hairdryer' – both blow hot air.[36] Similar meteorological conditions create the Californian Santa Anas, which bear down hot and fast from the Great Basin (bounded by the Rockies and the Sierra Nevada) to the coast, but the cultural responses are regionally specific. Experiencing these winds is part of living in California, or northern Italy, a sensory clue that builds over time to generate a feeling of familiarity and belonging with the particulars of the landscape, and a reminder of mountains.

These winds combine specific meteorological conditions, such as pressure changes, with associated phenomena and lived experiences. People often ascribe irritable moods, and headaches, to such winds. Janina Duszejko, the central character in Olga Tokarczuk's *Drive Your Plow Over the Bones of the Dead* lives on a plateau in the lee of mountains, and the wind affects her ability to think: she complains that 'when the foehn wind blows it is difficult to concentrate'.[37] I recognised this line from real life, delivered to me in Munich when my landlady explained the source of her headaches and general irritability. One study found a significant association between days the *foehn* wind blew and severe trauma incidents.[38]

Introduction

No one exploited wind's unnerving effects better than Raymond Chandler. In his 1938 short story *Red wind* the wind sets the Los Angeles scene. 'There was a desert wind blowing that night. It was one of those hot, dry Santa Anas that come down through the mountain passes and curl your hair and make your nerves jump and skin itch. On nights like that every booze party ends in a fight. Meek little wives feel the edge of the carving knife and study their husbands' necks. Anything could happen.'[39] These winds stir violent possibility.

In the Mediterranean, my friend Giulia recalled the cold Mistral spoiling Sardinian beach days by bringing the *medusas* (jellyfish) to the shore. By contrast the warm Scirocco brings anchovy to the surface where fishers wait. In Italy, the rains it produces are known as 'blood rains', as they fall laden with Saharan red sand. The returning presence of these winds has shaped ideas and behaviours in these regions; they have become part of place and culture, and when they blow in the present they carry history with them.

The winds in *Electric wind* come in off the Atlantic Ocean and North Sea. They often blow with great force. Coastal communities have weathered these winds through time. Another way of 'reading the wind' is through language that reflects its presence, and the beliefs, superstitions, and behaviours that communities have developed and attached to wind. These are highly localised, and often 'embodied' forms of knowledge – information passed down through traditional songs and rituals and learnt through practices which engage with winds: fishing, farming, walking, navigating. The cultural resonance of such knowledge is especially tangible in places like the Outer Hebrides, the Orkney Islands, and Shetland, where indigenous culture has been fought for, protected, and consciously cultivated. The location of many of the technological advances of British wind energy in these same places is no coincidence: the presence, and resonance, of wind in these communities informed their identification as suitable test sites for wind technologies, shaped their development as 'energy-rich' places of speculation and opportunity, and in some cases also informed local resistance to government and industry interventions in the form of 'big wind'. The wind in this history is more than a resource to be harnessed, or input into an enviro-technical system. It has actively shaped the ideas, people, sites, and technologies that together constitute wind energy. It blows through this book, sometimes a whisper, sometimes a roar.

This history of energy takes its cue from some of the groups and characters it discusses, who framed wind power as alternative. Alternative, as it was discussed in parliamentary debates on how to provide electricity to remote communities after the Second World War: a choice, an option, a contrast to the status quo. Alternative, as pitched by advocates of self-sufficiency in the 1970s: embracing difference, a little radical, a way of living and thinking. Alternative presents possibilities. With the stakes for thinking and acting on energy issues never higher, this history finds in the past ideas that expand our understanding of what wind energy is now, and what it could be in the future. By focusing on the places where energy technology has been encountered, and the people who inhabit them, it centres the environmental, social, and cultural dimensions of the transition from fossil fuel to renewables. Too often, Imre Szeman and Dominic Boyer write, 'these changes are envisioned as narrowly technical ones'.[40] This book is alternative in its approach, and also in its findings. The history of wind energy provides possibilities, multiplicities, and imaginaries to take forward in the 'collective challenge of planning what comes next, and in the fullest way possible'.[41]

Chapter 1 shows how industrial revolution and the rise of coal created the conditions for the emergence of electric wind, as engineers and inventors explored the potential for wind-powered machines. In Chapter 2 we see how scientific and meteorological knowledge of wind fed technological progress, and how a new national geography of wind began to emerge through the early twentieth century. Chapter 3 takes us to Orkney, a critical site for wind energy, where experiments after the Second World War conjoined the ideology of the welfare state with energy planning. Longstanding traditions of living with wind on the edges of the nation met with new technologies. In the 1970s and 1980s, when state and industry attention to wind energy disappeared, a commune in Wales kept a dream of 'alternative energy' alive. This do-it-yourself approach to wind energy (Chapter 4) was a crucial bridge between early state interest, and the later rise of wind as commercial venture, against the backdrop of Thatcherite neoliberalism and privatisation (Chapter 5). A dominant model of renewable energy emerged, as did a range of protests against wind. Resistance to the growing presence of wind energy in the British landscape is explored in Chapter 6, which takes us beyond 'NIMBYism' to explore the tensions between communities and energy infrastructure. Chapter 7 takes us offshore, where wind energy scaled up and opened up new avenues for critique. And in Chapter 8, examples from wind energy history offer starting points for more experimental, speculative, and ambitious approaches that build new energy imaginaries.

1

Experiments

On the side of the Newton Street electricity substation in Glasgow is 'Generation Green', a mural by the Australian artist 'Smug'. In photorealistic style, it depicts a child crouched in grass in a typical Scottish upland landscape. He grips a wind turbine, planting it in the soil, plastic spade at his side. Produced with Scottish Power in 2021 to mark the event of the 26th United Nations Conference of the Parties (COP26) in the city, the child is 'planting a greener energy future'.[1] (He could, in a different reading, be ripping the turbines out, though such infrastructural rage would sit strangely among the upbeat offerings of the City Centre Mural Trail, designed to 'brighten up lanes and streets'.) The substation sits on the banks of the River Clyde, which in the nineteenth and early twentieth centuries was a global centre of shipping and ship-building. The mural speaks of a 'greener energy future', but that idea, and its location on the Clyde, draw meaning from Glasgow's past as a cradle of the Industrial Revolution. It is a good place to begin exploring wind energy because, paradoxically, it was in the age of fossil fuels that wind's power and potential became a subject of new interest.

The Industrial Revolution was fuelled first by coal, later by oil. Coal had been used in small quantities for centuries in parts of China, France, and England, too.[2] But wood remained the main fuel source, until the confluence of the identification of great coal seams deep beneath the ground, and the development of technologies that put it to work, aligned in eighteenth-century Britain. Where a pre-modern town needed access to a large hinterland of forest to meet its fuel needs, coal packed 60 million years of giant Carboniferous vegetation into a dense, carbon-rich mass that was accessed vertically, not horizontally.[3] Coal burnt steadily and slowly, and once extracted it could be transported – and stored. This made it ideal for the engines being developed that heated water to create pressurised steam that turned rotors that powered other machines – spinning, weaving, threshing, grinding, motoring – that in turn 'projected the fossil economy out of Britain' and around the world.[4] The work that these machines could do 'liberated a good chunk of humankind from the drudgery of muscular toil and from the poverty imposed by the limits of (the old regime)'. [5] Put to work in the name of empire, those same machines enabled the subjugation of many others.[6] Coal transformed Britain's industry, economy, and society through the nineteenth century, and powered its colonial expansion.

Victorians perceived coal's significance to their period. William Stanley Jevons wrote in 1865 that 'the coal we happily possess in abundance is the mainspring of modern material civilisation'. Even in its midst, it was clear to Jevons that he lived in 'the Age of Coal'.[7] Traditional energy history – focused on economics and technology – has seen this as a decisive shift, one so marked that we can view everything before c. 1800 as the Age of Solar Power, and everything since as the Age of Fossil Fuels (building on Jevons' terminology).[8] By 1890 coal had overtaken biomass – mainly timber – to become the world's primary fuel, and wouldn't be overtaken by oil until 1965.[9] A sense of stagism inevitably can pervade these big histories, but Andreas Malm has shown that when coal was adopted by northern English cloth manufacturers it wasn't because it was suddenly cheap and plentiful. In fact, it was expensive, at least more so than the water that powered most mills for free. But coal allowed mill owners to detach production from those hillside streams and their resident skilled workers and relocate factories to new urban locations replete with a poor, unskilled, desperate – cheap – workforce. Coal concentrated power and profits in the hands of industrial capitalists.

Coal consumption grew at pace. But pre-existing sources of what has been called 'organic' power – timber, water, solar, wind – remained. A neat line drawn between one age and another belies the reality of all energy transitions, which is that one fuel doesn't suddenly or comprehensively replace another (no matter how much more abundant, accessible, or efficient). As Ian Miller and Paul Warde note: 'The global history of energy transitions is better read as an aggregate increase and intensification.'[10]

Steamships illustrate how fuel sources overlapped and coexisted. The first circumnavigation of the globe by steamship occurred in 1847, by HMS Driver – a ship equipped with both paddles and sails. In early steamships, steam was a supplementary form of power to their sails. They continued to ply the established trade routes that had themselves been set by prevailing air and ocean currents in the age of sail. As engines became more efficient, masts were removed. This untethered them from wind-bound sail routes. The new constraint became how much coal (and later oil) they could carry and how much distance lay between refuel stops. As Greg Bankoff notes, these new possibilities 'wrenched trade in new directions', and empires (British, American, Japanese) grew against the wind, where pre-modern empires (Spanish, Portuguese, British, French) had gone with it.[11] By the 1880s sailing ships had been eclipsed by ships with engines commercially and militarily, but the transition from sail to steam was neither immediate nor absolute. Steamships heralded a new age of industrialised shipping, but sailing did not disappear.

Was wind energy replaced by coal? It was certainly affected. Wind energy did not power major manufacturing in Britain, like water did, but it did have a significant role to play in food production and land use. The rise of the steam engine impacted how and where traditional windmills and pumps were used. But it also played a role in the rise of wind energy's next incarnation.

The history of energy is, at its simplest, a history of people making life and work easier by replacing human effort with other means. Take the treatment of grain, for example. The nutritious content of edible grains is unlocked by breaking through the rough outer husk. Tools for grinding grain have been found at some of the earliest human settlements. Ancient peoples used coarse sandstones and schists for querns and millstones in neolithic settlements. In Shetland and Orkney you can encounter such tools, smooth round and stone heavy, at the neolithic settlements of Skara Brae and Jarlshof, though very occasionally they appear randomly from the earth like ancient eggs, as a large quernstone dated to 3600–3200 BCE did in an Orkney field in 2021.[12] In Pompeii, destroyed in 79 CE, there are remains of rotary mills, where the human work of the grindstone had been replaced by horse power to draw the wheel. In tenth-century Sistan (a Persian region in what is now southeast Iran and southwest Afghanistan), stationary clay and wood windmills with upright sails woven from straw were used for milling. These fixed, vertical (uni-directional) constructions were built in the path of the '120 day' strong summer wind that blows north to south along the present-day Irani–Afghan border. The machines, known as *asbads*, caught the desert winds to drive a vertical axel to grind grain. Some remain and have been submitted by Iran to the UNESCO Tentative List for heritage status.[13]

Some theorise that that the windmill was transmitted to Europe from Sistan via trade through the Mediterranean, or up through Russia and the Baltic. By the time we have the first records of European windmills in the twelfth century, though, they have a very different shape. Richard L. Hills, a historian of windmill technology, argues that it is more likely that in Northern Europe experience of sailing with wind at sea was transposed to working with wind on land. There were no windmills recorded in the Domesday survey (1080–1086) though there were some 5,624 watermills, but by 1155 there is an account in the *Testa de Nevill* of a windmill given by Hugo de Plaza to the monks of Lewes, in Sussex.[14] This mill, and the many that quickly followed it, had vertical sails which turned a horizontal shaft, and the specificity of this form to England, France, and Flanders means that it was likely indigenous. By the thirteenth century, according to Hills, windmills had been built in Germany (1222), Denmark (1259), Holland (1274), and in Sweden (1300), Russia and Latvia (1330). These mills did what the ancient quernstones did: amplified the energy available to ease the human labour involved in making food.

The vertical windmill would be altered and improved through the following 500 years. However, there was a continuity in design and use that rooted these technologies into the surrounding landscapes so that they became emblems of the regions that they proliferated in, like East Anglia and the Netherlands. Windmills became part of the landscape, and the agricultural practices which shaped it.

Windmills were used primarily to mill grains into flour, and to pump water to drain land. This explains their prevalence in eastern and southern England, the flattest lands, good for arable farming and susceptible to inundation. They were, however, found all over Britain, from Cornwall to northern Scotland, Wales, and particularly in the east of England. Agriculture was not their sole use. Windmills were used for grinding flints (for pottery), crushing chalk (for cement), and, from the late seventeenth century onwards, draining water from mines. The need to keep mines from flooding motivated mine owners to sponsor inventors and engineers to design increasingly sophisticated technologies, some driven by wind. In a neat historical twist, it was this race to improve mine safety and productivity that also produced the steam-powered engine. Thomas Newcomen's atmospheric engine of 1712 produced steam to push a piston to propel a pump. In 1776, James Watt's design radically improved the efficiency of the engine. Richard Trevithick, chief engineer of the Ding Dong mine in Cornwall, built his own steam engines (not least to dodge Watt's patent fees). He also developed a locomotive engine, which used steam pressure not to pump but to propel forward. On Christmas Eve, 1801, the 'Puffing Devil' engine travelled with six passengers on board. A Cornish folk song still celebrates 'going up Camborne Hill, going down/ the horses stood still, the wheels went around/ going up Camborne Hill, going down'. Motorised transport had arrived.

The proliferation of steam engines, with their glowing hearts of burning coal, did impact the various types of wind-powered mills. The ever-industrious Trevithick designed small portable engines to be used on farms; to thresh corn, for example, and to drive millstones. One advantage of the engine was that it could work in any weather. Traditional flour mills worked intermittently according to when the wind blew and were limited in size: sails too large would break in very strong winds. With engine-driven milling machinery, flour mills could scale up and mill continuously.[15] For drainage, too, the consistency of the engine compared to the wind pump meant an ability to maintain the water table at a steady level, allowing more predictable and reliable yields for farmers. Engines, then, led to a decline in the use of wind through the nineteenth century, but not its total demise. For farmers and millers who already had the equipment, wind remained a free resource, worth using. For those wanting to maintain a smaller scale of activity, wind continued to work fine. Working with the arguments made by David Edgerton in *The shock of the old: technology and global history since 1900*, one can understand the Industrial Revolution through the narrative of invention and innovation, with the arrival of new technologies that transformed traditional practices. This narrative supports a sense of progress, and of British dominance and exceptionalism. Or, one can look beyond innovation to focus instead on use, and in a use-based history continuity features as often as change. With the lens adjusted slightly, we see that wind energy continued to be harnessed, in Britain and elsewhere, through the nineteenth century and into the twentieth. It remained a usable, abundant resource, with relatively simple technologies that could be worked, mended, and maintained with basic engineering knowledge. And so while the steam engine proliferated, and in some cases replaced windmills and pumps, those older technologies didn't disappear, and wind was not suddenly made redundant or obsolete.

While traditional energy history made the case for large-scale transitions, recent energy history views transition less as a 'discrete, punctuated shift from one stage or system to another' and more as an 'ongoing transformation', to borrow from Stephen Gross and Andrew Needham.[16] This nuance complements use-based history and is essential for connecting the rise of coal with the rise of wind. The rise of coal would seem to be a story that leads us *away* from wind – one of the energy sources of the old regime. But in fact, the use of traditional wind energy continued, impacted but not eradicated by the advent of fossil fuels. Furthermore, the Industrial Revolution created the conditions for wind's next phase, which was not organic, but electric. Concern among some industrialists about the finite supplies of coal placed wind in contradistinction to fossil fuels, a categorisation which would prove persistent. And the ever-increasing appetite for more energy that industrial capitalism engineered in consumer societies found a bright new outlet: electricity.

Resources and their limits

A rare item hangs at the entrance of the School of Earth Sciences at the University of Bristol. A huge map of Britain made in 1815 by William Smith, with swathes of pinks, blues, greens, and yellows across its interior, depicts – for the first time – the geology of an (almost) whole nation. Smith had started mapping what lies beneath Britain's soil in nearby Bath in 1799, and it took him fifteen years to cover England, Wales, and southern Scotland. I did say *almost*: his work as a mineral surveyor gave him opportunity to travel and study, but the mapping he did mostly in his own time and with his own funds. We find, then, that the area around Bath and Bristol, where he was employed by the Somerset Canal Company, is very detailed; northern Scotland and Northern Ireland, some of the most geologically rich landscapes in the world, are missing from the map as Smith did not travel there, but neither did he conjecture: better to leave space for future surveys to fill. About 400 copies of his map were printed; fewer than 10 per cent are known to still exist. Five are kept in the Natural History Museum; another hangs in the corridor of the Geological Society (est. 1807). Students and staff pass by Bristol's on their daily routes to and from lecture theatres and offices.

Smith's map represents a new understanding of what constituted the nation: what lay beneath its surface. Geology had grown as an amateur pursuit through the seventeenth and eighteenth centuries. But by the beginning of the nineteenth century, a case was being made – by landowners, engineers, and surveyors – that the industrialising nation needed salaried professionals to scientifically analyse the Earth, for it contained valuable raw materials in unknown quantities.[17] Germany and France had established formal mining academies, and Britain followed. A key motivation was to ascertain where Britain's coal seams lay, how deep they went, and how much they might contain.

British industrialists marked their luck that a deep coal seam bisected the mainland from south Wales up to northeast England and southern Scotland.

The rapid rise of steam power could not have happened without this geological gift. But they also feared its limits. Historian Nuno Luis Madureira calls this 'the anxiety of abundance': no sooner than coal had been identified and extracted, than concerns over its scarcity were expressed.[18] Debates over the amount of coal, and the speed at which it was being used, took place in Parliament and among landowners, engineers, scientists, and merchants.[19] When William Stanley Jevons published *The coal question: An inquiry concerning the progress of the nation, and the probable exhaustion of our coal-mines,* he presented coal as 'the material energy of the country – the universal aid– the factor in everything we do'.[20] Calculating the total quantity of Britain's coal-bearing strata, Jevons worried that with yearly increasing consumption, an estimated 2 3/4 millions of tons would only last 212 years. It is clear, he wrote, that 'long before complete exhaustion takes place, England will have ceased to be a coal-producing country on an extensive scale'; other nations with larger reserves – namely, the USA – would overtake. Improving efficiency wouldn't solve the problem by reducing consumption either, because, as Jevons argued (the Jevons Paradox), greater efficiency would decrease the cost of energy and raise demand.[21] In the midst of abundance, concerns of future scarcity took hold.

Jevons, through his writings on coal exhaustion and resource scarcity, became one of the founders of neoclassical economics. As Frederick Albritton Jonsson and Carl Wennerlind explore in *Scarcity: a history from the origins of capitalism to the climate crisis,* his focus on efficiency and production was narrowly economic, without discussion of the ongoing political struggles for democracy and organisation for worker's rights that were also a hallmark of this period and its industrial turn. Exhaustion happened to resources, not the people who extracted and produced them. Jevons' audience was his fellow elites. Firmly among that class was William Thomson, who made his name and fortune through practical science applied in the name of empire.

As a scholar, Thomson worked on the mathematical theory of electricity and the dissipation of energy. Professor of Natural Philosophy at the University of Glasgow from 1846 to 1890, he set up the first university physical laboratory in Britain. But as his biographers note, 'scientific knowledge meant wealth for Thomson'. He was an intellectual capitalist, self-articulated, for whom 'scientific wealth tends to accumulation according to the law of compound interest'.[22] Thomson made his expertise available to commerce, earning a baronetcy (he was known best as Lord Kelvin) by overseeing the laying of transatlantic telegraph cables for the Atlantic Telegraph Company.[23] Like Jevons, Thomson was concerned with British reliance on limited coal stores, and its impacts on

Britain's global standing. As a hands-on scientist and engineer, who professed the value of practical experimentation and observation, he was attentive to how energy was being used. 'When we look,' said Thomson

> at the register of British shipping, and see 40,000 vessels, of which about 10,000 are steamers and 30,000 sailing ships, and when we consider how vast an absolute amount of horse-power is developed by the engines of those steamers, and how considerable a proportion it forms of the whole horse-power taken from coal annually in the whole world; and when we consider the sailing ships of other nations ... and throw in the little item of windmills, we find that even in the present days of steam ascendency old-fashioned wind still supplies a large part of the energy used by man.[24]

Thomson noted the limits and graduations of the use of fossil fuels. He also looked beyond it. 'When the coal is all burned,' his 1881 lecture to the British Association for the Advancement of Science continued, 'or long before it is all burned ... it is most probably that windmills, or wind-motors in some form, will again be in the ascendant and wind will do man's work on land at least in proportion comparable to its present doing of work at sea.'

Thomson was enthusiastic about wind energy because he connected it, crucially, to electricity. Advancements in electrical and chemical engineering in the later decades of the nineteenth century sparked a so-called second phase of the Industrial Revolution, and this was very much the world that Thomson himself moved in and contributed to.[25] In 1847 he met Michael Faraday, and James Prescott Joule, and the scientists debated a major issue with electrical current: its loss of heat when conducted.[26] By the 1880s, gutta percha cables, dynamos, generators, and transformers allowed electricity to be produced and transmitted more reliably. In 1881, the year of his speech, Thomson supported Joseph Swan, inventor of the incandescent lamp, in business, and became aware of Camille Faure's 'accumulator' for the storage of electrical power. Thomson understood that wind could be compatible with emergent electricity-generating technologies, and that battery storage could allay the great disadvantage of wind energy: its intermittent nature.

While Joseph Swan had succeeded in producing an electric lamp, over the Atlantic Thomas Edison and his team were making lamps that wired together to create an electrical system. Edison's ability first to imagine, then to build, an interconnecting means of providing electricity not just to individual objects or users but to households, towns, entire cities, was his greatest and most enduring contribution. We still imagine electricity today using the language of the system, the grid, and the network, which can be scaled up and down, be opened or closed. The provision of power from one central source through cables and wires via substations to our homes remains the essential model of electricity provision today.

Ambitious and entrepreneurial, Edison founded several companies to support and promote his work. The Edison Electric Illuminating Company of New York was incorporated in 1880 and built the first central generating station – on Pearl Street, in New York City – to supply the charge for the lighting systems that were installed in offices, shops, and restaurants nearby to attract customers.[27] A year later in 1881 – the same year as Thomson's speech – Edison displayed his electrical systems at the first International Electrical Exhibition in Paris; interest across Europe was immediate. It is also worth noting that, also in 1881, a year to the month that the Pearl Street generating station opened, a public supply of electricity to power streetlights was opened in Godalming, Surrey (funded by the borough Lighting Committee). The source of this, the world's first public supply of power? A water-wheel at the Westbrook Mill.[28]

The rise of electricity as a publicly accessible and useful form of energy would create an appetite for power that fuel sources and networks could barely keep pace with. The thermal model, essentially massive steam engines which burnt coal to heat water into steam, which turned turbines that generated power, became dominant. Coal and gas power plants today employ the same basic technology, as do nuclear power stations, which also run on steam. Electricity further propelled the rapidly increasing consumption of coal and oil that had begun with manufacturing and transport. But Godalming's public, water-powered supply of energy shows us that non-fossil fuels played a part in the emergence of electricity, too. This was not solely a fossil achievement. Wind could not produce the heat which powered a steam engine. But it did offer kinetic energy that could turn a dynamo and generate electricity. Demand for electricity opened the doors for wind energy as an alternative source of power.

Edison attempted to introduce an electrical system to London in Holborn in 1881, but his financial backers were frustrated by a cautious government.[29] While there was great interest in the new electrical technology, Britain's politicians and law makers took time to work out how they would allow its widespread operation in the capital. Berlin and New York tore ahead, illuminating at pace. When an electricity station opened in Deptford in 1889, engineered by Liverpudlian Sebastian Ziani de Ferranti, it placed the centre of electricity production on the banks of the Thames, within easy reach of coal barges and at some distance from consumers. Government by this time had implemented legislation that granted tenure for private companies to provide electricity to consumers at guaranteed rates, making the provision of electrical power a commercially viable venture in Britain. A proliferation of municipal and private undertakings developed from the late nineteenth century through to the 1920s that offered electricity to paying customers through networks. Electricity grew piecemeal, through towns and cities where population density ensured that the outlay costs of constructing transmission centres and substations and laying cables could be recouped through many paying customers. Rural communities offered fewer customers, greater area to connect (needing more materials and labour), and thus less profit to the undertakers. An urban–rural electrical divide emerged early and would remain for decades.

Rural people could see the benefits of electrical lighting no less than city dwellers. Indeed, they could arguably use it more, given that few farmsteads or villages could boast the gas lights that incandescent bulbs replaced in cities. Enter a range of inventors and entrepreneurs in the USA, Denmark, and Britain, who looked for alternative ways to power rural communities, and connected wind to electricity in practice, as William Thomson had in theory, to create localised power sources in the absence of widespread electricity provision.

Electric wind

William Thomson's invitation to make the wind electric was not fantastical or futuristic, but an idea already in motion. Robert W. Righter, historian of wind energy in the USA, notes that in 1860 Moses Farmer patented a device to convert wind into electricity, but he was so far ahead of the curve on this that there was little wider demand, or profit to be had.[30] (Farmer, a prolific inventor, also patented a platinum-strip incandescent lamp in 1859, decades ahead of Edison and Swan.)[31] The commonly attributed 'first' use of a large windmill to generate electricity is to an American, Charles F. Brush, from the winter of 1887 onwards.[32] Brush was an already successful inventor of electric lights, and it was at his home on Euclid Avenue in Cleveland, Ohio, that he constructed a 60-foot tower with an enormous 56-foot diameter wheel made of 144 wooden blades, that was attached to a generator.[33] It was large and functioned well enough to power '350 incandescent lights, 2 arc lights, and a number of electric motors'.[34] In the UK, a Glaswegian and contemporary of William Thomson, James Blyth, devised a wind generator just ahead of Brush, though it was far smaller. In 1880 Blyth was appointed Professor of Natural Philosophy at Glasgow University – like Thomson, who retired in 1899. Thomson makes no note of Blyth in his papers, but Blyth mentions Lord Kelvin's speech on wind in his; the men shared an interest in electrical engineering and were part of the same intellectual and civic milieu. In July 1887, Blyth installed a 'small windmill for supplying electric light by means of storage cells' in the garden of his holiday home in Marykirk, Aberdeenshire.[35] The tower stood 33 feet above ground and supported four canvas sails attached to wooden arms. These turned a horizontal axis and flywheel that was connected to a dynamo by a length of rope. Blyth offered to supply power this way to the village of Marykirk, which turned him down on account of a general belief that electricity was the work of the devil. Instead, he installed a wind machine to supply emergency power to the Lunatic Asylum, Infirmary and Dispensary of Montrose (now Sunnyside Royal Hospital).[36] Blyth's wind machine in Marykirk was demolished in 1914.

Recent research by Philippe Bruyerre suggests that an Austrian, Jospef Friedländer, beat both Brush and Blyth (though not Farmer). Friedländer connected a 'Halladay' wind turbine supplied by the US Wind Pump and Engine Company to an electric dynamo and displayed the device at the 1883 Vienna International Electric Exhibition. The installation powered twenty-five lamps and a threshing machine, though a steam-powered traction engine was also on site to provide power in the absence of wind.[37] Friedländer took an existing windmill turbine – of a type manufactured and used throughout the American continent, but particularly in the mid-west for 'traditional' wind pumps and mills – and made it electric. There was a functional continuity between the traditional and the new, the organic and the electric, in these nascent stages of wind energy.

Experiments were also underway in Denmark by the end of the nineteenth century. Poul la Cour, a scientist and teacher working at a rural school for adult education in Askov, built a wind turbine that provided electricity to the school in the early 1890s. Convinced of the value of wind-generated electricity for rural communities, and of its commercial viability, he founded the Society of Wind Electricians in 1903 which trained rural electricians to install the simple, reliable direct-current (DC) machine he was producing (which he called the *Klapsejler*). As a result, rural Denmark was home to an early decentralised electricity network, later replaced by a centralised high-voltage grid. After the Second World War, DC-producing turbines were replaced by alternating current (AC)-producing power plants, but a tradition of wind engineering was established and taken forward by Johannes Juul, who had trained as an electrician under la Cour.[38]

American windmills and pumps were imported and available in Britain and Northern Europe in the late nineteenth and into the twentieth century. As with American customers, they appealed to rural households and farmsteads in need of functional technology, and the small metal turbines were a not-unusual sight in rural landscapes. The possibility to connect these machines to electric dynamos opened up new markets for existing companies – and allowed new businesses to emerge. The Mills Archive in Reading has a rich collection of marketing materials produced by companies like the Wind Motor Electric Company operating out of Montana, USA, but also J.G. Childs (London), Lucas Ltd (Birmingham), and the Glasgow Electrical Engineering Company (GEEC), from the 1910s to the late 1930s, to name a few.[39] These companies produced brochures and catalogues to promote and sell their wind devices to the public, and the way wind energy is described and visualised allows us to analyse how it was understood at the time, with some themes appearing consistently through the literature.

In 1909 J.G. Childs and Company, of Willesden Green, London, advertised wind turbines and electrical equipment. Their brochure noted they were contracted to the Admiralty, the War Office, and the General Post Office, but the brochure pitch was firmly to the domestic customer. On the first page they describe how wind turbines in conjunction with storage batteries could supply current for lighting, cooking, and heating, as well as dairies, plantations, and mines. Childs & Co told the potential customer that 'there is power blowing to waste' all around them. This idea of wind as free energy is picked up by the Patent Lighting Company's 'Ventimotor' marketing materials (Figure 1.1), promising 'electric light in your homes from the natural power of the wind', and was embedded in the very name of Lucas Ltd's 'Freelite' device. Wind as a free resource was contrasted to the expense and inconvenience of coal. The GEEC's 1927–28 brochure for their Garty 'Apex' Wind Dynamos sold them with a strapline: 'No Fuel, No Smell, No Trouble.' Unlike dirty coal that had to be bought in, wind was clean and convenient. It was also safer, with brochures noting the danger of fire from engine exhausts or explosive petrol or oil.[40] Still on the fence? Childs & Co did the maths for you: 'with coal at £2 per ton, a wind turbine of 100ft diameter will do work requiring coal of the value of £1,500 per annum – and upwards'. It was a tantalising offer, though few if any domestic turbines would have run to a comparable size.

1.1 The Ventimotor brochure, Patent Lighting Company, 1924. MA Mildred Cookson papers.

One of the selling points of wind, then, was as an alternative to coal. Its small scale was also marketed as help, not hindrance. The Ventimotor brochure is illustrated, with a photograph of the machine and drawings of various rural and suburban settings – a village church here, a cottage there. The machine itself was not pictured in these places, but the implication was clear: this was not simply a functional piece of kit for the working farm, but a suitable addition to any home. Childs & Co advertised that their technologies were already in use by the company: 'for some time past we have been lighting our works from a wind-turbine plant with most satisfactory results', but not only lights; also: 'a complete set of electric cooking and domestic utensils', an oven capable of roasting a large joint, saucepan and steamer, toaster and grill, electric laundry iron, cigar-lighter, shaving-pot, and ladies' curling-tong. Even one's Electric Carriage (car) could benefit from wind power, according to the tempting pitch of Childs & Co. The first electric car was produced in 1842, and by the First World War there were no less than 565 different brands available.[41] Electric cars were quieter, simpler, and more reliable than combustion engines (fuelled by either steam or gasoline) and used rechargeable batteries, but were limited to a range of 30–40 km. Already known and appreciated for 'convenience and cleanliness', Childs & Co's Electric Carriage could be parked in a garage where wind fed the recharging plugs. 'We anticipate that the adoption of wind-turbine plants will greatly encourage the use of Electric Carriages', they wrote in 1909 (Figure 1.2). Prescience aside, the message was that the entire home could (potentially) run on wind. The utility of a power supply for everyday items was central to the sell.

This power supply, the sales materials made clear, was suitable for isolated dwellings. The Apex Wind Dynamo was specifically described for use for mansions, farms, and outlying buildings 'where public supply mains are not close at hand'. This framing of wind energy continued through the twentieth century, as later chapters will show. It was not only remote reaches of Britain, but also the extended periphery of the British Empire that presented sales opportunities. Childs & Co marketed their machines directly to imperial agents, but not imperial subjects. In the 1909 sales materials we see illustrations of colonial bungalows, surrounded by palms and well-tended gardens. Three dark-skinned men wearing loincloths or shorts stand in the middle distance; two white-skinned men wearing white suits and sun hats stand in the foreground. A wind turbine rises in the centre background. The scene is purposefully non-specific: this could be India, Jamaica, or east Africa. Wind power would

Refrigerators for food and drink are a necessity in hot climates. They are now made of all sizes—from that suitable for a household of two, and upwards. They require power of some kind to work them, however, and here again a wind-turbine plant would supply the necessary electric current.

The foregoing are merely some of the forms in which electricity may be applied to the domestic uses of a household in hot climates.

Copyright]

ELECTRIC MOTOR CARS.

The convenience and cleanliness of the Electric Carriage are well known and appreciated by all who have used it. But for the cost and difficulty of obtaining a suitable supply of electric current for charging purposes, particularly in Suburban and Country districts, the use of this form of carriage would be much greater than it is at present. The wind-turbine plant removes these limitations to Electric Carriages entirely. When the chauffeur, on returning from a run, places his car in garage, he inserts the generator plugs in his battery, and any wind available will recharge it, without attention on his part. In fact, as far as recharging is affected, no further attention need be given to the car before it is required for another run. If a large supply of current is required, it will be well to have an auxiliary battery placed in the garage, which would be charged by the turbine at times when the car was either absent or fully charged. This additional battery would be available whenever the wind was insufficient for direct charging from the turbine. The automatic switching arrangements fully protect and control both the battery and the generator under all conditions of wind. We anticipate that the adoption of wind-turbine plants will greatly encourage the use of Electric Carriages.

1.2 Illustration of an electric carriage in 'Electricity from the Wind' sales brochure, J.G. Childs and Co, Willesden, 1909. MA Mildred Cookson papers.

make a useful addition to a colonial home. The GEEC were more place-specific: they included images of government buildings and 'natives at work' in Accra, Ghana, with no wind technologies yet in sight but the implication that they could soon be.

These adverts and sales brochures show that there was interest in wind's capacity to generate electricity for the home and for the small business in the early twentieth century. Wind was distinguished by its contrast to coal, and by its availability in places where mains electrical infrastructure had not yet reached. The scale of the machines and their suggested uses was small, and consistently domestic. At prices such as £45 for a ½-kilowatt dynamo and switchboard, and £14 for a mast (GEEC, 1927–28) these were by no means common objects within reach of the general populace. But neither were they extraordinary, or the 'preserve of the curious inventor' as they had been only two or so decades previous, when Edison, Thomson, Brush, Blyth, Friedländer, and de la Cour had been experimenting.[42] The move from the highly experimental to the reliably functional was underway, but the crucial step up in terms of the reach, scope, and significance of wind energy was still ahead: the ability to supply electrical power to public supply grids. Coal, specifically, and the category of fossil fuels more broadly, played a central role in delineating between old and new forms of wind energy. The traditional uses of wind for milling and pumping did not disappear due to the rise of steam power but they became artisanal in an industrial age. The use of wind continued, and demand for electricity provided a new application for this abundant resource. No fuel, no smell, no trouble? Wind energy was on its way, but there was still a way to go. As the next chapter shows, developing the technology was only part of the challenge. The wind itself had to be better understood, and it was not an easy subject of study.

2

Where the wind blows

The men of industry discussed in Chapter 1 brought wind into conversation with machines. For them, harnessing wind's energy was a challenge which technology and ingenuity could solve. But wind was no passive input into a machine that could be contained and stored, stockpiled and traded. Intermittent, localised, and unpredictable: what made it powerful also made it problematic. Productive reliable turbines had to withstand the weather. And to withstand the weather, wind's role and behaviour in it had to first be understood.

Much of the available scientific knowledge of the wind came from meteorology: the science of the weather. Studies of wind at sea and on land amassed methods of recording the wind, but also noted the limits of scientific observation in the face of a tempestuous subject. Using records from the UK's Meteorological Office, this chapter shows how scientists recorded and described the wind through the nineteenth century and into the twentieth. Through this process many found both science, and language, wanting. Neither could amply express the true nature of the wind.

The wind that turned Brush's and Blyth's turbines and powered Ventimotors and Freelites was also the wind of weather lore and storm memory. Following it took scientists out of the laboratory and onto hillsides and cliff tops; it introduced them to communities who lived with the wind and possessed different forms of knowing, recording, and articulating it. Only by reckoning with this wind could wind energy move from being the 'preserve of the curious inventor' to the domain of state-sponsored research and development – a crucial step in its development.

The wind is weather

Viking: southeasterly 6 to gale 8, occasionally severe gale 9 in southeast, occasionally 5 in northeast; sea state: moderate or rough, becoming rough or very rough; weather: occasional rain; visibility: good, occasionally poor ...[1]

29

The words of the Shipping Forecast drip through the radio, a soothing balm for insomniacs and a daily necessity for ship's captains, fishers, sailors, and coastguards. Through Cromarty, Forties and Fisher, Biscay, FitzRoy, and Fastnet, we listen to winds and waves articulated through very specific words, in very specific order. The Shipping Forecast offers one response to an enduring challenge: how to measure the wind (and weather more broadly), and how to describe it accurately. Much of how we intuit weather is subjective and experiential, and thus hard to systematically quantify. Wind is felt – but how to describe this to another person, outside of the moment of experience? This question of translation opens up a world of understanding and living with wind, and even the possibility for the wind to write itself.

Broadcast on BBC Radio 4 at 00:48, 05:20, 12:01, and 17:54 daily, the Shipping Forecast always starts with a description of the wind, followed by sea state, weather, and visibility. The words used correspond to the Beaufort wind force scale. This system of describing wind strength and its effects was designed by Francis Beaufort (1774–1857) during his time as Admiralty Hydrographer, a research position within the Royal Navy that he held from 1829–55. Weather was a strategic issue in the age of sail, and the Royal Navy had established a scientific arm – the Hydrographic Office – in 1795 to study oceans and coasts.[2] Beaufort began to develop a system to describe different wind states, but subjectivity and language were issues. One sailor's 'gentle' breeze could be another's 'fresh' breeze, with successful sailing contingent on the potentially large differences between them. A standardised scale of reference was needed to make weather reports reliable and widely comprehensible.

In a sea of constant change, the ship offered a point of surety. Beaufort thought to use the architecture of the ship as a gauge, correlating wind strength to the amount of sail a fully rigged ship could use. In a gentle breeze, therefore, a man-of-war could use full sail; a fresh breeze pushed it to the maximum amount of wind that full sail could endure. Still, the difference was subtle to the non-sailor! But for seafarers it created a common language for the wind understood through daily practice rather than additional study. In his study of Beaufort, the geographer Simon Naylor suggests that this solution effectively turned the 'ship into an instrument of science'.[3] And by making the daily recording of weather observations in ships' logs part of the duties of ships' lieutenants, sailors themselves became data collectors on these mobile weather stations that stalked the seas of the empire.

Beaufort's scale needed adjustment for use on land, and at sea on ships without sails. The original attention to rigging was replaced with observations of the effects of wind on water and land. It is still through reading these territorial and maritime clues that we can assess the state of the wind. So, a Light Breeze (force 2 on Beaufort's scale) is wind that can be felt on the face; that makes leaves rustle; that moves a weather vane; and that raises small wavelets on surface water. Jump two steps on the scale up to a (force 4) Moderate Breeze and the wind is now strong enough to raise dust and loose paper; move small branches; and make small waves with frequent 'white horses'. Another two steps up the scale again (force 6, Strong Breeze), and an audio clue is added to the visual signs. As well as moving large branches, the wind can be heard to whistle in telegraph wires. (At sea, without this audio infrastructure, one can detect it by seeing large waves with extensive foam crests.) The sensory signals of the Beaufort Scale as it exists today allow people to describe the wind by observing and describing its interactions with, and effects on, land and sea – without working knowledge of a sailing ship. We read environmental effects: the wind itself remains largely invisible. For the force 12 Hurricane at the very top of the scale, Beaufort had no language. The scale point simply read 'Hurricane!', as no sails (or sailors) could survive such winds and so there was nothing to observe. Even today, Hurricane remains briefly described on the Beaufort scale. It reads, simply: 'devastation. Air filled with foam and spray, very poor visibility.' Only at this extreme does wind does finally become visible, full of matter it has drawn up from land and sea.

Beaufort's scale has been in use for almost two centuries. It provides a linguistic apparatus to describe the wind at sea that is valued by ships' captains and poets alike. But while competition for naval dominance pushed the study of wind at sea, attention to the behaviour of wind on land lagged behind, a situation that the Royal Meteorological Society (established in 1850) attempted to redress by encouraging the development of more accurate measuring devices, or anemometers. Simple wind vane anemometers, which measure wind speed and direction, had been in use for some time – the Italian inventor Leon Battista Alberti produced one in 1450 that was reworked first by Leonardo da Vinci, and then Robert Hooke. In the eighteenth century the Scottish physician and naturalist James Lind developed a new device, a u-shaped tube filled with water; it span in the wind and the level of the water gave a measure of wind force. (Lind also experimented with electricity, using it to re-animate the muscles of dead frogs in experiments. At the time he tutored Percy Bysshe Shelley at Eton, who immortalised him in poetry as the wise teacher Zoronas. Some suggest that Shelley's stories of Lind were a source of inspiration for Mary Wollstonecraft Shelley's *Frankenstein.*)[4]

Nearly all British wind records of the nineteenth century were captured using a Robinson cup anemometer, designed by Thomas Romney Robinson, astronomer and director of the Armagh Astronomical Observatory, a research institution that has collected weather records continuously since 1789.[5] Robinson's anemometer gave mean wind speed measurements, a breakthrough for dealing with the fluctuations of the wind, where, Robinson wrote, if enough observations can be given, a definite reading 'can be disentangled from the seeming chaos'.[6] This extraction of order from chaos offers a metaphor for not only the development of better wind measuring devices, but the meteorological science of wind more broadly.

By the twentieth century, the anemometer of choice for meteorologists was the Dines model, designed in 1892 by William Henry Dines. The device used pressure differences created by the wind blowing over horizontal and vertical tubes to cause a float to rise and fall, proportionate to the wind speed. A pen mechanism transformed this movement into a line on graph paper. The device was a step forward in recording wind, providing more accuracy than earlier cup and vane anemometers, and by 1914 twenty-five were installed around Britain. Ten of these were on aerodromes, places with vested interest in accurate measurement of wind speed; one sat atop the Royal Meteorological Society headquarters in Kensington. With their pens, Dines anemometers allowed the wind to write. Instead of numerical readings, anemograms showed linear graphs of black ink that moved up and down on the page according to the wind speed, much like a cardiogram – but where we might expect to see steady atrial pulses, we find instead the gusts and flurries of the air in motion. Some of these wind charts are kept in the National Meteorological Archive in Exeter. They make for a curiously moving reading experience. Wind is one of those elusive historical subjects that leaves little trace of itself and can be hard to articulate (as Beaufort found). To see the writing of past winds conjures the imagination of experience. To compare the steady, open scrawl of a stiff South Kensington wind (70 mph, 8.15 pm, 12 January 1930) with the blotted extremes of a gusty Scilly storm (111 mph, 7.20 pm, 6 December 1929) or the sure black lines of a Lizard gale (92 mph, 4 pm, 9 January 1936: see Figure 2.1), offers a glimpse into time and place, an accessible feeling of the past.[7] Like children practising their handwriting in exercise books, these winds expressed character through the lines they made. As I read their writing, their strengths and shapes felt real. Instead of scrabbling for words to describe them, I could follow their own, self-written, lines. They left me their autographs to read.

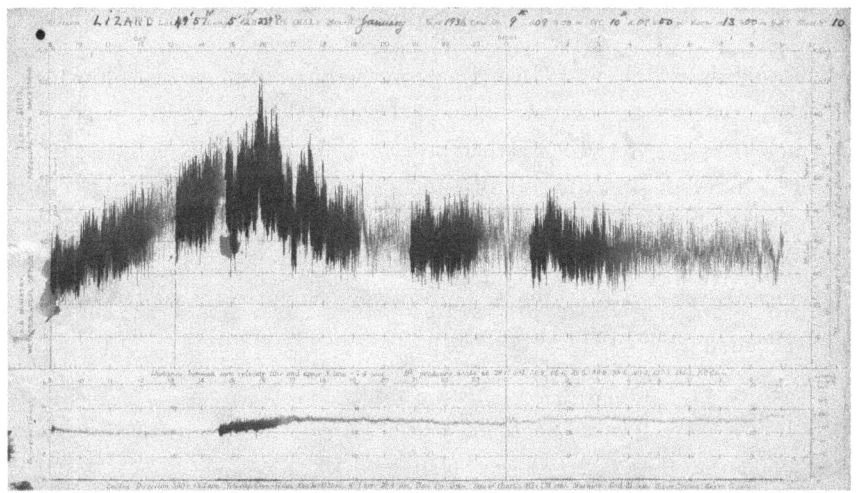

2.1 A wind's autograph: anemogram of a 92 mph wind at the Lizard, Cornwall, at 4 pm on 9 January 1936. Gold, 'Wind in Britain', Plate xix.

Ernest Gold, the president of the Royal Meteorological Society from 1934–35, was captivated by these records too. In his 1936 Presidential address, he spoke about recent advances in wind measurement, and how this was building new knowledge about the behaviour of the wind. But, he confessed, he wanted to show some wind records 'for their beauty'.[8] He showed an anemogram from Spurn Head, inviting the audience to see 'the rhythmic rise and fall' of the wind. Another, from Bell Rock, depicted 'a curious uncertainty about the wind'. One record was of 'a more Gothic type', where one 'might exclaim with Lear: Blow, winds, and crash your cheeks! Rage! Blow! You cataracts and hurricanes, spout!' Gold, the weather scientist, looked into the winds and found Shakespeare looking back at him.

The wind, usually a felt presence, had become visible via data capture. Gold meditated on this reconstruction. The Dines instrument, he said, had given us 'a real picture of the wind: it makes a direct appeal to the imagination … we see the wave-like blows and the relations of the long rolling clouds, and the dance of the gusts … we can picture the storm … we can hear the whistling and the moaning and the roars.' Nonetheless, even anemograms could not capture the full experience of the wind, which was 'not merely a velocity and a direction', but a 'sound as well as a feeling'. To capture the wind required all senses. Even the wind could not write what it was like to experience it in full.

The topographical effect

In his 1936 speech, Ernest Gold clearly wanted to enrapture his fellow meteorologists with the power and vitality of the wind that he felt. But he also had research to report. Meteorologists had been studying the wind using the anemometers in different sites around Britain and had collated interesting results. Beaufort had been a student of the wind at sea, where it blew over vast distances, whipping up waves and building the fetch of a swell. There is a symbiosis between oceans and atmospheric currents, the engines of planetary weather patterns. The poet Emily Dickinson intuited this relationship:

> I think that the Root of the Wind is Water –
> It would not sound so deep
> Were it a Firmamental Product –
> Airs no Oceans Keep –
> Mediterranean intonations –
> To a Current's Ear –
> There is a maritime conviction
> In the Atmosphere –[9]

Anyone who has stood on a beach or cliff, face to a strong wind blowing in from the sea, can appreciate that 'maritime conviction'. Meteorologists had data to show it. Between 1909 and 1935, the Royal Meteorological Society studied the wind at thirty-nine sites in Britain, and five in Ireland, to build a better understanding of the wind in Britain. Bar a few anemometers placed in strategic inland locations, such as the military training area on Salisbury Plain, and major cities such as Birmingham and Manchester, the majority of sites traced the coastal edges of the nation and its islands: South Shields, Holyhead, Scilly, Orkney, Tiree, Bell Rock (the oldest surviving sea-washed lighthouse). One was placed on the Lizard peninsula in Cornwall, the most southerly point on the British mainland, on a pole 25–40 ft above the ground. But the records moved from showing a 'very good exposure' to a 'very bad one'.[10] A row of coastguard cottages nearby created an eddy in the wind, which caused the measuring device to swing around, and the wind speed readings to oscillate wildly. The scientists had to raise the pole to 75 ft to overcome the effect of the local architecture.

This finding gave Gold pause. 'Consider what we want an anemometer to record – nominally it is the wind. But the wind at a particular point depends not merely on the geographical situation of the place, but also on the obstacles in the immediate neighbourhood … the effect of obstacles is to increase gustiness.'[11] Wind, even or especially that which had travelled over long ocean fetches, reacted to the presence of land and solid objects. The maritime conviction picked up over water fractured into unpredictable gusts. The wind was an affective entity which changed the environment around it, as noted by the Beaufort scale. But it was not impervious to affect itself and moved differently according to the shape of the land and the presence of natural and manmade objects. This identification of a 'topographical effect' and the particular gustiness of coastal winds meeting landforms had clear consequences for meteorology and the industries it served: aviation, the military, communications, architecture. Wind's potential as an energy source was not, at this point, under consideration. Through the nineteenth and into the twentieth century, wind was a subject of interest for inventors and entrepreneurs and for meteorologists – but the two remained largely separate realms of enquiry. As wind energy came more fully onto the radar of the state, which commanded the study of weather at the national level, the relationship between wind and land and its meanings for potential energy production could be further explored.

The wind is welfare

Demand for electricity drove early twentieth-century explorations in wind energy. As Paul Brassley, Jeremy Burchardt, and Karen Sayer note in their book *Transforming the countryside*, electricity's rapid spread and now ubiquity is 'a reflection of its remarkable properties as a source of power'.[12] It can be converted (into light, heat, movement, sound) and distributed easily, through insulated networked wires. Wiring also makes it safe, and it is clean, especially compared to the smoke and smuts of a coal fire. Through the early decades of the twentieth century, electricity proliferated in towns and cities. Access to electric light, heat, and power became an industrial necessity (to the extent that some industries built their own generating stations), and a feature of a modern lifestyle, enjoyed by those who could access it and desired by those who could not.

The Edison model of private electricity provision rather than the Godalming public one shaped the early industry in Britain. Until 1927, electricity was provided by individual local monopolies – lots of them. In 1925, there were 572 separate electricity undertakings, responsible for 438 generating stations.[13] These companies sunk capital into building the stations and networks and then made profits by charging customers for the power supplied. Each network operated independently. This was administratively complicated and did not breed efficiencies of scale. Take London as an example: the amount of power being used by Londoners by 1926 was equivalent to what four of the newest power stations could produce. Seventy different electricity companies oversaw the supply – and in two different (direct and alternating) currents![14] Regulation was desperately needed. The Baldwin government acted to bring electricity provision closer under state control with the 1926 Electricity (Supply) Act and effectively began its nationalisation. A Central Electricity Board (CEB) was established to oversee powers stations and construct a national connected transmission system, nicknamed the 'gridiron', or grid, that supplied standardised alternating current. England, Wales, and Scotland were subdivided into eight large geographical regions whose supply was managed by Area Boards. A further Act in 1931 created a state-appointed Electricity Board for Northern Ireland.[15]

Efficiency in electricity generation increased. In 1920, 1 ton of coal produced 631 units of electricity; by 1930 that was up to 1566 units.[16] Electricity had moved from being a luxury, at the end of the nineteenth century, to a basic industrial need and an increasingly standard feature of the modern home – if that home was in a town or a city. Labour-saving and health-improving electric lightbulbs, ovens, and fires were advertised widely, to rural women and men as well as their urban counterparts. But if the grid did not extend to their region, they could not access the power, no matter how much they could afford to pay for it. Some farms bought their own electricity generators, but their size and expense could not be borne by most households. The southwest of England offers a good illustration of how access to electricity varied depending on where you lived. Plymouth and Devonport electrified in 1899. By 1926 (and the establishment of the CEB), nearby Exeter (1923), Torbay (1924), and Dawlish (1926) were all connected to electrical power. But large parts of Cornwall, West Devon, Dartmoor, Exmoor, and the Mendips were not. Even by 1953, 42 per cent of the South West Electricity Board area remained unconnected.[17] This unequal geography of electricity was not confined to the southwest by any means – rural Wales, and in particular the Scottish Highlands and Islands, were similarly unconnected. Electrification continued through the 1930s, but it remained uneconomic to sink costs into installations in sparsely populated areas. The industry justified lack of rural provision by arguing that even if they did sink costs into new lines, people could not afford to be connected, thanks to economic depression.[18]

Where the wind blows

By the mid-1930s, there was discontent among those sections of the public which did have access to electricity, over tariff disparities, and discontent among those who did not. The government, led by Stanley Baldwin in his third term as Prime Minister, appointed a Committee on Electricity Distribution, which made a strong case for full nationalisation.[19] The build up to the Second World War interrupted those plans. As historian John Sheail notes, the presence of a national grid and fourteen large, efficient power stations that generated the bulk of power, despite the hundreds of undertakings, itself proved crucial to the war effort.[20] Industrial mobilisation relied upon it. In the domestic sphere, the introduction and impact of blackout regulations on the civilian population is its own testimony to the place of light, by then much of it electrical, in British homes and towns by this period.[21] The return to nocturnal darkness at the onset of war was a difficult shift for many, with a raft of accidents and incidents reported.

The vast scalar gap between national electricity policy, meteorological studies, and individual wind energy experiments seems too big to bridge at this point in history. Energy was core national policy, central to industry, society, and victory in war – and administered accordingly. A new Ministry of Fuel and Power was established in 1942. Fuel was power, and Britain's main fuel source continued to be coal. Miners were exempted from military service to keep the giant furnaces of power stations and steel factories burning. But the war also challenged an industry that had contracted through the depression of the 1930s: it demanded an increase in production. With ageing pits and labour shortages (despite military exemption, many miners joined up), and an industry run by private owners that were seen by government as obstinate and intractable, it was only the reduction of exports that 'staved off the ever-lurking threat of a coal crisis' through most of the war.[22] Towards the end of the war, coal shortages led to public electricity blackouts, as power generation faltered.

In comparison to the huge capacity and quantities of the coal industry when it came to electricity production, wind wielded no comparable power whatsoever. In 1947 nationalisation brought 1,200 coal pits, worked by 700,000 people, under state ownership – assets worth £390 million at the time.[23] There were no wind turbines generating electricity for public supply at this time. Wind was the realm of speculation, experimentation, fanciful optimism – not of real, blackout-busting kilowatts that could make any impact at the national scale. And yet, it is in this period – during the war, and immediately after – that we see wind energy come into political view. The birth of wind energy in Britain and the welfare state are entangled.

During and immediately after the war, there was a broad political movement to extend welfare provision. William Beveridge's 1942 Report made the case for a comprehensive social insurance scheme that would address five 'giants' the populace faced on the road to reconstruction: Want, Disease, Ignorance, Squalor, and Idleness. All who could would contribute, and all would benefit. Expenditure on fuel and electricity came into the costings needed to meet basic living standards.[24] Also in 1942, the government Committee on Land Utilisation in Rural Areas was planning for postwar recovery. It viewed electricity as an 'essential service which ... should be in the home of practically every citizen in town and country alike, at no higher price to the consumer in the country than in the town.'[25] Like the McGowan Committee in the 1930s it recommended nationalisation of the industry and further grid expansion. Political discourse of the 1940s added a principle of equity to the older argument that electricity improved health, work, and living standards. Electricity had become ubiquitous enough for some that it was part of everyday life, but for many (rural) others, this basic necessity remained out of reach. The National Union of Agricultural Workers lobbied government for rural electricity as an 'urgent national necessity'.[26] The lack of electricity for rural people was forging a major inequality in British life that was out of step with the political momentum to centre principles of welfare in policy that swept Clement Attlee's Labour government to electoral victory in 1945.

This is where power runs into (or out of) place. Grid construction was ordered apace, but with shortages of critical materials (such as copper and timber), progress was slow. Decisions made in Whitehall found their limits in peat bogs, granite-studded moors, and immoveable mountains. The hard realities of geography were an impediment to the principles of the new welfare state.[27] In the gaps that emerged between what was promised, and what could be delivered, engineers and politicians started to consider wind more seriously as a potential energy source. It had the distinct advantage of being very present in precisely the parts of the country hardest to reach by the centralised power grid: the high places, and the coastal edges.

Moving north

This shift towards considering wind as an alternative energy source, particularly for remote places that lacked other options, particularly focused on Scotland. In 1943 the MP for Argyll, Duncan McCallum, spoke in the House of Commons about the potential of wind energy in Scotland, where 'Atlantic gales [are] more frequent than breezes' and 'could generate sufficient electrical power to furnish [the Highlands and Islands] with electricity'.[28] The debate was the 1943 Hydro-Electric Development (Scotland) Bill, which established a new energy provider for the far north. If, in the rest of Britain, regional energy boards were struggling to bring electricity to rural areas, you might be forgiven the inclination to spare a thought for the Highlands and Islands of Scotland, with huge expanses of moors and peat bogs, firths and tides to contend with. But in northern Scotland in this period, out of the most challenging of landscapes and circumstances, grand ambitions connecting politics, engineering, and environment were formed.

The model of electricity provision in the rest of the country – sinking initial capital costs to build networks and connect homes, recouped through electricity charges – was doomed in a region that had so much land, and so few people. The cost–profit ratio, to a financier, spelt failure. But Tom Johnston, Labour MP for West Stirlingshire (appointed by Churchill as Secretary of State for Scotland in 1941) refused to accept that geography would determine rural Scotland's access to power, and with it development. Taking inspiration from the Tennessee Valley Authority's series of projects in 1920s and 1930s America, Johnston built a political, economic, and social case for hydro-electric development in the Scottish Highlands overseen by a new electricity board. A bill to establish the North of Scotland Hydro-Electricity Board (NSHEB) came before parliament in 1943, and Johnston argued that the provision of electricity to rural communities was a social responsibility. It was also an environmental responsibility: a 1941 bill to empower the previous commercial supplier, the Grampian Electricity Company, to construct two large dams at Glen Affric and Glen Cannich was withdrawn after intense opposition from both sides of the House to the 'vesting of monopoly powers over great natural resources to a private company'.[29] The Highlands landscape was considered a national asset and private commercial development threatened it.

Johnston rejected the notion that development and natural beauty were incompatible, by centring socialist principles in the plans for the NSHEB. There were ongoing debates in this period about the need to balance industrial development with the preservation of amenity in the countryside – the right to take enjoyment, healthy exercise, and spiritual nourishment from the outdoors.[30] These debates also fed into the movement towards the establishment of National Parks, which finally manifested in 1951 following decades of campaigning. No sooner were national parks established in England and Wales than conflicts arose over the aesthetic and amenity impacts of the siting of electric pylons in them.[31] When a programme of nuclear power station construction got underway in the 1950s, the Central Electricity Generating Board (CEGB) employed landscape architects specifically to improve the siting of power stations sensitively in surrounding landscapes.[32] The best-known was Sylvia Crowe, who worked as Landscape Consultant for Wylfa, the nuclear power station on Anglesey, and Trawsfynydd, the first inland nuclear power station in Snowdonia/Eryri National Park. That there could be a place for energy infrastructure within national parks was something Crowe advocated for in her book *The landscape of power*. The distinctions between preservation, conservation, and responsible development played out in these debates and many others centring on town and country planning in Britain in the postwar period.

Johnston agreed that the presence of industry need not disfigure or desecrate landscape. There was a deference to the technological sublime in NSHEB plans: this was infrastructure at its most muscular, with hydro-electric dams carved out in great sheets of concrete through water, soil, and peat. This kind of grand-scale construction as a means of economic stimulation and expression of centralised state power characterised high modernism around the globe – the Tennessee Valley Authority, and later in the twentieth century, in India, Pakistan, and Egypt, where involvement by the World Bank in megadam projects added an international-developmentalist element.

Johnston's vision of hydro-electric power in Scotland centred Scottish interests, needs, and conditions within a national energy model that usually took England as its centre. He questioned the emphasis on amenity in landscapes that had been emptied through forced clearances, dominated by aristocratic sporting estates, and whose residents lived in poverty. Johnston invoked a strong sense of social justice when he said that use of these landscapes should not 'begin about 12th August [the traditional start of the grouse shooting season] and last only until the deer stalking and salmon fishing seasons are over'. The chief amenity he wanted to see in the north of Scotland was 'the amenity of social security, the right to work and the amenity which derives from remuneration for a useful service in the world'.[33] It was hard to see the beauty in a landscape preserved only for amenity, and not for the people who lived in it. Johnston's point was not simply that if development of the Highlands was needed, then better it be Scots who did it; it was that a publicly owned utility, which through the terms of its own foundation was required to serve the needs and interests of the Scottish people, would pursue a more responsible and equitable development on their behalf than commercial interests ever could. Hydro-electricity was a way to make the landscape work for Scotland.

The Hydro-Electric Development (Scotland) Act was passed in 1943, bringing the NSHEB into being. It set about a programme of dam-building and grid connection by hundreds of workers from all over Scotland, known as the 'hydro boys'.[34] In popular and political imaginations the NSHEB was seen to be producing affordable Scottish power through Scotland's natural resources. Dams like those of the Affric-Beauly scheme were transformative in landscape terms, but unlike campaigns against Thirlmere in the Lake District or, later, Trywyryn in North Wales (both reservoirs created to provide drinking water to Manchester and Liverpool, respectively) they were widely seen to benefit local communities, the Scottish economy, and give a boost to Scottish identity too. According to Emma Wood, author of *The hydro boys*, the cost of supplying electricity to the Highlands could only have been met by the 'inspired inter-ventionism' that created the NSHEB. By 1960, 80 per cent of farms and crofts in the north of Scotland were connected to the grid.[35]

These political debates around energy, social deprivation, landscape, and amenity brought to wider attention the fact that alternatives to the (southern) models of power generation and distribution existed. They also carved out space within political discourse to consider water, and wind, as valuable national energy resources. This shift was crucial in drawing attention to the possibilities of wind energy as an alternative source of electrical power at the national scale. Hydro-electricity could be generated easily through mountainous rivers in the Highlands, but the Islands lacked major waterways. Members for Parliament such as Duncan McCallum (Argyll) and Major Neven-Spence (Orkney and Zetland) demanded that the NSHEB explore wind as a means of supplying island communities with power. It was as a potential solution for the intractable issues of providing constant electrical power to remote islands that wind energy moved firmly onto the state's energy radar. The NSHEB had not only the ability and the inclination, but also the sense of responsibility, to explore how that might work in practical terms.

It was at this precise moment that the weather-wind, the dynamic and unpredictable force that so animated meteorologists like Gold, came up against the energy-wind, the unlimited power source waiting to be tapped. To harness the latter, the former had to be properly confronted. Enter the British Electrical and Allied Industries Research Association (ERA), a government research organisation based at the Institute for Agriculture at Harpenden, which undertook the first national wind survey between 1948 and 1954. This work was not the by-product of routine weather monitoring, but a purpose-built effort by the ERA in conjunction with the electricity supply authorities to categorically answer the question of where the wind blew strongest in Britain – and where could wind turbines be placed? It is a testament to wind's difficulty as a subject that, in 1947, following victory in war and the development of sophisticated national meteorology systems and nuclear science capabilities, the question of where the wind blew strongest could not be answered. By 1951, it could.

Britain was not the only nation seeking answers to questions about its winds. The USA surveyed wind from 1940 to 1945 in Vermont to support a wind energy experiment by Palmer Cosset Putnam and the S. Morgan Smith Company at Grandpa's Knob, Virginia.[36] A large wind turbine, over 200 ft high, successfully generated 1–1.5 MW of electricity from 1941 to 1943, and for a short time in 1945 until a series of technical faults finally disabled the project. The US Government offered no support, and Putnam turned his technical skills to nuclear science, placing his turbine patents in the public domain.[37] France, too, approved a programme to select wind power test sites in 1946; 150 anemometers were installed around the country, including on the Eiffel Tower, at varying heights.[38] In 1948 Britain's wind survey was in line with that of its allies. A mix of nationalised industry, political commitment to welfare provision, and Scottish energy innovation came together to create the conditions for Britain to edge ahead, for a brief time in the 1950s, to the forefront of global wind power development. This didn't happen in the centre of political power. It happened at the windiest, wildest edges of the nation. It happened in Orkney.

3

Electricity at the edges

There is a photograph in the Orkney Library and Archive haunted by a wind. Its angles are awkward, surprising – the horizontal lines of a familiar rural landscape (fields, roofs of a distant village) are jarred by off-kilter verticals which pucker the image like stitches in a wound. In the foreground, remnant patches of snow melt in the sun, which casts forth the shadow of the photographer, standing, head to one side, observing the scene. It is 1951 and this is the Rendall road, near the Norsemen garage, a pencilled note on the back records. Those not-verticals are electricity wires and poles, blown over by a gale. The unknown photographer has stopped to capture the scene, a landscape both familiar and strange, a moment in which time and reality are stationary. Snow, never melting; power, suspended in the sky. The wind has been here, and this is what it left (Figure 3.1).

In Orkney, wind is a near constant presence. The islands sit 16 kilometres north of the Scottish mainland, with the North Atlantic Ocean on one side and the North Sea on the other. Ferries are routinely cancelled because of high seas and gale-force winds. Low-lying, the islands appear to hunker down in the cold clear seas. There is no lee to be found. The winds approach from all directions.

Living with the wind has always been a fact of island life. Words to describe minute changes in its behaviour developed in Norn, the language derived from Old Norse which was spoken in the islands for almost a thousand years, and in the Orkney dialect in use today.[1] Old Norse loaned words to Hebridean Gaelic and Shetlandic, too, some of which Robert Macfarlane catalogued in his *Landmarks* glossaries. We find *skub*, a Shetland word for hazy clouds driven by the wind; and *ultaichean*, strong rolling gusts of wind in Hebridean Gaelic, among other terms.[2] Macfarlane shows how language makes place, and how place can be recovered through language. Hugh Marwick, scholar and founder

3.1 OA L5834/1. Photograph, Rendall Road, Orkney. Undated and photographer unknown. Orkney Archive.

member of the Orkney Antiquarian Society (established 1922) thought along similar lines when he wrote, while compiling his books of place names, farm names, and weather words, that the climate of Orkney 'is one of the vilest under heaven'. This was not derogatory: it made a place especially rich in language, with myriad words for rain, snow, and wind.

Some of the words Marwick recorded as in use on Orkney were Scots, but with specific local applications. One example is *skyelly*, to describe the sky when 'covered in bright glittering white clouds', and a local pronunciation of the Scots *scaly*.[3] *Scuther*, a strong, short, windy shower (in Scots, *scudder*); *cool*, and *grey*, which on Orkney mean a light breeze. In Scots, *holler* means to howl or roar in an angry outburst; on Orkney, the term – tellingly – describes a gusty or blustery wind. Another acoustic term, this time Orcadian in origin, *skolder* means an outburst of loud talk and a strong, dry gale. Some words move, as people did, between Northern Isles. *Skub*, which according to Marwick in Orkney denoted a light shower, is used slightly differently by James Stout Angus (collector of Shetland words): *a skubby hask hings, icet-gray* were hazy clouds driven by the wind, in Shetland.[4]

Language bent and flexed to hold the full breadth of island weather. Wind so finely described is wind observed and used. Orcadians used windmills from at least 1763, when a deed survives for a commercial mill in Stromness.[5] It was not uncommon for individual crofts and farm buildings to host wind sails on their roofs, similar in shape to the miniature foil windmills children use to anoint sandcastles on the beach. This 'windy gear', as it was known, was used to grind malt, oats, and barley (Figure 3.2).[6] It is mostly out of use now, but I was told of a farmer on Hoy who repurposed his windy gear to power his television set, long after electricity came to the islands. These archival traces, words, and stories provide a cultural record of wind in Orkney that continues to be enriched. Research in the 1940s and 1950s added new layers to this environmental archive.

In 1948 the Electrical Research Association appointed a Wind Power Committee and set about a programme of work to supply the NSHEB with useable data. Edward William Golding was its Technical Secretary and became an influential documentarian and advocate of wind energy in Britain.[7] His book, *The generation of electricity by wind power*, would in later decades become a handbook for do-it-yourself turbine enthusiasts. In the 1940s and 1950s, he worked at the heart of a team of state-employed engineers and physicists studying wind energy. They did data analysis, laboratory experiments, and international research, but first and foremost came the work to find suitable

3.2 OA L3868/3 'Westray. Example of windmill for driving threshing mill.' Orkney, undated. Photographer unknown.

sites for wind turbines – 'the first step towards any reasonably accurate estimation of wind power potentialities in these islands'.[8] The ERA set up a national survey, which ran for 6 years, assessing 102 sites around Britain and Northern Ireland selected for their windiness, but also for having 'steep, smooth' hills, devoid of trees or buildings (remember the effects of those cottages on the Lizard wind …), with fairly flat tops and a usable road for access.[9] These criteria showed the need to move beyond theoretical and meteorological understandings of wind and pay attention to the reality of operating wind turbines. The key questions were: could a wind turbine be put there and, if so, how much power might it generate? The survey provided answers.

Orkney, which had recorded high winds in the Royal Meteorological Society's wind studies, was selected for the survey. Photographs recorded the placement of a 120 ft survey mast with anemometer attached at Costa Hill in 1948.[10] The ERA relied on the assistance of local people who helped haul the machinery through snow by tractor. At Slieve Tooey in County Donegal, Ireland, this was done on horseback; at Mynydd Anelog in North Wales, with a small tank-like vehicle with tracked treads. Local cooperation was essential, and Golding credited farm workers, shepherds, postal workers, mountaineering club members, and others living near the sites as having a 'considerable natural aptitude for the semi-technical work of attending to the wind-measuring instruments'.[11]

The scientists were looking for wind speeds that could produce an annual output of 4,000 kWh per kW installed.[12] Calculations were made according to assumptions that the wind turbines would have a blade length of 50 meters; an efficiency of 30 per cent – that is, an electrical output that is 30 per cent of the wind power passing through the area swept by the blades; and that they would be positioned 400 metres apart. If, under these conditions, the winds could power 4,000 kW, this would be 'economic'. This was not to say profitable – both ERA and NSHEB were state-funded, after all – but rather, would comfortably justify the initial outlay and any subsequent maintenance costs of installing wind turbines. The survey supplied data to work out the amount of power that could be extracted from a site with an 'excellent' rated wind speed of 33 mph, and average of 26 mph, versus a rated wind speed of 21 mph, and average of 17.5 mph. The first could produce 1,210 kW; the second, only 312 kW.[13] That 12 mph difference in wind speeds had a huge effect on capacity and underlined the need to locate wind turbines in the right, windy environments.

If we think of the national wind survey as an unofficial competition to find Britain's consistently windiest place, Orkney won. Its prize was to be chosen as the location for the NSHEB's test wind turbine, that would produce power for the local supply grid. Orkney supplied the steadily strong winds, coastline and smooth (treeless) hills that produced the best conditions for turbines, and, in return, received Britain's first wind-powered public electricity. Orkney's islandness here was also useful: the island grid served as a proxy for the national grid. Testing the capacity of the turbine to feed the local grid on the small island of Orkney was a pilot study for mainland UK. Islands are often valued highly for biodiversity and social studies because they offer a naturally contained sample; for electricity, too, they presented a real-world simulacra of a much larger and more complex national system.

The Orkney grid, though, was still a work in progress. In 1951–52 the NSHEB laid cables in Kirkwall and Stromness, the two largest towns, to other mainland parishes, and laid a subsea cable to connect Gairsay and Shapinsay. Other islands – South Ronaldsay, Burray – petitioned the island council to be included in the grid expansion.[14] Communities were eager to access power, something the NSHEB encouraged by opening a shop in Kirkwall where it showcased electric appliances and held cookery demonstrations.[15] In May

1951 the NSHEB built and opened a diesel-powered generating station in Kirkwall. Tom Johnston attended the opening and spoke of the NSHEB commitment to 'make life more bearable and happier in rural areas, and stem the tide of rural depopulation'.[16] Orkney's Provost praised the 'magnificent' new power station building, 'the finest one we have in Orkney after the Cathedral'. Electricity in Orkney had the blessings of church and state. The point was not, through Orkney, to prove the redundancy of fossil-fuelled power generation. For NSHEB the point was to provide power to the population, and in Orkney wind was a resource too good not to use.

The NSHEB commissioned shipbuilders John Brown and Company to build the Costa Hill turbine. Their vast Clydeside metalworks ordinarily produced ships' hulls and enormous propellors. Constructing 50 ft turbine blades and a 135 ft tower used existing capacity and was perhaps also seen by the company as carving out a future direction. The machine was installed in 1951 by John Brown employees, who were stationed in Orkney along with some ERA colleagues through 1951 and 1952 to maintain and monitor its performance, drawing expenses from the company bank account and, by all accounts, enjoying their time in Orkney (Figure 3.3).[17] Installation was reported in local and national newspapers. In the *Manchester Guardian*, Mr C.W. Marshall, deputy chief engineer of the British Electrical Authority, said the long-term view was that 'wind power would become essential to eke out our diminishing irreplaceable fuel resources'.[18] Wind's framing as an alternative to coal continued to shape its reception.

This was especially true in the economic case for wind. The cost of wind-produced electricity was calculated not as 'firm power' – i.e., the quantity of electricity being generated by turbines and supplied to the grid – but, rather, the fuel cost that would be saved by use of wind power instead of coal-fired thermal power stations. This reflects a reality in which wind energy would supplement the existing electricity generation system, and it tied the value of wind energy to that of coal.

Using a general value of 0.4 pence per kilowatt hour, Golding calculated that sites with a mean annual wind speed of 20 mph or more would be economic for large-scale wind power generation in Britain, saving money by saving coal. If the fuel component reached 0.6 pence, sites with mean wind speeds of only 15 mph would be economic.

The coal industry, recently nationalised, was well understood by energy policymakers to be a time-limited fuel source, and postwar coal extraction never exceeded the levels of the interwar years.[19] The Ministry of Fuel and

3.3 OA L6954/1 Engineers work on the test turbine constructed on Costa Head by John Brown and Company. 1955, photographer unknown.

Power was interested in the wind experiments and sponsored a comprehensive design and costing study by Folland Aircraft Ltd.[20] It extrapolated data from the Orkney turbine to test the relationship between size and cost. There was a scale economy to be achieved with a bigger rotor/blade diameter, but also a limit to what available materials and manufacturing techniques could manage – machines, as the Orkney turbine had shown, had to withstand extreme gusts and high torques, and size increased vulnerability to damage. The study assumed a forty-year lifespan (longer than today's thirty-year norm), with blade overhauls every ten years and regular minor repairs. It found that for a machine of 225 ft in diameter, producing 3670 kW in a wind regime of 35 mph, the overall construction cost would be £150,462 (1951 prices), with annual running costs of £9,544.30.[21] This challenged the perception, prevalent in marketing materials and speculative discourse, of wind as 'free'. The machinery and maintenance required to transform wind into electrical energy incurred costs. The comparison to coal, which also required machines and, more significantly, labour (miners were and are famously organised and aware of their value) was nonetheless still in wind's favour.

The news of the survey results and wind turbine tests were met, in the rapidly electrifying Orkney community, with enthusiasm. 'Costa: Windiest Place in Britain', the *Orcadian* crowed in 1949; 'Power "Windmill" is first in Britain', it proclaimed again in 1950. There was a note of pride that Orkney weather had been recognised. Winds that were lived with, tolerated, endured, and enjoyed had been measured and found outstanding in their category. This sense of Orkney winds as extraordinary can also be seen in newspaper accounts of a hurricane which blew through the islands in the early hours of 15 January 1952. A display of the 'merry dancers' (aurora borealis) was followed by a severe storm. An estimated 501 agricultural buildings were damaged or demolished and 2,459 agricultural buildings unroofed or partly unroofed. The poultry industry, which brought in £1 million annually to the local economy, was wiped out: 76,541 birds were lost to the hurricane winds; along with ten cattle, sixty-six sheep, twenty pigs, and one horse.[22] As the *Orkney Herald* noted, it was 'almost incredible that (it) resulted in no (human) casualties', probably because nearly everyone was in bed at the time it struck.[23] Local people interviewed about the storm noted it's particularly 'freakish' strength that 'battered us like shrapnel'. Orkney residents prided themselves on not exaggerating wind strengths – unlike 'the leafy Lothians who are inclined to speak of a breeze of thirty miles as an "awful gale"'.[24] They knew that this storm was exceptional. 'In the North of Scotland and especially in the isles, and also in the fishing ports, we have cause to know the violences of nature. But very seldom, fortunately, is the wind so devastating as yesterday.'[25]

The wind turbine, and its on-board anemometer, confirmed this. For over half an hour the wind blew at 100 mph; the turbine registered gusts of 115 mph, at which point the needle went off the recording chart. Too strong to record, with estimated gusts of 120 mph, it was the strongest wind recorded in Britain to that point. Local papers added this technical specificity to the wide-ranging emotional registers of their coverage. Islanders didn't need wind readings to tell them that Orkney weather was exceptional; but the data affirmed their experiences and shows how the wind turbine fitted into island traditions of weather experience. In the event, local people proved far hardier than the turbine, which was badly damaged. It was repaired and continued to be tested despite issues with the plywood skins of the blade cracking under pressure when run at full speed in the autumn of 1952. The NSHEB persevered with the experiment though – it was 'all useful information', and they authorised an extra £4,000 for repairs. John Brown & Co submitted design patents and soon received enquiries about buying machines from Buenos Aires and Israel.[26]

The feeling among those involved in the wind experiments and research in this period was optimistic. State interest had opened up funds to pursue real-world turbine tests that were proving wind could directly power public supply grids. The machines had problems, but every fault was giving the engineers more information to work with. And a spirit of common endeavour animated international knowledge sharing. At ERA, Golding was in correspondence with leading Danish wind engineers like Johannes Juul. By 1954 Denmark was the country that had made the most continuous progress in wind turbine design. Windmills were commonly used for irrigation and drainage – over 15,000 were in use in 1936 – and while many of the early electricity-generating machines had aged out (not least because they produced direct current, and a new national alternating current network was being built), a new research programme was underway. Post-Second World War this was led by the South-East Zealand Electricity Supply Company. Golding noted that their Danish 45 kW wind generator was simple, relatively cheap, and robust. He wrote in 1954 that scaling up this production was the next step and that 'it seems certain that in Denmark the production of electricity by wind power ... will be developed on a significant scale in the near future'.[27]

Interest in wind energy went wider still. Between 1950 and 1952, the Organisation for European Economic Co-operation held four meetings in Paris and London of a Wind Power Group that had been started following an offer by the ERA to share its preliminary research and exchange knowledge with other nations.[28] Australia, Austria, Belgium, Canada, Denmark, France, Germany, Greece, India, Ireland, the Netherlands, New Zealand, Northern Ireland, South Africa, the United Kingdom, and the United States of America were all represented. Edward Golding, and R.J. Brearley, the Canadian representative, suggested publishing the proceedings as technical papers. Thanks to them we have a snapshot of early international collaboration on wind energy. Nations were at different levels of research and development, but principles of free exchange of information and of cooperative research were seen by the experts in attendance to be critical to developing wind power at national levels. The international committee agreed on several key points: wind could make a significant contribution to the economic life of some countries; larger scale developments were the inevitable next step; developments would be helped through continuing to share research. However, the Organisation for European Economic Co-operation (OEEC) could not fund further work and lack of support elsewhere meant that an intention to establish an International Wind Power Association at this stage was, as far as my research has found, not taken forward.

The outlook for wind energy in this mid-twentieth century moment was positive. There was momentum in turbine research and development, and experiments had shown the ability of wind to supply the electricity grid. Here was proof that wind could supply not just individual homes but whole communities. But wind energy in Britain did not move to the next stages that had been so readily identified and discussed by its advocates – that is to say, large-scale installations, numerous turbines in operation, more state-supported research, and a gradual move towards playing a functional part of a national electricity generation system.

There are a few factors we can reach for to explain this, and they relate – as so often with wind – to other energy systems, and a changing political context. Britain continued to rely on coal for most of its electricity, railways, and for a lot of domestic heating. Its health and environmental impacts were well documented by this stage, and the 1952 'Great Smog', which was largely caused by accumulated coal smoke and contributed to the premature death of 4,000 Londoners, spurred on clean air legislation. However, the industry remained politically powerful and had a deeply embedded social presence, sustaining communities from South Wales to South Shields and beyond. The quantities being extracted may have been less than government and the CEGB wanted, but coal *was* still being extracted – and for a national electricity system that had been built around coal, it remained the easiest source of power. It may have been cheaper per unit, but wind could not compete with coal in quantity, consistency, industrial might, or social capital.

Speaking at an OEEC meeting, Thomas Haldane, an electrical engineer (and 1948 President of the Institution of Electrical Engineers) sounded a cautious note on wind's potential as a source of large-scale power. British coal stocks could maintain contemporary levels of production for two centuries, but energy use was rising and was set to enormously increase in the future: Britain had 'not more than a few decades in which to find sources of energy alternative to coal'. He chose an example industry which had achieved 'astonishing' economies due to mass production: the motor industry.[29] Intentionally or not, Haldane's example reflected the increasing dominance of oil.

In interwar Europe oil was not yet a major fuel source – it provided 10 per cent of Europe's primary energy needs. But the 1950s and 1960s were its 'golden decades', when cheap oil flooded European markets, and the oil share rose from 10 per cent to 50 per cent.[30] Britain had a majority share in the Anglo-Iranian Oil Company (AIOC, later British Petroleum) which had been in Iran since 1913. On 1 May 1951 Iranian Prime Minister Mohammad Mossaddegh announced the nationalisation of the industry, cancelled the AIOC concession, and reclaimed its assets for Iran. The UK and the US promptly embargoed Iranian oil and set about undermining Iranian self-determination. The democratically elected Iranian government was toppled and the Shah reinstated by a US-led coup in 1953, aided by the British secret service.[31] In 1956 Egypt nationalised the Suez Canal, the main entry route for Middle Eastern oil to Europe, amid a complex regional situation in which a newly created Israel, the USSR, the USA, the UK, and France jostled for influence. An Israeli military invasion of Egypt was supported by France and by Britain, though prime minister Antony Eden was widely denounced at home for this foreign policy. The move also displeased the US, which led the UN opposition to the war. With its currency price collapsing, Britain agreed a withdrawal from Egypt in return for US support of sterling.[32] The crisis left petrol prices high, Eden unwell and soon to resign, and Britain weakened on the world stage. Iran and Suez both underscored that Britain's access to oil was determined by volatile geopolitics, and, thus, a strategic risk. Britain had yet to establish the presence of (yet another) geological gift horse: its own reserves of North Sea oil. So, while oil use was rising across Europe, it did not present a secure and reliable source for future national electricity generation.

Britain's domestic politics was also changing. Attlee's Labour government had 'started, but not completed' widespread social and economic change, and lost the 1951 general election to the Conservatives, led by an ageing Churchill.[33] The period of immediate postwar reconstruction gave way to a decade of 'consensus' politics, with differences between Labour and Conservatives less acute than in other periods. Within this broader sea-change, the spirit of wind-as-welfare which propelled the NSHEB experiments waned.

A brief detour from Orkney back to Glasgow in 1951 offers a sense of where the state thought it would get its future energy from. The Festival of Britain was the postwar Labour government's proclamation of national recovery from the war through art, architecture, and design. As well as Festival Hall and the Southbank development in London, events took place across the four nations. Its major Scottish incarnation was the Exhibition of Industrial Power in Glasgow's Kelvin Hall. The exhibition offered a narrative journey through Britain's industrial past. In the Hall of Coal a Soviet-style mural of muscular miners was hewn out of the coal face: coal was (still) the bedrock of industrial might. The exhibition reinforced the significance of electricity and the role of the national grid in national life through numerous displays, including a replica power station and two replica crofts – one supplied by electricity and one without, an invitation to view and compare.[34] Visitors moved through a Hall of Steel, and Hall of Hydro-Electricity, towards the Hall of the Future. There, among the installations, was meant to have been a 'mobile made of metal representing energies capable of harnessing the wind', designed by Allan Farmer. Wind had been given a place in this forward-looking industrial narrative – but it was accidentally destroyed by workmen the day before the exhibition opened. Nevertheless, it was not the main attraction. The Hall of the Future was all about atomic energy.

The Exhibition of Industrial Power was thought a good fit for a city where 20 per cent of the population worked in heavy industry, but in the event only around 280,000 people visited, a third of the estimated number.[35] A surviving sketch of the Atomic display shows a rather abstract depiction of atoms in motion, with electrical current flowing outwards and silhouetted faces lit by the brilliance of nuclear power. Nonetheless, it pointed to where Britain's energy focus was at this time.

The detonation of atomic bombs in Alamogordo, Hiroshima, and Nagasaki in 1945 marked a new world order in which nuclear power was key. As soon as it became clear after the war that American would pursue an isolationist atomic policy, Britain began to develop a nuclear programme. As Jonathan Hogg and Kate Brown summarise, the British government mobilised money, scientific knowledge, people, and military–industrial capacity to create both an independent nuclear deterrent and the ability to generate electricity from nuclear reactors.[36] This expensive and vast techno-political project was mostly top secret, and central to Britain's Cold War strategy. Britain detonated its first atomic bomb in 1952 at Monte Bello, off the northwestern coast of Australia. In Britain in 1953 work on Calder Hall, a so-called civil nuclear power station, began. But the entwined nature of military and civilian nuclear power is also illustrated succinctly by Calder Hall (which was located at a former military base at Windscale in Cumbria, now known as Sellafield). Its four electricity-generating Magnox reactors were trumpeted in 1956 as world-firsts and the answer to the nation's energy needs, but the real purpose of the site, and where nearly all the electricity it produced went, was the production of weapons-grade plutonium. The development of nuclear-fuelled power plants by the British government in the 1950s legitimised domestic nuclear facilities. It also built a narrative that connected complex themes of technological superiority, prestige, and national identity.[37]

Nuclear historian Jonathan Hogg describes the 1950s as a pivotal decade when public nuclear knowledge began to increase and anxieties, slowly, to build. A disaster at Windscale in 1957 certainly contributed to this. A fire in one of the reactors burned for three days, releasing a radioactive plume that spread across the region and over the sea to Ireland, contaminating pastureland. Among the isotopes spread by the plume was iodine 131, which is linked to thyroid cancer, particularly in children. Contaminated milk from a 200-square-mile zone was deemed unsafe for public consumption and 'destroyed' (in reality, it was dumped untreated in the Irish Sea). A British Pathè public information film 'Atomic Milk' (1957) informed audiences of the measures taken to contain radioactivity to restore confidence in British produce. It showed the Milk Marketing Board collecting the milk and pouring it down the drain, reassuring audiences that 'the danger is already past'. A worker who helped to put out the fire at the plant, Stan Ritson, is shown with his wife looking at a newspaper cutting of himself. 'He was radioactive for four days,' the RP voiceover informs the viewer, 'and couldn't even kiss his wife!' The tone is efficient and jaunty, but the event registered 5 on the International Nuclear Event scale, as 'an accident with wider consequences'. Only two events have reached 7, the highest point on the scale: Chernobyl and Fukushima. While news of the event was heavily censored by the state, which did not want confidence in its nuclear capacities to be damaged, it was also necessary to report the danger to avoid a public health disaster.

Despite the risks, and the problem of what to do with nuclear waste (an issue that wasn't addressed until much later, and which is still a work-in-progress), the great appeal of civil nuclear power to the state – as well as its ability to support military nuclear power – was that it promised grand scale. Just as atomic bombs dwarfed other munitions, the scale at which nuclear power reactors were being planned was huge – indeed, to make them cost-effective and safe, they *had* to be large. While wind power in 1951 was being developed at the scale of individual 100 kW turbines, Calder Hall's magnox reactors were 180 mW apiece. That said, nearly all the power they produced was used on site for plutonium production rather than feeding into the grid, but in terms of planning for a future in which electricity demands were rising, the capacity to generate large amounts of power through a relatively small number of nuclear powers stations around the nation was seductive to politicians. Through the 1950s, more nuclear power stations (Berkeley on the Severn estuary and Bradwell in Essex) were announced as plans for nuclear grew and grew. In his history of nationalised electricity Leslie Hannah noted that, due to security, the British Electricity Authority was largely shut out of these expansion plans, which were pushed by the UK Atomic Energy Authority which lobbied to expand the projected capacity through the 1950s. After Suez, the government tripled its commitment to nuclear power, seeing it as a 'technological lifebelt' from the impacts of oil insecurity.[38] This escalation, and plans for nineteen power stations, committed enormous capital investment into the next decade. Using conventional non-nuclear technology, capital expenditure on the electricity supply from 1956–57 to 1965–66 was estimated to be £2.58 billion. With the nuclear programme, it increased to £3.35 billion.[39]

Nuclear power stations tend to take longer and cost more to build than originally planned. Bradwell and Berkeley came online two years late in 1962, along with Hunterston; a fourth, Hinkley, ordered in 1957, was delivered in 1965, as was Trawsfynydd (ordered in 1959). Delays meant more interest to pay on capital and gave room for price increases to impact delivery too. In Hannah's analysis, the overall cost per kWh of electricity generated in the first two Magnox stations in their early years was nearly two-and-a-half times that of the best coal-fired power stations which the CEGB was commissioning.[40] With Hinkley Point C today under construction, well behind schedule, running to a budget increased from £18 billion to £32.7 billion, and due to produce the most expensive electricity in the British grid, many of the same issues that played out in the mid-twentieth century continue to dog the industry in the twenty-first.[41] Today, it is nuclear's perceived consistency compared to other low-carbon energy sources (wind, solar) that underpins its ongoing place in national energy planning, with an ability to 'plug the gaps' should prolonged periods of calm or cold affect renewables inputs.

Early excitement of energy 'too cheap to meter' was always misplaced, and nuclear power did not deliver on its initial promise. The atomic glow of the Hall of the Future had begun to fade, and by the end of the 1960s the government was effectively in retreat from its own nuclear policy. For wind energy, the timing and scope of nuclear power planning in Britain, along with other shifting energy and political contexts, was detrimental. Wind benefitted from a brief window of welfare-driven energy experimentalism that opened political eyes to the potential for non-fossil-fuelled energy systems that used abundant, renewable resources. In the context of nationalisation and welfare reform, the creation of the NSHEB gave an outlet for ideas to take tangible shape, and for wind energy (along with hydro-electricity) to deliver power for the public good. State research bodies such as the ERA supported industrial and technological development and, for a brief window, a turbine in Orkney fed the power grid, political imaginations, and international discussions about the future of wind energy.

But the fate of wind was tied to coal, oil, and nuclear power. For a national grid constructed around an unending supply of hydrocarbons, wind could not yet deliver at a comparable scale to reliable, if dwindling, coal. It remained inconsistent and unpredictable in nature. Uncertainty around oil pushed the British state further towards the perceived geopolitical security of nuclear power. And the willingness of individuals like Johnston and Golding to seriously explore the alternatives to the energy status quo, and test the ability of wind technology to provide power for the grid, were replaced by a politics of consensus. I don't often foray into counterfactual history, but I do wonder what might have been achieved had Britain invested even a small part of its nuclear power budget into wind energy research and development into the 1960s. Keeping up with Danish turbine refinement (which continued), sharing research, building capacity – this was a moment in which Britain relinquished a powerful international lead. In the event, the state turned away from Orkney, its turbines, and its winds – though the story of wind energy finds its way back to the islands eventually. The willingness to experiment and to explore alternatives moved out of mainstream politics and into new communities – who cranked up the 'alternative' dimensions of wind power and disavowed the role of the central state in energy development. The future of wind energy in Britain was taken up by hippies, idealists, and drop-outs. From the 1960s through to the late 1980s, if you wanted to generate electricity from the wind in Britain, you'd have to do it yourself.

4

Do-it-yourself energy

In July 1975, an old slate quarry in mid-Wales opened to the public. Nestled in the lush, green Powys landscape, over two years a group of environmentalists had transformed the site from one of old industry to new off-grid living. But this was no hermetic cult disconnected from the real world. At the Centre for Alternative Technology (CAT) an experimental community intended to act as a 'test bed for technologies and ways of living that could demonstrate workable alternatives to the mainstream'.[1] While state interest in wind energy had ebbed, and pause had been pressed on further industrial development, CAT cultivated a community of engineers, activists, enthusiasts, and visionaries who not only promoted their belief that wind energy could power a functional, thriving society: they *lived* it.

How important can a small community be to the history of energy, usually written at the scale of the national and global? What can an old slate quarry and a few wind turbines tell us about the transition from the old fossil regime to a cleaner energy future? CAT deserves a place in this history.[2] The group kept renewable energy alive in discourse and practice during a period when major investment and development had all but dried up. They worked hard to place energy at the centre of the popular environmentalism and subsequent environmental politics, which was growing in Britain in the later decades of the twentieth century. They remind us that technological expertise and environmental knowledge resides beyond the mainstream. But perhaps, above all, they show that a community can make a difference. In a time of global environmental crisis, there's hope to be found in a community which believed, and showed, that an alternative world was possible.

When Gerard Morgan-Grenville first saw the place that would become the Centre in 1973 it 'was a bit of a jungle, scattered with ruinous buildings from which birch trees grew in profusion'.[3] Neither the quarry, nor Morgan-Grenville, appeared at first glance to have the makings of a radical new vision of self-sufficiency and environmental innovation. The great-grandson of the last Duke of Buckingham and Chandos, Morgan-Grenville's early life unfolded in Establishment tradition: born in 1931, schooled at Eton, national service in the Rifle Brigade, a career as a businessman.[4] In his thirties he underwent an environmental awakening, becoming 'acutely aware' of environmental issues, and visited the United States to immerse himself in counter-culture. Time with Californian hippie communes offered instruction on what to avoid, as much as what to aspire to. 'An anarchic commune,' he wrote in 1979, 'consisting principally of unskilled couples, mostly in their twenties, often of transient loyalties to each other and the commune, apathetic about hard work, serves as an education as to how mankind could slip quietly back to the Stone Age.'[5]

But Morgan-Grenville also recalled how 'a transparent and almost infectious honesty showed in the way they thought and lived'. He admired their 'closeness to the earth' and commitment to causing no harm to people or environment. A perceived 'fragility' to their way of life was offset by a 'good in the people which shone forth'. Their concerns over the dangers of nuclear power ('it represented all that was authoritarian and secret') chimed with his own developing ideologies of anti-authoritarian 'usefulness'.[6] He returned to the UK convinced that a less environmentally deleterious way of life was achievable, and that practical skills were the missing ingredient at the communes he'd visited. In the USA he had been joined by Diana Brass, a friend who shared his privileged background and environmental concerns. With Steve Boulter, an American postgraduate with an interest in ambient energy systems, and with £20,000 from Morgan-Grenville's wealthy half-brother farmer in Kenya, the three committed to setting up a 'practical project' in the UK and scouted for possible sites. News of a 30-acre quarry with a landowner, John Beaumont (another Etonian), amenable to a 'useful' project, reached them through word of mouth. The site was secured on a hundred-year lease with a peppercorn rent of 1 shilling a year, and a group assembled around the principle of demonstrating the tools for self-sufficiency. 'In such seclusion, so far from the pressures under which most people live,' Morgan-Grenville reflected in 1985, 'I had the feeling that something new, some fresh and saner way of living might be demonstrated.'[7]

As word spread about the project, people who shared the aims and ideals of CAT began to arrive. Involvement at the Centre was on a live-in, voluntary basis. The early years consisted of making the site safe, productive, and ultimately liveable. Hydro-power was provided by a stream; gardens were dug; roofs patched and buildings repaired; and solar panels and wind turbines installed. Morgan-Grenville was not a permanent presence, alternating between his family home (Burgate House, a Grade II listed Queen Anne period house) in Surrey, and a house close to the Quarry lent to him by Eirene White, Labour peer and Minister of State for the Welsh Office. Morgan-Grenville's social connections spared him the deprivations described by the early volunteers. He continued to fundraise for and promote CAT remotely, while the group in Wales grew more autonomous. Decisions were made collectively by those on site, and wages were equal for all. Roderick James, who left his job as an architect to join the group, was appointed Director from 1975 to 1980 and Bob Todd, a former lecturer at the University of Sheffield, was Technical Director.[8]

The Centre demonstrated alternative technologies and lifestyles in a variety of ways. Volunteers were encouraged to join the group and work in return for accommodation, food, and a share in the discussions that took place. This strategy was so successful in the early years that a system had to be introduced whereby volunteers booked in advance and paid a deposit, and a cap of six at any time was introduced.[9] By 1985, 160 volunteers were participating in the Centre a year. The movement of short-term volunteers in and out of the Centre was a challenging dynamic for some of the longer-term members, but Peter Harper, the Volunteer Co-Ordinator in 1985, remarked that in terms of fulfilling CAT's educational ambitions, 'the "vols" may be our most effective export'. They left with a working understanding of small-scale renewable energy systems, able to apply and promote that knowledge beyond the confines of the quarry.

The Centre was designed to be a visitor site, where people could see technology at work in an everyday setting and contribute financially to the project through admission fees, a café, and a shop (Figure 4.1). The community and its infrastructure were the attraction: through exploring the site and talking to members, visitors were shown that 'alternative technologies', old and new – water-wheels, wind turbines, solar panels – worked in a domestic setting. In 1975, the first year of opening to the public, 15,000 people made their way to Machynlleth. In 1976, 35,000 people came. By the end of the decade, 59,000 people annually passed through the Centre.[10] These included school groups, and a specialist Education team produced resources for children and for teachers to use in classrooms. Press coverage overseas raised the profile of CAT abroad. Articles in *The Western Australian,* several Canadian newspapers, and Dutch and German press attracted visitors and volunteers from those countries and

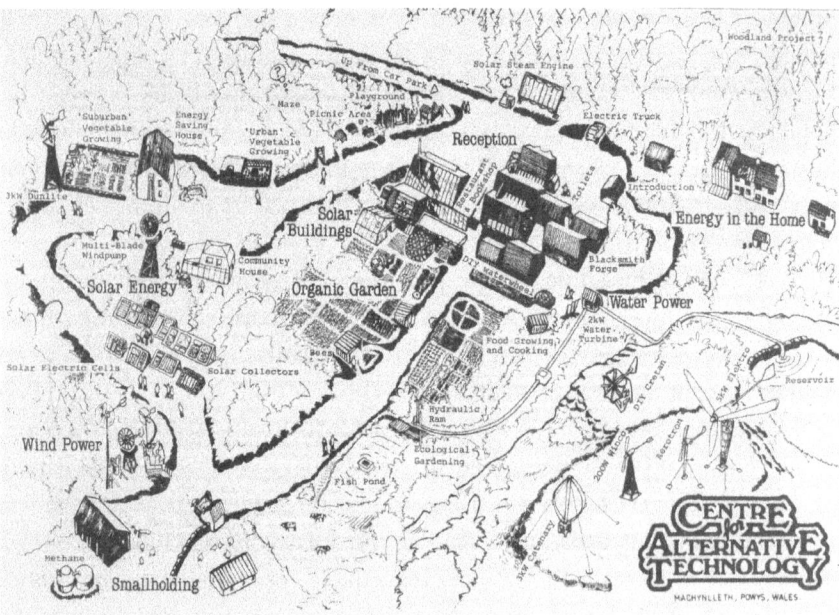

4.1 NLW CAT. Map of the Centre for Alternative Technology produced for a visitor guide.

beyond. Visitor numbers reached their peak in 1992, the same year that Britain's second commercial wind farm was built in mid-Wales, when a total of 93,500 people made their way to the Centre.[11] These numbers attest to a growing public interest in the Centre and the technology and ideas it promoted. They also show that the Centre succeeded in spreading the word about renewable and non-nuclear forms of energy to an audience that far exceeded its own members and its immediate rural surroundings. In terms of engaging people in environmental discourse, the combination of practical demonstration, lived experience, and invitation to get involved was a successful one.

CAT promoted do-it-yourself energy. They compiled up-to-date resource lists detailing what wind turbine tech was available to the individual consumer (available for purchase for 50 pence plus postage); they maintained reading lists for those who wished to do independent research; and published manuals and guides to making simple home tech, such as a small wind device made out of a bicycle wheel connected to a dynamo (as seen in action on site). This emphasis on home-spun problem-solving of global environmental issues was not unique. CAT echoed to a great extent the 'appropriate technology' movement that was active in North American environmentalist circles at the time, which critiqued industrial capitalism and its impact on the planet and sought new ways of living within identified means. The *Whole Earth catalog*, the American mail-order handbook for do-it-yourself environmentalism, was its secular bible, and CAT's modest resource lists pay homage to it in spirit, if not in scope and quality.

There are long traditions of rejecting mainstream capitalist society and going 'back to the land' in search of authenticity, skill, and comradeship that CAT could be situated within. In the nineteenth century, for example, John Ruskin and a group of followers attempted to create a new type of self-sufficient community and craft-based economy on the shores of the Lake District.[12] Like CAT, Ruskin's group sought a new model of social and economic relations through practical skills. Unlike CAT, they looked only to the past for those skills, eschewing modern technologies in favour of traditional crafts. But reflecting in 1999 on CAT's twenty-five years, members firmly placed themselves within the recent upwelling of popular environmental consciousness that occurred in North American and Europe in the 1960s and 1970s. Gerard Morgan-Grenville cited Rachel Carson's *Silent spring* (1962) and E.F. Schumacher's *Small is beautiful* (1973) as influences on his thinking prior to setting up CAT (unlike most readers, he met Schumacher at a dinner hosted by Prince Philip at Buckingham Palace, such were the social circles he moved in.)[13] Peter Harper was an affiliate of the Centre from 1983 onwards, had been actively publishing and participating in environmental discourse in the 1970s, and claims to have coined the phrase 'alternative technology' in 1972.[14] That same year, the Club of Rome's report *The limits to growth* (1972), and Edward Goldsmith's *A blueprint for survival* (1972) were published, which Harper credited as influential texts. Also in 1972 was the UN Conference on the Human Environment in Stockholm. Harper was there, as part of the 'fringe', staging an 'alternative technology' exhibition.[15]

In 1972 the Apollo space missions photographed Earth from space. Surrounded by the darkness of the galaxy, the planet was a 'blue marble', colourful and alive. The extra-terrestrial perspective of the image, together with the earlier 'Earthrise' photograph (1968), conveyed a sense of planetary vitality, but also a smallness, a fragility. The finite planet was a continuous theme in the publications and conferences of this period, which historian Emma Schroeder argues 'solidified the "Earth" as a political concern'.[16] Simultaneously, the Cold War pushed the world's nuclear powers to unprecedented levels of 'scientific' surveillance and monitoring. Geopolitical fears unlocked new understandings of Earth as a functioning ecological system.[17] With the need to maintain strategic advantage, responses to identified problems of pollution, population growth, (over) consumption, and impending nuclear disaster by environmentalists in the global north became more technological in focus.

This was far from the only type of environmentalism developing at this time, nor was it the only influence on British environmentalism. A look to South Asia in the same period, for example, reveals a wealth of environmental activism and philosophy which connected social with environmental justice and promoted bottom-up activism, not least centring the role of women.[18] Ghandian non-violence and filtered elements of South Asian spiritualism had been prominent in British hippie culture in the 1960s. Satish Kumar – the Indian-British anti-nuclear campaigner and environmental activist who undertook an 8000 mile 'peace walk' from New Delhi to Moscow, Paris, London, and Washington DC in 1962 – was a leading figure in British environmentalism by the time the CAT was active. From 1973 onwards he edited *Resurgence* magazine, a key publication for emergent British 'green' politics (it later merged with *The Ecologist*). CAT featured regularly, and members published articles promoting their work and outlook through the 1970s. According to Jane Bryant, 'if anyone could have been considered a guru at CAT it would have been Satish Kumar'.[19] He didn't join the group in Wales, however, as it 'couldn't accommodate his cow'.[20] Kumar settled with his family in North Devon, where he still lives.

On one hand, CAT was a product of its time – a Welsh reworking of a North American style of environmentalism, with international reference points. It made real beat poet Gary Snyder's vision of a planet on which the 'human population lives harmoniously and dynamically by employing a sophisticated and unobtrusive technology – in a world environment which is "left natural"'.[21] Snyder could have been describing CAT when he lauded the 'inherent aptness of communal life: where large tools are owned jointly and used efficiently'. But for all the *Whole Earth* flavours of their outputs, there are lines of connection to less self-consciously alternative or counter-cultural traditions of sustainability already at work in Britain. Take the CAT bicycle wheel turbine, for example – it used the same basic homespun technology as the 'windy gear'-powered televisions on Hoy. The emphasis on practical energy solutions places CAT within a British tradition that first identified wind as a useful 'alternative' for remote communities, as well as in an environmentalist tradition of do-it-yourself fixes. And while there were shared values and visions with the North American appropriate technology movement, there was a conscious positioning by the British collective as distinct from it.

'Alternative' carried with it a sense of a lifestyle, one more on the fringes than 'appropriate'. It underscored the choices involved as viable – a genuine alternative. Zoe Gardner characterises the movement as one that fundamentally re-examined the role of technology in modern life as 'an ecological way of critiquing the power structures of post-war society'.[22] But the use of 'alternative' also echoed the specific language used by technocrats to describe different energy systems in the middle decades of the twentieth century, suggesting that the group was not as closed off to mainstream energy discourse as might be expected, or indeed as they themselves might have thought. The trajectory of CAT bears this theory out.

Since state interest in wind power developed from the 1950s in Britain, it was discussed by government and industry as an 'alternative' energy form. Wind (and solar, wave, and tidal) energy as 'renewable' did not come into common parlance until the 1980s. The Hansard archive of parliamentary debates is a good record of when particular terms make their way into mainstream political discourse – whatever politicians say in debate in the Commons and Lords goes on record, creating a core resource for historians of British politics. There are occasional references to 'renewable resources' in the context of energy: Lord Boyd-Orr discussed timber, hydro-power, and solar energy as 'renewable resources' in the House of Lords in 1954; and with some deft wording Lord Merrivale framed nuclear power as a 'renewable natural resource' in 1959.[23] The first mention of 'renewable energy' in parliament was by Anthony Nelson, the MP for Chichester, to again describe nuclear energy;[24] and later that year by Tom King, MP for Bridgwater, in relation to the Severn Barrage proposals for tidal energy being debated at the time – edging closer to the familiar usage of renewable energy, but not quite there yet.[25] A debate in the Lords in 1975 gives a sense of how 'alternative' was used in relation to energy at the time: Lord Hannam called for more expenditure to be 'directed towards developing alternative energy resources, such as solar, wind and wave power and geothermal power'.[26] Alternative, in the mid-1970s, encompassed all that would go on to become known later as renewable energy.

When Peter Harper and CAT named their environmentally beneficial practices 'alternative technology', they aligned it with a way of thinking about energy as offering practical solutions to problems of supply and installation that was familiar to those working on energy issues and part of the political discourse of energy. This would eventually move from 'alternative' and towards 'renewable', tapping into a different energy sensibility than mid-century technocracy. CAT proved able and willing to work with both state and industry to raise the profile of wind energy and push an alternative energy agenda. At flashpoints where concerns around the safety of nuclear power in particular heightened interest in wind and other energy forms and triggered public debate, CAT acted as effective lobbyists.

There was a tension between CAT's intended autonomy from authority and its willingness to work with the state and within the frameworks it laid out. The do-it-yourself approach sat comfortably with Gerard Morgan-Grenville's hardline anti-government stance – he described the state's 'army of bureaucrats' as 'social parasites', and justified acceptance of the dole by counter-cultural hippies as an antagonism against the uses public funds were put to.[27] There is no evidence that other members of CAT shared these views, and the do-it-yourself approach also fitted with a less politically hardline emphasis on generating popular interest and capacity in wind energy that could lead to state investment rather than follow it. Why wait for state progress when a movement could be built from the ground up by generating popular interest in, and demand for, wind energy?

Whether actively anti-state or ambivalent to state-led innovation, this approach did challenge the pathways to growth favoured by government and industry in which centralised funds supported research and development by experts based at universities, research organisations, and within industry itself.[28] This was the route being taken in Denmark, where the government had formulated a strategy in the mid-1970s to reduce oil imports by building up wind capacity. A holistic approach was developed that supported producers, consumers, and suppliers. The state supported research and development support at the Risø Laboratory, in Roskilde, where manufacturers could test small wind generators designed for use in homes, farms, and institutions such as schools and hospitals. Machines could be tested for three months and be advised on technical improvements free of charge. A package of financial incentives was provided for people buying wind machines.[29] The purchase of a small wind turbine was supported by a subsidy of between 20 and 30 per cent, and value-added tax, then at 20 per cent, refunded. Lastly, the Danish electricity utilities agreed to purchase electricity from private wind turbines, at one half the unit sale price paid by the consumer. Through these policies, not only had wind energy been supported as a specialist discipline and industrial sector, but also a good relationship was established between manufacturers and the public, and small operators could benefit financially from their investment in wind technology. By the early 1980s, there were twenty manufacturers of small wind turbines operating commercially in Denmark, and, while the total market remained small at that point – about one machine per hundred households or institutional buildings, according to the Risø lab – industry, state, and public were 'all optimistic about future business'.[30]

It would take another decade for Britain to develop policy mechanisms to bridge the do-it-yourself approach with electricity as organised at a national level. While the (at least early) shunning of the state shaped the outlook and outcomes of the do-it-yourself energy movement, the reality was that energy was shaped by politics. When I spoke to Hugh Piggott, a self-taught wind turbine engineer who occasionally taught at CAT and established his own settlement at Scoraig in Scotland where he demonstrates homemade energy technologies, he attributed the Danish success to a willingness – a humility? – to develop small-scale wind technologies. The UK and the US, he argued, both held a perception that 'in order to be of any use at all you had to be generating hundreds of kilowatts or megawatts of power … trying to run before you can walk'.[31] The Danes built lots of small machines, tested them, improved them, consolidated designs, and – if the machines had been tested in the state facility – publicly shared the feedback. A functioning industry grew incrementally, but not slowly. An emphasis on practical use and testing at the small scale aligns with the outlook of CAT, but the sustained collaboration between state, industry, and private individuals in Denmark contrasted with Britain through the 1970s and 1980s.

At the beginning CAT's importance lay in showing, rather than saying, what was possible with wind and other alternative energy systems. There was a deliberate positioning of wind turbines, solar panels, and other energy technology as something that could, and should, be part of everyday life – as familiar as a garden composter or bicycle. Encountering the technology in person was a way to demystify it. It worked for many of the thousands of visitors, but not everyone came away from Machynlleth enthused about self-sufficiency and practical living. A journalist from *Harpers and Queen* stayed at the quarry in 1975. 'The people involved in this unique socio-technical research project insist that they are neither idealists nor survivalists. But, having spent a night at Llwyngwern Quarry, I am bound to tell you that survival, when there is no alternative to Alternative Technology, could be hard going unless you are something of an idealist.'[32] The journalist was relieved to leave after one night. Some of those who were there long term found their endurance tested. Jill Whitehead joined in 1974. She remembered the first summer, 'working for two months in a permanent downpour, hacking out from slate bedrock … with – well not quite bare hands, but pickaxes designed to transfer the watery contents of the trench to your face, day in day out, and retiring at the end of the day to a leaky caravan dragged from its grave in a nearby dump.'[33] One can almost feel the damp seeping through the memories.

Physical hardships were overlaid by ideological differences: 'endless candlelit discussions of "alternative" versus "appropriate" technology, anarchy versus democracy, manual versus mechanical labour ... coloured toilet paper versus white ... one member got so fed up with the hours devoted to this discussion that he festooned the loo roll holders with sprays of stinging nettles, thistles, etc; the debate never resurfaced.' Judy Williams joined in 1980 and stayed for four years. For her, 'the yawning chasms between some of our stated ideals and our actions, the rheumatism from near-zero office temperatures ... the never-ending cycle of paperwork ... and the long-standing community hassle of T-Chest hygiene, site children, etc. all got pretty wearing at times'.[34]

These women recalled the sensory dimensions of self-sufficient life, stripping away the comforting gloss of nostalgia to describe life hewn from the wet stone walls of the quarry. The difficulties of building and living in a community bound by a commitment to environmentally beneficial energy systems could have edged out small pleasures, but plenty of the accounts also describe parties, shared meals, building relationships, and a gratifying sense of purpose. Nonetheless, there is a hard edge to the memories. An intensity ran through activities. 'Things have not been as clear to me since,' said Jill Whitehead, 'and grey areas have crept in.'[35]

The clarity of purpose that CAT encapsulated, and cultivated, perhaps explains why its work, in the end, could not be constrained to the site (Figure 4.2). While the quarry could contain a community, it could not shut them off from the outside world. Members looked outwards and actively worked to promote wind energy as a viable energy system among a range of formal and informal networks of enthusiasts (technical, environmental, lifestyle). They also responded – of course they had to – to the changing politics of energy, and an international order being reshaped by fuel.

As we know, energy had long been on the minds of nation states and their changing governments. By the 1970s, the extent to which their programmes of continued economic growth depended on access to abundant, cheap fuel had deepened. The 'great acceleration' of human activity that had started in the nineteenth century took off after 1945 to reach unprecedented, planet-altering levels. Whether measured across population, GDP, fertiliser consumption, motor vehicles, international tourism, water use, or the number of McDonald's restaurants, the graphs all leap in the same upwards direction, at around the

4.2 NLW CAT 16/7. Promotional poster for the Centre for Alternative Technology. Undated, c. late twentieth century.

same mid-century marker.[36] Fuelling this expansion was, increasingly, oil. This was true of Western Europe, which, in 1952, consumed 124 million tons worth of oil (in thermal coal equivalent units); that figure had more than quadrupled to 628 million tons by 1972, 80 per cent of which came from the Middle East and North Africa.[37] Oil had accounted for only 8 per cent of Britain's energy requirements in 1950, and supplied 48 per cent by 1973.[38] Environmental movements were responding to the increasingly tangible impacts on the planet. Protecting the energy that fuelled economic growth became a political priority for national governments.

Europe had come to rely on oil from the Organisation of Petroleum Exporting Countries (OPEC), established in 1960 by the Republic of Iran, Iraq, Kuwait, Saudi Arabia, and Venezuela. By 1973 Qatar, Indonesia, Libya, the United Arab Emirates, Algeria, and Nigeria had also joined. Arab attempts to take control of domestic oil were routinely sabotaged by the West (see the Anglo-American organised coups in Iran (1953) and Iraq (1963), for example).[39] OPEC offered an economic means to leverage power by consortium, negotiating the prices at which its members would tax oil sold to the major companies. The companies had been powerful enough to dictate these prices. Conflict (not least the 1967 Arab–Israeli war), pipeline sabotages, and embargos (by Qaddafi in Libya) broke this ability. OPEC demanded a general increase in price, which also suited oil companies looking to compensate for loss of control in the region. The outbreak of war between Egypt and Israel in 1973 and subsequent cuts to supply hiked prices further. The result was the 1973–74 oil crisis, which, in the words of Timothy Mitchell, 'collapsed the postwar petroleum order and the prosperity it brought'.[40]

In Britain, oil prices quadrupled just as a National Union of Mineworkers strike began.[41] The two fossil fuel pillars of Britain's power supply, coal and oil, were in turmoil. Winter power cuts ensued. Add to this soaring inflation, and the crosshairs of finance, labour relations, energy production, industrial capacity, and social discord brought down Edward Heath's government in 1974. The legacies of this period cast long shadows in this history, some of which I'll discuss in more detail in the next chapter. But in the shorter term, the crisis created a scenario in which energy dominated political discourse.

CAT was determined that wind was not overlooked. They lobbied ministers with memos and publications that made a case for wind energy as a viable energy source at a national scale. An opportunity to make a more public intervention presented itself in 1977, when a planning application to Cumbria County Council and Copeland Borough Council was made by British Nuclear

Fuels for a plant to 'reprocess' nuclear waste from the Windscale and Calder Hall works. The waste processing plant was rebranded as Sellafield by British Nuclear Fuel Ltd in 1981.[42]

Anti-nuclear activism was not *de facto* environmental – there were strong moral, philosophical, and spiritual dimensions, for example – but there were close alignments with British and international environmental groups, with Friends of the Earth and Greenpeace spearheading anti-nuclear campaigns, for instance.[43] CAT made their anti-nuclear stance known through their self-published literature, but when the British Nuclear Fuel planning application to build a new processor at Windscale triggered a public inquiry in 1977, it created a public platform on which the limits of fossil fuels and the dangers of nuclear energy could be challenged. CAT submitted a published pamphlet, *An alternative energy strategy for the United Kingdom* as written evidence to the inquiry. It made a case for phasing out fossil fuels and nuclear energy and investing in wind, wave, and hydro-power.[44]

Through *An alternative energy strategy for the United Kingdom* we see a different dimension of CAT. While visitors to the site encountered alternative-energy-as-alternative-lifestyle, the CAT that engaged with government and industry bodies worked as a think-tank and aimed to intervene in national energy planning. No do-it-yourself advice here. They were speaking directly to the concerns of governments and elites. Sir Martin Ryle, the Astronomer Royal and recent recipient of the Nobel Prize for Physics, said in the preface: 'we have become accustomed to believing that our standard of living and full employment depend on an ever-increasing consumption of energy … if we continue in this belief, the energy shortage initiated by the exhaustion of the world's oil reserves will, by the end of the century, forcibly curtail the present trends in the worst crisis civilization has yet experienced'.[45] What followed was a case to develop wind, wave, and tidal energy to 'not only solve our own energy and economic problems, but contribute to a safer future for the world'. One can't help but notice that, while the oil crises were a complex fusion of postcolonial power struggles, ideological and actual warfare, labour demands, and corporate interests, the solutions proffered by CAT were focused on the sources of energy, and not the means by which it would be managed, supplied, or used.

The strategy reframed energy not along lines of supply and demand, but in terms of 'capital' (fuel reserves), which was finite, and 'income' (the flow of energy into the Earth from the sun) – also technically finite, but abundant and large. Unlike fossil fuels or nuclear energy, the energy income from 'ambient', 'renewable', 'unconventional', 'alternative' sources of power, it said, 'is inexhaustible, diffuse, non-polluting, and seldom dangerous'.[46] It promoted wind, wave, hydro, and biomass sources of power, and suggested the widespread uptake of heat pumps (which are only now becoming more available in the UK, though widely used in the Scandinavian countries). By 2025 wind and wave energy (categorised together) could supply 130 TWh/year, it estimated. Anticipating arguments that the loss of fossil fuel and nuclear energy systems would result in high unemployment, the strategy made a case for combining renewables and coal to create a stabilised energy provision in the short term: 'a first step in the inevitable, long-term adaptation to living in balance with income energy sources'.[47] The strategy underscores how central anti-nuclear sentiment was to the CAT. The group were not pitching renewable energy as the low-carbon alternative to high-carbon fossil fuels so much as the clean and safe alternative to nuclear technology. Their most enduring ideology, though, was belief in practicality. If making alternative energy work meant partnering with coal, then so be it.

This was also demonstrated by the success of several businesses which started out at CAT. Those who worked more on the technical side of things, putting up and maintaining turbines and such like, became highly skilled in an area that had been largely neglected in the wider world. A box of papers in the National Library of Wales documents seven years of commissioning and operating a new prototype wind turbine, the MS4, in the 1990s. Error reports, faxes to the manufacturer, software and mechanical issues show a machine that turned out to be – to use the description in the papers – 'a lemon'.[48] The papers 'stand as a memorial to Tim B and the other engineers who dedicated themselves to this elegant but dysfunctional machine'.[49] The turbine technology was imperfect, and those who worked on it had to be electricians, mechanics, and engineers with bags of patience and determination. When the single turbine tripped the circuitry, or blew a fuse, or leaked oil, the members fixed it themselves. This gave them a skillset that would become more commercially valuable as the technologies became more available.

In 1982 centre members started an electronics company called Dulas Engineering, making the control equipment for renewable energy systems. In 1988 it became an independent, employee-owned company and in 1990 it moved to the village of Eglwysfach. Dulas has now been in operation for over forty years, supplying the renewables industry with wind monitoring equipment, data instruments, and logging systems. It installed its first off-grid solar photovoltaic systems in 1993, and the first grid-connected solar systems in Powys in 2003.[50] It also has a hydropower arm of the business. Because CAT was developing and working on renewable technologies before a commercial industry was in place, it got a head-start in identifying what issues, and fixes, were needed to keep the technology running. When the rest of the UK caught up, Dulas and others were primed to offer their services.

Perhaps the best-known and most important of the CAT commercial offshoots was Ecogen, formed in 1991 by two ex-CAT staff along with members of the Cornwall Energy Group. Tim Kirby, who had worked at CAT, became the company Chairman and had a long career working in renewables. Ecogen married CAT's belief in wind energy with an eye for its commercial promise. It operated at scale, constructing large wind farms, including one in Powys that became an early focus of debates on the visual impact of turbines in the landscape (see Chapter 6). Ecogen effectively proved CAT's broad principle: that small-scale energy development, use, and expertise led to successful large-scale energy infrastructure. It built wind farms, but its founders had started out fixing single turbines.

Through these businesses, CAT made a significant impact on a nascent British wind industry. The years of mending, tinkering, and improving available wind turbine technology had not been wasted. In fact, they provided the technical expertise and training to support others ready to invest in wind as viable energy source. The move to a more commercial mindset was reflected at CAT, which had a new Director by 1988. Roger Kelly led an organisational 'gear change' which saw CAT become a public limited company and issue £1 million worth of shares.[51] The money was invested in repairing and improving the site, which left behind its 'living experiment' sensibility – more staff lived off-site and visitors could no longer look around the houses. CAT moved away from its communitarian roots and towards its current incarnation as an educational charity 'dedicated to researching and communicating positive solutions for environmental change'.[52] Still at Machynlleth, today one could opt to do a short course on organic farming or woodland management, or a postgraduate degree in sustainable architecture. Renewable energy still features, but sustainability (a broad and malleable category) is the central theme. It is, perhaps unsurprisingly, a more professional operation these days.

CAT serves as more than a quirky footnote in the history of wind energy. It shows that valuable knowledge and expertise have been generated from grassroots organisations and collectives when state and big business have been too short-sighted, distracted, or invested elsewhere to do what is needed. The capacity for innovation to spring from small groups is under-appreciated in today's wind industry, where the emphasis stays firmly on scale, moving towards ever-bigger (turbines, farms) as the factor in building ever-better energy systems. But, as past and recent energy crises have shown, the energy industry serves markets which operate to make profits for shareholders, not better systems for societies. The record-breaking profits enjoyed by oil and gas companies in the wake of soaring bills in Britain in 2022 emphasised how little agency or choice most people still have when it comes to how they heat and power their homes. CAT's do-it-yourself model of energy generation holds new appeal and potential at a time when 'consumers' are beholden to companies who do not work in our, or the planet's, interests. One roof of solar panels, or one small turbine in a field or garden, might not change much. But a national, joined-up, supportive system in which ordinary people can contribute to clean generation of electricity? That could be transformative. The following chapters show how conditional the dominant 'Big Wind' model was on the political ideology of the aftermath of the oil crises and the neoliberalism of the late 1980s. CAT reminds us that alternatives always exist.

5

Turning a profit

From my childhood bedroom window, I could see the UK's first commercial wind farm. I didn't realise this at the time. I knew it just as Delabole, where the wind turbines stood on a ridge locally known for being very consistently shrouded in cloud and drizzle. The village is intersected by the B3314 road, off which routes to the surfing beaches and fishing villages of north Cornwall peel, but Delabole has so far largely avoided the gaze of holiday makers and the affliction of second homes that follows them elsewhere in the county. The community has a church, Methodist chapel, primary school, fish and chip shop, and a rowdy annual beer festival. Strung out along the road, the village maintains a defiant greyness, an affinity with the mizzle and the purplish slate quarried there.

It's a windy place, only a mile or two from high cliffs that rise out of the Atlantic. In the age of sail, ships passing in and out of the Bristol Channel would give this rocky coast a wide berth if they could, fearing shipwreck. Prevailing southwesterly winds, ocean swells, and strong tides create a dynamic, energetic shoreline. Like Orkney, the Hebrides, and West Wales, winds that have gained strength over the long fetch of open oceans hit land with force. The trees grow low and bent on the southwest – northeast diagonal, wind-shaped, and bowed.

In November 1991, ten tall Vestas turbines were raised in Delabole, visible for miles around. The first commercial wind farm in Britain was situated on a traditional farm, owned by the Edwards family, who sold their dairy herd but still grew organic oats and horse feed on site. Paul, Philippa, and their son Martin became interested in alternative energy following a proposal to build a nuclear power station at Luxulyan in central Cornwall in 1981. It triggered protests and debates in the county, which at the time imported all its energy. Paul Edwards began to explore possibilities for producing electricity through wind turbines on his land and visited Denmark in 1983 to learn more about wind power. Discussions with the South West Electricity Board in the 1980s raised the practical challenges facing wind power enthusiasts: 'there were no grants, the payments for surplus electricity were tiny, and the machines available were too small. It would have been totally uneconomic.'[1] That changed when the electricity industry was (re)privatised in 1989–90.

Hydrocarbons flow in

Several significant energy and political developments created a context in which re-privatisation could occur. The first was the opening up of domestic oil and gas from the North Sea. A gas field had been identified off the Gröningen coast in the Netherlands in 1959. This raised the interest of oil companies that the North Sea geology could also hold large amounts of gas and oil.[2] Oil was first struck in 1969 by Phillips Petroleum Company, an American company working in Norwegian waters. The Ekofisk oil field lies around 320 km southwest of Stavanger and remains one of the most productive in the North Sea. (If you've ever thought that the story of North Sea oil deserved a *Mad-Men* style period drama treatment, then, as with the oil, the Norwegians got there first. Allow me to direct you to the excellent television drama *Lykkeland*, broadcast on the BBC as *State of Happiness*.) Norway developed its domestic oil and gas industry to create a state-owned company (STATOIL) to control development and channel profits into a national fund. The Norwegian Government Pension Fund Global (commonly known as the Oil Fund or *Oljefondet*) invests wealth from the petroleum industry into international financial markets, so as to remain independent from the Norwegian economy. It is the world's largest single sovereign wealth fund, and in 2019 its value passed 10 trillion kroner ($1 trillion). This wealth funds the nation's social costs and is worth over 2.5 million kroner (c. $250k) per subject.

Oil from Britain's Forties field came on-stream in 1975, flowing into Cruden Bay in Aberdeenshire. The year before, Edward Heath's Conservative government had been defeated at the polls and felt themselves 'humiliated' by striking British mineworkers exerting political power through the oil crisis.[3] The main party manifestos from the 1974 election reveal how energy had assumed a central place in discussions of industrial policy and economic growth. The Conservatives spoke of an 'urgent need to make Britain as self-sufficient in energy as possible', while Labour were determined to ensure that 'North Sea and Celtic Sea oil and gas resources are in full public ownership'.[4] 'We cannot accept,' Labour argued, 'that the allocation of available world output should continue to be made by multi-national oil companies and not by Governments. We will not permit Britain's resources to be parcelled out in this way.'[5] But even after a Labour electoral victory (albeit with a majority of just three seats), full nationalisation along Norwegian lines never materialised. The British state was heavily invested in the existing oil companies – it held a majority share of BP and Shell operated as a partly British company on the global stage. Oil historian Giuliano Garavini argues that because of this close relationship, 'the resistance of fossil capitalism against state intervention was much stronger' than in other industries – and in turn the state more accepting of that resistance.[6] BP and Shell unsurprisingly pushed back hard against any attempts to redirect their lucrative new revenue streams to the public purse.

Harold Wilson's government also wanted to keep the coal industry on side, which was nervous that oil would reduce their power and influence. In the end, the government shied away from the proposed fully nationalised National Hydrocarbon Company, to instead establish the British National Oil Company (BNOC). This was a state oil firm of sorts: it had a right to buy 51 per cent of the oil produced in the North Sea fields at market prices from the companies, but no control of the extraction process. The political discourse moved from public ownership to public 'participation' in oil.[7] This new national – but not nationalised – resource eased reliance on imports and positioned Britain as an energy exporter. The 'right to purchase' and access to markets as a substitute for ownership of infrastructure and/or the site of production is something we see again as a market for renewables was developed.

By the next election in 1979, the Conservatives used oil as a prime example of how private enterprise could create jobs and wealth 'for the nation' through generating taxable private revenue.[8] Re-elected under Margaret Thatcher's leadership, the government pursued a politics of neoliberalism, whereby, to quote the historian Thomas Turnbull, 'competition could unleash the "general pressures" of the market upon nationalised industries'. Competitive free markets would drive the creation of wealth instead of state-operated industry.

By 1983 the Conservative neoliberal project was fully underway. Britain was the world's fifth largest oil producer and the North Sea success story was pitched as 'a triumph of private enterprise for the nation's benefit'.[9] This wasn't hyperbole: the year before, in 1982, the contribution to the UK economy that energy as a sector made peaked, at 10.4 per cent, thanks to the oil and gas influx.[10] Juan Carlos Boué has calculated that had the United Kingdom followed the Norwegian model of state ownership of its oil resources, the nation would have benefitted between 2002 and 2015 alone from $324 billion fiscal reserves.[11] Instead, the oil companies profited. The North Sea gave Thatcher a consistent source of fossil fuels that pleased the financial markets and secured electricity generation and industrial activity, thereby weakening the negotiating power of the Coal Board and National Union of Mineworkers. She and her energy minister Nigel Lawson could pursue their project of privatisation of state industry, starting with British Telecom in 1984, followed by British Gas in 1986, and electricity in 1989.

Privatisation split the electricity industry into its component parts. The Central Electricity Generating Board was broken up into two companies: National Power and Power Gen, which accounted for 60 per cent and 40 per cent of conventional generation capacity respectively. Meanwhile the twelve functioning nuclear power stations were placed in a state-owned holding entity, Nuclear Electric. (Nuclear was a complication in the process of privatisation, for reasons I'll go into below.)[12] The grid network had to be separated out from the rest of the industry, with shares taken by the twelve regional electricity companies, which in turn were sold to the public in 1990.[13] The UK government retained a 40 per cent stake in the grid at this point, which was sold in 1995. Once on the open market, British electricity companies were later snapped up by other national utilities, with PowerGen now E.ON UK, owned by E.ON (Germany), National Power split into businesses owned by German utility company RWE and French company Engie, and Nuclear Electric now, via a series of splits, EDF Energy, wholly owned by the French state company *Électricité de France* (EDF). As well as diverting the profits of oil to the pockets of oil company shareholders, (re)privatisation stripped the existing national assets of electricity generation and provision and sold them off.

A market had been created where companies competed to generate electricity and sell it. This was something that wind energy supporters had been crying out for as a way to make wind energy profitable. They had not received the levels of state investment, incentives, and subsidies – nor the mechanism to sell power to the grid – that had successfully stimulated the Danish wind industry over a decade earlier. Here, at last, was one of those things. An electricity market where multiple suppliers were buying power from multiple providers made it newly possible, in theory, to sell wind-generated electricity, thereby covering the costs of buying a turbine. As long as supply met demand, it didn't matter how the electricity was produced – there was no distinguishing between coal-fired or nuclear-powered or wind-generated electricity once it was in the grid system.

If we turn our attention back to Delabole and the Edwards, their plan for a wind farm began to look viable. They still faced the challenges of finding financial backing and obtaining planning permission, as well as negotiating the contract with the supplier, the Department of Energy, and the Office of Electricity Regulation. But in principle, if they could secure a decent rate for the electricity they produced, they could 'farm' the wind for profit – producing a commercial product that could be sold to customers, no different (though of course very different) to milk or beef or oats. A European Commission grant of £300,000 shored up the finances of the scheme; National Power and South West Electricity Board (SWEB) also took shares. The Edwards projected that with each of the ten turbines making profits of 9 pence per kWh of energy, the £3.5 million investment should pay for itself by 1998.[14] It wasn't completely smooth sailing: a planning application to North Cornwall District Council generated two public meetings, visits by council officers to the farm, and visits by two councillors to a Danish wind farm before it was passed.[15] But it did succeed and ultimately with the strong backing of the chairman of the district planning committee, Peter Wonnacott, who declared that 'these experimental projects have to be got going'.[16]

In interviews the family were modest in their ambitions for the farm, perhaps to soothe concerns over large-scale landscape transformation. Paul Edwards, quoted in the *Guardian*, was circumspect. 'We get regular storm damage to buildings here and the wind is sometimes a real nuisance,' he said, 'It will be nice to get something back for a change.'[17] Ten turbines were needed to make the wind farm financially viable, and ten turbines were put up. In 2011, the wind farm was 'repowered' and the old Vestas replaced with newer, bigger machines. Today, four Enercon E70 turbines generate 9.3 MW, more than doubling the 4 MW produced by the ten earlier models. But in their day, the Vestas were some of the largest and most powerful turbines available. 'All our decisions have to be taken on a strictly economic basis, there is no money in farming to subsidise the turbines or vice versa,' said Paul Edwards at the time. 'We do not expect to get rich but we think it will work.'[18] The margins for both failure and profit were slim. The wind farm had to stand on its own feet.

A privatised electricity industry created a market in which power generation was bought by distributors and sold on to consumers. This changing context was key in establishing a wind industry whereby some individuals, like the Edwards, and, increasingly, large companies could begin to turn a profit from the wind. But before we hail the power of the market, there was one other critical mechanism at play. Like so much of this history, it relates to other energy sources.

Market obligations

Thatcher was not an advocate of wind energy. She wanted to replace coal with domestic oil and gas – and more nuclear power. Energy scholar and government adviser Dieter Helm suggests that 'nuclear power held a fascination for her: as a scientist, for its technical achievements; as an advocate for a strong defence policy; and, as an opponent of the miners, in the form of an insurance policy'.[19] But nuclear power remained, as it always had been, very expensive. It took a lot of time and money to build nuclear power stations, making capital investment costs high and returns slow. To finance their construction, the government had always committed to very long contracts that locked in guaranteed prices for the power produced. The need for stringent health and safety protocols and the issue of waste materials meant that operational costs stayed substantial too. For all Thatcher's belief in a free market economy, electricity produced by nuclear power remained (and remains) significantly more expensive than that produced by coal. It couldn't compete on the open market. And, *glasnost* notwithstanding, nuclear power sites remained strategically sensitive. So, while other industries were privatised, nuclear was separated out as Nuclear Electric and remained under state control until 1996. At this point, the five newer gas-cooled reactors were privatised as British Energy, but the market would not accept the seven old Magnox reactors and the government had to use public ownership to secure these stranded assets.[20] Government support for nuclear power, and its commitment to a competitive market economy as a mechanism for stimulating trade and industry, had nothing to do with a stimulation of a renewable energy boom. But both things were consequential for a nascent wind industry.

The miner's strikes and international oil crises didn't turn Britain away from fossil fuels. In fact, reliance on fossil fuels deepened. A coal embargo to power stations on one hand, and the availability of North Sea oil and gas on the other, in the short term resulted in many of the power stations switching to oil. In 1984–85 the amount of diesel fuel burned by power plants increased from 131,000 tons per week to 650,000 tons per week as the strikes drew to a close.[21]

The promise of North Sea oil and gas was darkened considerably by a disaster in the North Sea in 1988, on the Piper Alpha platform northeast of

Aberdeen. At the time the world's single largest oil producing platform, Piper Alpha accounted for 10 per cent of all North Sea oil and gas production. It exploded into flame on the night of 6 July 1988, killing 167 men on board. Only sixty-one men were rescued from the sea. It remains the world's worst offshore oil and gas disaster and Occidental Petroleum, who owned the platform, never faced criminal charges for safety lapses. Occidental's owner Armand Hammer was a personal friend of Thatcher, who thanked him for his 'warm humanity and generosity' around the disaster.[22] A public memorial was opposed by Occidental and self-funded by the Piper Alpha Families and Survivors Association and Aberdeen City Council and designed by Sue Jane Taylor. She recalls that it was a struggle for the Association to raise the funds, and to save embarrassment the Scottish Office stepped in to meet the £100,000 target. Only £14,000 was donated by all the companies operating in the North Sea at the time.[23]

Longer term, it was gas that fuelled a major change in British electricity production. In a privatised system companies looked for the cheapest way to supply electricity to consumers and industrial customers. Gas had been seen as a 'premium' fuel suitable for domestic heating and cooking and too limited for large-scale power production. But the development of large gas turbines for energy production in the US, and Britain's own North Sea reserves, made gas a newly attractive and cheap form of power generation. In 1989 there were no combined-cycle gas turbine power stations (CCGTs) in the UK. By 1993, there were fifteen in operation or under construction, providing 8.9 GW of generating capacity.[24] Smaller than the coal or nuclear power stations, CCGTs had low capital costs, were fast to build, and gas prices were low. The 1990s 'dash for gas' was precipitated not because of demand as such, but because gas was so competitive on the market.

Another dimension also fed the dash: growing concern around emissions and particularly the effects of acid rain (caused by sulphur dioxide: SO_2). The European Union introduced a Large Combustion Plants Directive in 1988 to cap SO_2 emissions, and in 1994 the UK signed the UN Convention on Long-Range Transboundary Pollution which committed it to a 70 per cent reduction on 1980 levels of SO_2. Around 70 per cent of the UK's SO_2 was emitted by power station chimneys.[25]

Unlike coal-fired power plants, CCGTs emitted virtually no sulphur, ash, or dust. (They do emit carbon dioxide.) While cleaning equipment could be fitted to 'scrub' existing coal plants and be incorporated into new coal plants, it was cheaper to switch to gas to meet the targets and build new CCGTs.

Power companies went for fuel 'switching' over fuel 'scrubbing'. Other perceived benefits were that the CCGTs were smaller and so less impactful in landscapes; and gas was piped in, so they produced little road traffic. There was relatively little public opposition to the arrival of multiple gas-fired power stations to the UK energy map in the 1990s, while government supported them on both public health and environmental grounds.

The privatised electricity sector suited gas. Nuclear power, by contrast, struggled to compete – its baked-in expenses a turn-off for a competitive energy market. But it was too expensive, and too symbolic, to abandon – and so Thatcher and Lawson rigged the system. The Non-Fossil Fuel Obligation (NFFO) was introduced by Sections 32 and 33 of the 1989 Electricity Act. It required a certain amount of public electricity supply to come from non-fossil fuel sources and was intended to guarantee a market for nuclear power: energy suppliers *had* to buy a percentage of their electricity from nuclear power stations or face a fine.

Renewables advocates saw a golden opportunity. The category was 'non-fossil fuel', not 'nuclear power', and this opened up the possibility of including other low-carbon energy sources. The wind industry grabbed it and lobbied for official extension of the policy to include their sector. The European Commission also requested their inclusion, in line with its competition policy.[26] The twist in the story of British wind energy is that the complex politics of fossil fuels and nuclear power created the opening that gave low-carbon energy a commercial future.

The NFFO underscores the selectivity of the neoliberal logic that markets self-regulate industry. It was applied to some industries, such as coal – where it eroded decades of political capital and labour protections, and gas – where it led to rapid growth, but not the nuclear industry. It also shaped the emergence of a profitable wind industry in some particular ways. It created a competitive market where prospective wind schemes could bid against each other in an auction to secure contracts for power generation. And it created incentives by applying penalties to electricity suppliers who failed to meet their obligations that were paid back to those that did. The competition drove down generation costs, as bidders kept their pricing low in order to win the contracts (even though this decreased the chances of making profit) – so far, so free-market! But it also meant that a significant proportion of proposed projects did not materialise, as if the market prices changed and profit looked unlikely, a sensible successful bidder – who'd likely already pitched low, to win the auction – would pull the project. Policy analyst Paolo Agnolucci gathered data on the rate of non-completed projects: in 1991, 33 per cent did not materialise, rising to a high of 61 per cent in 1998. Even at the lowest rate of non-completion (in the first year of the NFFO, 1990), one in five proposed projects were not carried forward. It meant that many of the proposed wind energy schemes existed in principle but were never actually built.

The NFFO succeeded in creating a market for wind power. But with a high project incompletion rate, it failed to massively alter the proportion of renewable energy being produced in England and Wales. In 1990, under 2 per cent of electricity supply came from renewable sources; by 2004, that had risen only to 3 per cent. Compared to its European neighbours of Denmark and France, Britain undoubtedly expanded its renewables sector, but it did not transform its energy portfolio in this period.

Critics also highlighted the bureaucratic system bidders had to navigate as a further factor in limiting renewables growth. A prospective wind project had to submit an expression of interest to the Non-Fossil Purchasing Agency, which was then assessed by the electricity regulator, with final reports made jointly by the Department for Trade and Industry (DTI) and the regulator, and a final price offer fixed by DTI. This was in addition to acquiring planning permissions. Transaction costs were quite high, and this coupled with the competitive nature of the auction meant that large industry actors with plenty of money and staff behind them were advantaged. Smaller wind energy projects – individual farmers, local cooperatives, community-run schemes – found it hard to navigate, let alone compete.

The members of CAT were more engaged with energy policy than most, keeping copies of white papers and energy policy papers – but their records hold a mountain of paperwork for lengthy negotiations with the Non-Fossil Purchasing Agency and the Office of Electricity Regulation just to receive consent for a single turbine.[27] The system had not been set up to help small enterprises and communities; it favoured large companies able to take risks and employ people trained to navigate the bureaucracy and process the paperwork.

Within in this context, the Edwards' achievement and their historic first commercial wind farm is one characterised by perseverance, over years of policy change, to finally realise a vision for wind energy. Visionaries have consistently driven wind forward when state and industry see no reason to pursue it – from Edward Golding, and his wind research unit in the 1950s, to the Centre for Alternative Technology group, to the Edwards family. Working in very different spheres, and at very different times, they shared an ability to imagine a world with wind energy, while living in a world without.

The Edwards' achievement at Delabole should also be recognised as atypical in that it remained a small family endeavour of the type structurally disadvantaged by the NFFO. This is not to say small-scale wind farms did not occur under these policies, but rather that they favoured businesses that could weather limited profit projections, relatively short-term contracts, and the uncertainty of the auction. The government strategy in favour of 'big' wind technology continued beyond the NFFO scheme, which ran until it was replaced by the Renewable Obligation in 2002. It rested on an assumption that the bigger the technology and/or scale of the scheme, the cheaper the electricity produced would be – and so better for the consumer, and the shareholder. But as energy policy analysts Catherine Mitchell and Peter Connor note, the total costs and benefits of technology development are not encapsulated within a price/kWh.[28] They highlight the way that large offshore wind farms often require additional major infrastructure development (roads, docks, transport links, grid connectivity) which, when costs are fully accounted for, may or may not alter their competitiveness relative to other technologies. (The Delabole wind farm did not require new roads to be built, and turbines were placed by hedgerows to keep productive farmland available.) An 'energy humanities' perspective can expand this further. If we understand 'costs' to include, but also go beyond, money and encompass other elements both vital and valuable to a successful energy project, we might consider landscape impact, engagement with stakeholders and communities, and effects on wildlife and ecosystems in assessments of 'costs and benefits'. In this richer reading of costs, a large wind farm produces more power but at more cost. Small-scale wind schemes are low-cost, and offer low-risk, but not large-scale, quantities of energy. British wind energy policy has consistently reinforced relatively narrow visions of large onshore and offshore wind farms as the dominant productive model, at the cost (pun intended) of micro-technologies and diverse uses.

The science and politics of energy

While mechanisms designed to control coal, nuclear, oil, and gas ultimately shaped a new place for wind energy in the national supply of electricity, the industry began to grow at a time when environmental issues were becoming more acute – and more prominent. In the early 1980s, Scandinavian countries had reported acid rain, caused by air pollution arriving on the prevailing westerly winds, damaging forests and rivers. The issue became a political one as international cooperation was sought, but not immediately given, to reduce carbon and sulphur dioxide emissions. In the US under Reagan, science and industry conflicted over the issue.[29] In the UK, industrial interests – the Coal Board – emphasised the 'uncertainty' of acid rain science, and the state called on its scientific organisations to study and accumulate their own data on the subject. Meanwhile, the issue struck a public nerve through reporting and environmental campaigning. Demonstrators dumped a coffin of dead fish outside the Royal Society, which was advising the government on the issue.[30]

One outcome of the acid rain issue was increased international discussion around emissions. West Germany and the Scandinavian countries proposed a 30 per cent club of nations who committed to reducing sulphur dioxide emissions by this figure. Thatcher's government was initially very cautious on the issue, questioning the science. The 1984 Select Committee on the Environment made its report on the matter, and having found the science credible and concerning, recommended joining the 30 per cent club.[31] By 1986, policy to cut emissions was introduced (increasing nuclear energy provision also spoke to this aim). Another issue shifting perceptions of emissions and global environmental change in this period was the discovery of a hole in the ozone layer over Antarctica. The link between chlorofluorocarbons (CFCs) and the depletion of ozone had been known since the 1970s, with some calls to ban CFCs for non-essential use such as in aerosols. In Britain, these calls had been seen to threaten industry and were not taken up. But the discovery of the ozone hole by the British Antarctic Survey changed that. The scientists had actually detected it in 1981 but could not believe their results; they eventually published in *Nature* in 1985.[32] Nations moved to agree tighter restrictions on the use of damaging chemicals. The Montreal Protocol (1987) agreed an international phasing out of CFCs.

Thatcher began to speak about environmental issues in her major speeches, firstly to the Royal Society, in 1988, and on the world stage, to the United Nations General Assembly in New York, in 1989. There she spoke about the 'scale of the damage we are doing' [to the planet], listing increased carbon emissions, the destruction of the rainforests, damage to the ozone layer, and rising human populations. 'Put in its bluntest form,' she continued, 'the main threat to our environment is more and more people, and their activities: the land they cultivate ever more intensively; the forests they cut down and burn; the mountain sides they lay bare; the fossil fuels they burn; the rivers and the seas they pollute.'[33] The issues mirror the topics that environmental groups such as Greenpeace and Friends of the Earth – critical of the government – were campaigning on. It is hard to parse Thatcher's commitment to neoliberal economic growth on the one hand, and her record on raising climate change and other environmental issues on the world stage on the other. Jon Agar, the historian who has worked most on the relationship between Thatcher and science, has found little engagement with environmentalists by her government, but sustained and close relationships with science in a period when environmental research and climate change in particular was becoming the leading issue. There were reputational benefits to be had. In her UN speech, Thatcher talks about 'a letter I received only two weeks ago from a British scientist on board a ship in the Antarctic Ocean', a canny way to convey an image of an attentive leader, in tune with the most-up-to-date science.

The environmental platform also allowed Thatcher to amplify her vision of a nuclear future, and bat down the environmentalists and activists who opposed it – a substantial number in the decade that had seen the Greenham Common protests (1981–2000), the Chernobyl disaster (1986), and the bombing of Greenpeace's anti-nuclear campaign ship *Rainbow Warrior* by the French state (1985). One of the key solutions to global environmental issues was, she argued, 'nuclear energy which – despite the attitude of so-called greens – is the most environmentally safe form of energy'.

Environmental politics is interesting in this period. Popular environmentalist groups in the West operated from a broadly leftist position: campaigns to protect rainforests, end commercial whaling, and call for nuclear disarmament critiqued overconsumption, rampant capitalism, and the political status quo. But environmentalism has never been the sole domain of the left. In the early twentieth century, tangled ideologies connected human health to nature and linked organic farming to eugenics, to feed white supremacy movements in Europe and the US. The Nazis famously invoked the idea of 'blood and soil' to support their racist hierarchies.[34] The Conservative political tradition in Britain has always drawn on notions of class-delineated land ownership-as-stewardship and, in the next chapter, we'll see how the arrival of wind turbines to the British landscape upset conservative (with a small c) attitudes to land use and some prominent Conservatives (with a big C) in particular, including one of Thatcher's aides. But Thatcher herself did not cede climate science to the left. She used it to shore up her programme for economic growth. 'Resist the simplistic tendency to blame multinational industry for the damage which is being done to the environment' she instructed the UN. Only they could 'generate the wealth to pay for the protection of the environment'.

It is worth remembering that by the late 1980s Thatcher's popularity was at an all-time low; politically she was being challenged from within her own party. In the meantime, environmentalism had emerged as a political presence. The Ecology Party renamed itself the Green Party in 1985 and in the 1989 European Parliament elections it won 2.3 million votes. Environmental issues were no longer niche. By publishing the first environment-focused white paper, *This common inheritance*, the Conservative government sought to join the politics of individualism and growth they had overseen for a decade with a position as a global environmental leader. The glue between the joins was sometimes visible: on Transport, for example, the white paper highlights the levels of carbon and greenhouse gas emissions coming from cars; it simultaneously asserts (in bold text) that 'wide car ownership is an important aspect of freedom and choice'. The solution? To aid consumer choice by providing information on fuel efficiency.[35]

Politics was changing at the end of the twentieth century. With the Berlin Wall, the old geopolitical divides of the Cold War were torn down. David Edgerton describes a sense, in 1989, that 'it was time to get rid of the grim old politics of production and embrace consumption'.[36] This fits with the changing social and political positioning of wind energy. While after the Second World War it fitted into narratives of rebuilding and recovery, a practical means to improve welfare through electricity, by the end of the century a commercial wind industry supplied power to a consumer society. It was not a production stop-gap anymore, but a growth sector. Added to this was the sheen of environmentalism. Pollution, rainforests, and whaling were emotive global issues and the subject of high-profile and innovative campaigns. As climate awareness grew, so too did the potential for wind energy to become part of the available toolbox, a means to respond to the issue of carbon emissions in particular. The industry was attuned to this. The threat to a planetary future provided a clear rationale for a wind-powered future.

Britain's wind industry had some catching up to do. Denmark's wind industry was well-established, and home to most of the technological and manufacturing expertise available. The turbines installed at Delabole, and many other UK wind farms since, were built in Denmark by companies such as Vestas. Denmark supplied turbines to the Californian wind boom of the 1980s. There had been no wind turbines in California in 1980. By 1991, the peak of the boom, there were 16,387.[37] Federal and state policies offered tax cuts for investment in wind energy, prompting a rush on land in the Californian interior where strong, hot winds blow consistently. The United States had launched a federal wind programme by the end of 1973, and spent $427.4 million by 1988, vastly outstripping Denmark's $19.1 million and Germany's

$103 million in the same period.[38] Most of the money went on developing megawatt turbines in a programme managed by NASA, with aerospace and military subcontractors such as Boeing, McDonnell Douglas, Lockheed, General Electric, and Westinghouse.[39] However, the American machines were plagued by breakages, and of the only 52 per cent of turbines that operated reliably in California in 1985, nearly all had been bought from Danish companies. Persistent machinery issues, and a reduction in state subsidies, meant that Californian wind contracted after the initial 1980s wind rush. Large wind farms remain in California, where coastal hinterlands meet the desert. In 2021, wind generated 7.8 per cent of in-state electricity generation, and (with imports) 11.4 per cent of the overall power mix.[40]

Renewable energy was also in the ascendant in West Germany, where a coalition of environmentalists, scientists, and members of the Social Democratic Party challenged the dominant energy system fuelled by coal and nuclear power and proposed an *Energiewende*. The oil crises and the Chernobyl disaster (which resonated deeply in German society) in particular fed this alternative energy paradigm, which refused nuclear power out of principle and rethought energy provision through decentralised systems that accommodated small private or collectively owned power plants. Renewable energy was judged favourably in terms of environmental impact and social acceptability, two key criteria. These new energy ideas didn't dislodge the existing energy model, which continued to provide power, but it changed the political discourse to one that was much more favourable to wind energy and that resulted in ongoing R&D investment across a range of renewables (that had begun, as elsewhere, in the 1970s), installation subsidies, and in 1990 the Electricity Feed In Law, which worked along similar lines to the NFFO in Britain.[41]

The British market-oriented approach to its onshore wind allowed for a gradual growth through the 1990s and into the early 2000s. Wind steadily became part of national energy ambitions. The Renewables Obligation, which replaced the NFFO, expanded the target amount of electricity that Britain would get from renewable sources, including solar, in 2020 to 20 per cent; the EU Renewable Directive pushed this further, with the discretion of government ministers, to an aim to supply 30 per cent of national electricity from renewables by 2020. In 2009, EDF – owner of British nuclear power stations – called for this to be limited to 25 per cent, but even this target acknowledged a major part for wind and other renewables to play in the UK energy mix. Crucial to achieving that level of contribution, though, was the expansion of offshore wind and, unlike the onshore industry, which was left to the mercy of the markets, government policy firmly directed the next stage of the expansion of British wind energy. For starters, the Department of Energy that had been abolished in 1992 following privatisation of gas and electricity was reintroduced as the Department of Energy and Climate Change (explicitly – but inadvertently? – linking cause and effect). The move offshore relied on state, industry, and crown to open up the seas to make more electric wind. It was largely through offshore wind expansion that the UK overshot the target set by the Renewables Obligation: by 2020, wind alone contributed to 23.8 per cent of the national electricity generation mix, and renewables overall made up 47 per cent across the year.[42] Electric wind exceeded expectations.

6

The ground and the grid: resistance to wind

Most of the people encountered so far in this history of wind energy have been advocates of turbines and their ability to eke electricity from the sky. But opposition to wind energy, or at least its physical infrastructural forms, has accompanied its development at every stage. What people disliked, suspected, and feared about wind energy is instructive, and requires us to step back from too close a focus on technological detail and policy shifts. We must look for turbines as they sit in wider landscapes – in farmland, national parks, and moorlands – and be attentive to how they appear on television and are discussed in newspapers and magazines. When we do so, it becomes clear that wind energy debates are never simply about technology or energy. They are about how people feel about place – and about change.

The act of viewing is central to the idea of landscape, a word that was introduced to the English language in the late sixteenth and seventeenth centuries from the Dutch *landschaap*, through art. Rather than as mere backdrop or scenery, seventeenth-century Dutch artists treated landscape as a subject in its own right (Figure 6.1). Their luminous depictions of rivers, fields, and waterways, painted to capture the breadth of low-lying horizons, brought a new perspective to European art and wider culture. These were not wilderness images but lived landscapes, where people skated on frozen ice, plied trade, and moved from town to distant town. Sometimes a windmill might give height and perspective to a scene, as it does in Jacob van Ruisdael's *Landscape with a Windmill* (1646). Its deep shadows and silhouette add structure to the airy willows and contrast to the radiant light of the sky.[1] It shows a landscape shaped by agricultural and domestic work, foregrounded by the mill and picked up in the middle distance by the glimpses of white linens bleaching in the sun. Such scenes conferred beauty and attention on the everyday rural and imparted an artist's way of seeing them, a lesson learned

6.1 Jacob van Ruisdael, *Landscape with Windmill*, oil on wood, 1646.

by British poets, artists, and landscapers, who developed Romantic sensibilities of the sublime and the picturesque. The rural scene became one worth framing, on a walk, through a window, in a sketchbook. It was where nature and history intertwined. The windmill was a component of the picturesque landscape, a gentle symbol of rural industry for those who rarely needed to participate in it.

The early presence of the windmill in rural landscape tradition makes wind energy distinctive from other energy infrastructures, which are symbols of modern industry. Some scholars see the hazy skies found in paintings by Turner and Monet as indicators of atmospheric pollution, rather than (or as well as) expressions of feeling. More certain depictions of fossil fuels can be found in paintings of industrial furnaces (like those at Coalbrookdale), of steam trains hurtling through the countryside, and etchings of rapidly expanding British cities that document factories, transport networks, smoke, and smog. Processes of fossil fuel extraction and the infrastructure needed to move and process coal and oil from source to consumer – oil derricks, pipelines, freight trains, refineries, container ships – created new views of industrialised landscapes, not always beloved. The Irish poet Seamus Heaney, whose life from 1939 to 2013 spanned the period of infrastructural change looked at here, described the shift from a pastoral rurality shaped by agriculture to one where

> that old sense of tillage and season and foliage has disappeared. Once trees and hedges and ditches and thatch get stripped, you're in a very different world. You're deserting the ground for the grid.[2]

Wind turbines span those two worlds. The old technology of the wooden mill sits comfortably in the ground, even though that ground was never static, and was drained and dug, enclosed and improved. The new machines, techno-trees with straight steel trunks and slender branches, exist for the grid. The terminology of the 'wind farm' invokes an agricultural affinity, a productive relationship between machine and land. But when electricity-generating wind turbines started to be installed in the twentieth-century landscape, as stand-alone experimental machines, it was into the uneasy discourse of grid expansion into rural spaces that they fitted.

The state programme of redevelopment following the Second World War didn't only encompass industry, health, and education. It was also concerned with land. The Town and Country Planning Act of 1947 recalibrated guidelines for building consents and gave local authorities powers to pursue urban redevelopment – and streamlined the use of private land for this purpose.[3] The 1949 National Parks Act for England and Wales enshrined in law new national parks, landscapes chosen for 'their natural beauty … and the opportunities they afford for open-air recreation', designated for use by the nation.

Britain was behind the rest of the world with its national parks. There had been a popular campaign to provide public access to open spaces through the nineteenth century into the twentieth, with numerous Parliamentary bills knocked back again and again by landowning Members of Parliament. A connection between health and access to green space and clean air was a driving principle behind the establishment of the National Trust by the social reformer, Octavia Hill, solicitor Robert Hunter, and clergyman Hardwicke Rawnsley in 1895, but this was a charity, not public policy or law. In the early decades of the twentieth century, working-class cycling and rambling clubs organised, particularly in the industrial northern cities, to assert the rights of ordinary women and men to enjoy the physical and spiritual health benefits of time outdoors in rural landscapes.[4] Politically socialist and communist, the groups challenged the status quo of private landownership which kept vast tracts of rural Britain out of bounds, ostensibly for the hunting recreations of the upper classes. The high moors of the Peak District, which sit between

Manchester and Sheffield, were particularly contested territory and famously the site of the 1932 Kinder Scout mass trespass. The folk musician Ewan MacColl took part and wrote 'The Manchester Rambler' in response to the protest and the violent reaction of gamekeepers to the walkers. 'I may be a wageslave on Monday/ But I am a free man on Sunday' framed recreation as vital respite from industrial capitalism for the masses.

Public and political momentum for recreational access to land grew following the Kinder Scout action, and while the war delayed legislation, it also created a consensus that a nation that had collectively borne the deprivations of war deserved parks for all. National parks aligned with principles of welfare by providing opportunities for healthful recreation. The 1949 Act was the culmination of more than a century of campaigning, and a reflection of the transformative politics of the immediate postwar period. But the breadth of the postwar political project which encompassed industrial regeneration as well as landscape protection led to tensions between those charged with expanding Britain's national grid – upgraded to the Super Grid – and those keen to preserve landscapes. Unlike elsewhere – the USA, for example – British national parks are not taken under federal ownership. Individual landowners continue to own and use their land for agriculture and industry, such as quarrying, under a national park designation. The Ministry of Defence is one such landowner and (controversially) conducts military training within the national park boundaries of Dartmoor and Northumberland.[5] This means that national parks are not exempt from having the infrastructure needed to connect communities to electricity running through them, and the presence of new pylons in places like the Pennines ignited clashes between different interest groups.[6] Organisations such as the Council for the Protection of Rural England, and its Welsh counterpart, campaigned against pylons and other energy infrastructure – such as power stations – in prized rural landscapes. One of their key criteria was the impact on the 'amenity' of a landscape – a term which marries a sense of agreeability and appeal with sense of usefulness, so that, as per the *Oxford English Dictionary*, applied to place it encapsulates 'an advantageous feature of a location serving to enhance its attractiveness as a place to live, work, etc.'.

It is telling that of the three major historical studies of the British electricity industry – those by Hannah, Sheail, and Luckin – two take the conflicts between grid expansion and amenity preservation as a central theme.[7] Preservationists positioned energy infrastructure as anathema to rural beauty, but the state was committed to providing electricity to rural people. I've mentioned previously the CEGB's use of landscape architects such as Sylvia Crowe to habituate the built environment of new nuclear power stations in the surrounding landscape. By 1960, there were seven operational nuclear power stations in Britain. This number was dwarfed by the sixty-plus new coal-fired power stations were built in England and Wales between 1948 and 1969 to provide 15,000 MW of electricity capacity.[8] With large concrete cooling towers, smoke stacks, and roads and power lines in and out, these constructions were visible. The electrification of the nation created new landscapes where modern industrial architecture found rural expression.[9]

As John Sheail notes, in terms of footprint power stations were an incredibly intensive and productive use of land, which required only 600 acres per annum in this period for their construction.[10] Opposition was less concerned with their footprint and more with their impacts on surrounding areas. The health impacts of pollution were a concern, particularly in urban settings where coal smoke hung over cities as smog. Visual impacts were a consistent concern across the board. There was support, and ambivalence too. A 1953 *Architectural Digest* article on the design of power stations suggested that 'five years from now enormous generating stations must stud the landscape … as windmills once studded the Dutch and English fens'.[11] This wasn't necessarily a bad thing – there was opportunity, as modernists like Nan Fairbrother argued, to create 'new landscapes' that moved beyond tired old pastoral tropes. With Sylvia Crowe, and Tom Johnston, among others, she shared a belief that the expansion of energy infrastructure in rural landscapes could be done well.

The *Architectural Digest* quote shows that windmills, in the mid-twentieth century, were still visual shorthand for pre-modern rurality. They were still of the ground, not of the grid. The introduction of new electricity-generating machines interrupted that default visual language. While the NSHEB was erecting the 100-kW turbine in Orkney in 1951, the British Electrical Authority (BEA) made plans to test its own, made by Enfield, on the top of Mynydd Anelog, a 191-m summit in the Llŷn peninsula in north Wales. While proposals for the Orkney turbine were welcomed, the Welsh machine required negotiation between several bodies to secure permissions to use the land. There were exchanges between the Ministry of Fuel and Power and the Ministry of Defence, which had an air force base nearby. It didn't object in principle but had planned to place a radar station at the same site and tried to convince the Ministry of Fuel and Power and the BEA to place the turbine elsewhere. Both pushed back, emphasising the need for optimal conditions for the experiment. No other summit or hillside would do.[12] The Ministry for Agriculture and Fisheries offered no objections. But the National Farmers Union objected on the ground that grazing rights on the summit would be disrupted.[13] And further objection, of a sort, was made by the Council for Protection for Rural Wales (CPRW). They wrote to the County Planning Officer that if windmills had to come, there was little that could be done about it, and they were 'less objectionable' than the hydro-electric schemes also being resisted at the time. But lest the planners felt off the hook, the CPRW continued that Mynydd Anelog was 'perhaps the worst place that could be chosen for the windmill, because it would dominate the whole headland'.[14] Like power stations and pylons, it was less the wind turbine's function, and more its visual presence, which was objectionable. The CPRW's objections in 1951 presaged the dominant cause of contention around wind turbines in the landscape. Their location on high, open hill tops maximises efficiency – and visibility.

Though it was awarded planning consent in 1952, the Mynydd Anelog turbine was never put up.[15] The compulsory purchase orders needed for the land were not approved by the Minister for Housing and Local Government, and the BEA did not pursue it. Possibly the availability of results from, but also ongoing repair costs of, the Orkney turbine experiment put them off. Lack of opposition to wind turbines for the next few decades, until the early 1990s, indicates only the lack of large-scale wind turbines themselves in this long fallow period for wind energy in Britain. When a commercial industry got going in the 1990s, critics voiced their concerns once again. Some of the same issues raised in the 1950s – land use, visual impact – resurfaced; but new complexities emerged, too. By this later period of flourishing, debates around the presence of wind energy in the countryside revealed the influence of environmentalism on public perceptions of wind and, not un-related, a political polarisation of the public discourse.

Delabole may have nabbed the claim to 'first' commercial wind farm in Britain, but Wales soon followed, with 'largest'. The Llandinam wind farm in Powys, built by Ecogen, had 103 turbines spread across 4 km of plateau, generating 30.9 mW of electricity, and was the largest wind farm in the world at the time, California excepted. It is still in operation today under Scottish Power ownership. If one turbine troubled the CPRW in 1951, it could be predicted that the large scale of the Llandinam wind farm (and others) would stimulate resistance. Companies like Ecogen were attentive to this and included view projections and landscape character assessments as standard in planning applications.[16] In fact, the campaign against the Llandinam installation focused on a different sensory affect of the turbines: their noise. Chris Lord-Smith, organiser of the protest against the wind farm, complained that he and others lived in a 'wind-shadow' which reduced the regular background noise of the wind, and thus the noise generated by rotating turbines could be heard more. An article in the *New Scientist* reported that in response to his complaints, Ecogen had re-tuned the turbines to reduce noise, and that seventeen visits to his house by environmental health officers had not registered noise at nuisance levels. Lord-Smith, however, found the 'mechanical droning' unnatural and irritating.[17] Another Welsh wind farm near Aberystwyth was featured on the 'Wales This Week' television programme in 1993. Here, too, noise was raised as an issue – 'sometimes it sounds like an aeroplane or helicopter. The most difficult noise to live with is when it is thumping, like an agitated heartbeat,' one campaigner described.[18] Where the visual pulse of wind had charmed meteorologists, the audible rhythms of large turbines, for some who lived near them, lent the landscape an irritating metre.

As well as featuring objectors to wind turbines, the programme interviewed farmers who leased their land to the energy companies. This is relatively unusual – the coverage of wind turbines in the early 1990s tended to focus on a duality of opponents/protestors, and energy companies and environmentalists as advocates. Landowners stayed somewhat out of frame, though they were making money from the leasing arrangements. But on 'Wales This Week' Dilwyn Jones and his wife Jackie presented the case for wind farms from a farming perspective. The sheep (who grazed around the bases) 'didn't mind one bit', and the Joneses received a new road and supplementary income of £6,000 a year from the lease. It wasn't surprising that farmers were in favour of wind farms said Jackie, who also said that opposition had come mainly from 'incomers' to the area.

This brief mention by Jackie, who identified herself as an incomer married to a local, is something of a Pandora's box that opens up the complex identity politics of rural places. Rural Wales, as we know from CAT, was attractive to those looking to escape some of the constraints of materialistic modern life. An off-grid community was a more radical version of a simpler life that was appealing to many (and was before – and remains today). This idea rested on particular understandings of the countryside as anti-urban, a place of slow change and nature. As the literary scholar Raymond Williams (who was born in Wales) identified in *The country and the city*, the rural and urban have worked oppositionally in British culture to construct each other, and cultural reproduction of the rural as pastoral often obscures the histories of work, oppression, and resistance that are more readily attached to the city as a centre of political engagement for elites and masses alike. In Britain, a further dimension of four-nations identity is also often present, in this instance in the form of incomers as English arriving into Welsh communities. 'Wales This Week' highlighted how expectations of rural Welsh life and landscape by English incomers, such as Chris Lord-Smith, differentiated from those such as Dilwyn Jones whose family had worked the land for generations. Lord-Smith complained that he felt like a 'guinea-pig', and that he had trusted what Tim Kirby and Ecogen had promised him about the noise levels. 'Tim Kirby is an environmentalist,' he said, 'and I am an environmentalist.' Lord-Smith expressed his environmentalism by moving to a rural Welsh small-holding for a quiet life; Kirby, through his green entrepreneurialism. Both men were English. The late-nineteenth and early-twentieth century revival of Welsh nationalism fought cultural erasure by a central English state, and land grabs by private and public English interests. These included the damming of Welsh valleys to produce water for English cities, for example, and use of Welsh farmland to train (mostly) English troops in the Second World War.[19] Kirby had lived in Wales for years and Ecogen was a Welsh–Cornish company, which had buy-in from Welsh farmers. The dynamics of national identity in this case swung in favour of wind energy – and against the 'incomer' English complainants. Another interviewee spelled out the elephant in the room: 'this is something people have got to come to terms with. People want renewable energy, people want these schemes, but they don't want them near them. Well, I can't understand that. It's the Not In My Back Yard syndrome.'

The Not In My Back Yard (NIMBY) characterisation of anti-wind farm protests occurred in this period of rapid development and proved a hard label to shake off. Media coverage of conflicts over wind farms framed the environmental case for wind energy in global terms. 'Wales This Week', for example, highlighted the concerns over acid rain that were widespread at the time. Wind turbines would save 25,000 tonnes of 'greenhouse gases' and 300 tonnes of 'acid rain gases'. The irony of people wearing 'the rainforest is endangered' t-shirts being interviewed about the incursion of wind energy in their daily lives, as in 'Wales This Week', was implicit in the coverage. So-called environmentalists might espouse green values, but object when the working alternatives to fossil fuels and nuclear power were situated in their vicinity. The geographer Patrick Devine-Wright, who has studied NIMBYism extensively, identifies how the NIMBY label became a succinct way of pejoratively describing local opposition to unwanted land uses.[20] The term carried a sense of opponents as small-minded and mean, which sometimes *was* the case – there was (and is) something uncomfortable and unfair about recent arrivals to a community organising protests against long-standing inhabitants' choices. This is as true in cities, where – for example – new neighbours object to established music venues on the grounds of noise pollution, as in the countryside. But the assumption that rural people are custodians of a timeless landscape that should remain unchanged for others to enjoy animated the preservationist movement in the 1950s and stayed visible in these later conflicts. It was a position rebuffed by Jackie Jones, who argued that 'a farmer is thought of as a custodian of the land, and therefore to be a custodian [s]he has to run a business and make it economic and make it viable, to look after the countryside'. Wind energy directly challenged the notion of the countryside as timeless and unchanging, and asserted its capacity to contain modern infrastructure. It also highlighted the different, competing visions of what responsible, sustainable land use looked like – and for whom. The rise of the commercial wind industry gave welcome revenue to hill farmers but also emphasised the power of landowners, a group able to make decisions about landscapes in which others inhabited. In this respect, at least, there was continuity with the past.

Media focus on wind farms emphasised conflict over consensus or critique. We see in this period a consistent delineation of wind energy as a polarised issue with people 'for' or 'against'. The British Wind Energy Association insisted its surveys found widespread public support, with 70–80 per cent of those surveyed in favour and 2–10 per cent wishing to see it stopped.[21] Rather than broad consensus, the perspective provided by newspaper coverage was one of pitched battle between 'greens' and anti-wind campaign groups. Prominent environmentalists such as Jonathan Porritt, and groups like Friends of the Earth UK (which Porritt had directed 1984–90), were regularly called on to speak in favour of wind; the other 'side' was provided by groups such as the 'Country Guardians'. Country Guardians was founded by Joseph Lythgoe in 1992 to campaign against wind power and provided resources and guidelines for groups and individuals to fight planning applications. By 1994 it had around a hundred members, including Bernard Ingham, journalist and former press secretary to Margaret Thatcher. Ingham became a vocal and persistent critic, who used his press contacts and regular columns in the *Hebden Bridge Times* and *Daily Express* to rail against wind farms, and delighted in upsetting 'the wind lobby'.[22] Wind turbines 'are a monument to energy do-gooders', he wrote. 'Forests of these infernal contraptions are springing up on the pristine

Pennine moors ... unless we blow up in revolt, we shall find every mountain, hill and cliff colonised by flailing pylons.'[23] Ingham was an unpopular character; his unrepentantly odious behaviour towards victims of the Hillsborough disaster remains a damning legacy. His stance on wind energy reveals that deep-rooted perspective of the rural as 'pristine'.

The growth of the commercial wind energy industry in this period should have been cause for Conservative celebration. Government policy had succeeded in creating a new, profitable market, which was growing and stimulating industrial development and investment. The NFFO commitment created an easy mechanism for the state to act on carbon emissions without radically changing direction elsewhere. Thatcher's public acknowledgement of climate change offered a moment for a Conservative–conservation alignment, in which environmental action worked alongside a paternalistic vision of stewardship of land, best done by those who owned it. Indeed, beyond the binary pro/anti lens that dominated the press, left-wing environmentalists criticised the form and shape the wind industry was taking as a result of government policy, with pieces in *The Ecologist* magazine, for example, highlighting the lack of community benefits from large wind farms and calling for policies to support smaller-scale, less acrimonious projects with more devolved decision-making.[24] This kind of nuance rarely made it into the national papers, which continued to focus on conflict. And the arrival of new energy infrastructure into British landscapes chafed at a primal conservative impulse to resist change. The more explosive critiques of wind energy from right-wing figures such as Ingham rested on a dislike of the role of the centralised state in stimulating and overseeing this change, as well as a deep-rooted, deeply conservative view of rural Britain.

The polarisation of wind energy as a left/right political issue deepened under David Cameron's Conservative–Liberal Democrat coalition government (2010–15), and Conservative government (2015–16). The latter in particular was the most politically hostile to wind energy since the expansion of the sector in the 1990s and introduced policy changes that produced an effective moratorium on onshore wind development that lasted until 2024. Under Cameron, government ministers intervened to disrupt the planning process by overriding local planning processes to reject wind farm proposals at national level, on grounds of localised dissent to schemes. Communities and local government minister Eric Pickles called in an 'unprecedented' number of planning decisions for his personal approval – so many, in fact, that he was accused in 2013 by Labour and LibDem politicians and energy firms of rejecting wind farms to win votes.[25] Figures at the time estimated he pulled 85 per cent of wind energy capacity out of the standard planning processes, for political approval.[26]

Driving this proactive oversight was the United Kingdom Independence Party (UKIP), which pursued a populist agenda further to the right of the Conservatives. Led by Nigel Farage, UKIP's political agenda in this period comprised of three main positions: it was anti-immigration, anti-European Union, and anti-wind farms. At their 2013 conference, Farage railed against 'ugly, useless and expensive' wind farms that were 'despoiling the British landscape'.[27] Farage has proved an effective political strategist. UKIP's stance appealed, as intended, to disgruntled rural Conservative voters. It drew a line of connection between an issue happening at a very local, landscape level, with a wider politics of right-wing populism. It positioned local protestors and councils as Davids fighting the Goliaths of state and industry. The strategy worked. The Conservative government rose to UKIP's bait and gave amenity-led local objections to wind farms a major national framing and a place in the 2015 party manifesto. Conservative peer Lord Berkely complained in the House of Lords that 'people who have been objecting in my area say that the only party that is representing little groups is UKIP'.[28] Party rhetoric shifted at the highest level. Cameron stated that people were 'fed up' with wind energy and that 'enough was enough'.[29] The re-elected Conservative government removed subsidies for onshore wind and introduced two planning 'tests' to the National Planning Policy Framework, so that councils could only approve wind farms on sites that had been clearly designated as part of a local or neighbourhood plan and where the proposed project had the backing of the local community. The result was an effective moratorium on new onshore wind energy that lasted several more Conservative prime ministers. One of the first actions of the newly elected 2024 Labour government was to lift the *de facto* ban on new onshore wind energy.[30]

Protests against wind energy fit into old, long debates around what and who the countryside is for. The nomenclature of the wind 'farm' alludes to the pastoral and the productive. Protests highlighted the tensions between these terms. My sense, from my analysis of wind energy protests through the twentieth century into the twenty-first, is that the modern three-bladed wind turbine has become somewhat naturalised in the landscape, in that it no longer stimulates the same strong views against visual impacts that it used to despite having demonstrably increased in impact thanks to larger, and more, turbines in the landscape. Key to this has been the alliance, in public discourse, between wind energy and environmental politics, that was in evidence in those 1990s polarised 'debates' weighing up the pros and cons of wind power. By bringing in Friends of the Earth, for example, to advocate for wind, the press effectively cemented an association between wind energy and green politics which has been sustained. This was not confection: Friends of the Earth, Greenpeace, and other environmental campaign groups really *did* support wind energy and were all too happy to use its coverage to raise their campaign agendas. Wind's environmental benefits remained a key attraction for investors and engineers. But wind energy as it took shape in the 1990s was also a neoliberal project which used the privatisation of electricity to build a new market, lucrative for some, in which to sell electricity made from the wind. The term wind 'park' is commonly used in other countries, and holds a telling ambiguity – is that a park for leisure, or a business park?

Opposition to wind energy has grown on right-wing political agendas while the alignment of wind energy and environmental action has strengthened as public awareness of climate change and global environmental crisis has increased. In 1997, only a year after Ingham and the Country Guardians were celebrating their capacity to halt wind schemes through letter-writing to local councillors in the national press, Britain and other industrialised/industrialising nations agreed the Kyoto Protocol which committed them to limit and reduce greenhouse gas emissions. The global response to climate change has been long, slow, and increasingly difficult in the wake of increasingly populist politics in the US, UK, India, Russia, South America, and Europe. Wind energy has been a singular area of success, as it has continued to grow and produce more low-carbon energy, outstripping industry predictions – a rare good-news story compared to, say, efforts to curtail oil extraction or address plastic pollution. But wind energy remains a point of political division. Across the northern hemisphere, new formations of right-wing populism double-down on a blue-collar 'petro-masculinity' in which conspicuous consumption of oil is both political statement (think, for example, of the monster truck and tractor blockades that have occurred in Canada, Britain, the USA, and France in recent years) and siphon to other issues.[31] In the Southern Hemisphere, the right to extract fossil fuels has been aligned with authoritarian politics of postcolonial self-determination.[32] Given the support that current energy policies give to corporate and capitalist interests, it should not be a given that the right have moved against wind. But as UKIP's lobbying in the 2010s demonstrated, wind energy offered a national platform and a way into debates that soon expanded away from energy issues into debates about immigration and nationalism.

As Patrick Devine-Wright and Susana Batel note, place attachment is important in explaining social acceptance of energy proposals.[33] A common mistake, made by government, industry, and many campaigners, has been to assume that responses to energy infrastructure, and place attachment, is only local in nature. It is the connection between local, national, and global understandings of place and environment which we can see at work both in the increasing acceptance of wind turbines and a gradual naturalisation of their forms into the landscape, and in protests against wind energy. In an age of widespread climate concern, the wind farm on the horizon is being more readily understood by many as a visual indicator of positive environmental change, rather than as an infrastructural blot on the landscape. But tensions remain in the relationship between ground and grid and where protests arise, they require understandings of history, politics, and culture – and sensitivity to how energy works across all three.

The developers of wind farms did not heed, for the most part, Sylvia Crowe's advice to settle the 'new tools of power' in existing landscapes of old industry, to blend new and old.[34] The high and windy places were not 'pristine', as some would have it, having been worked, grazed, deforested, and surveyed. Neither were they the places that traditional stout wooden windmills had been, serving a different purpose and requiring a more manageable wind. Wind precipitated a new energy geography, upon which the contestation of 'a new kind of beauty' unfolded.

Moorlands not turbines

Lewis, in the Outer Hebrides, has some famous bus stops. You can buy mugs, posters and t-shirts with them on in *An Lanntair*, the Stornaway arts centre.[35] Shaped like crosses, four vertical panels offer concrete compass points to shelter passengers from the wind no matter its direction. A slab on top covers the threat of rain. They are solid, sturdy, and unapologetically unromantic, but have also been described as 'dinky', appealing, and even 'cute'.[36] Designed by architect Alan Holling for the local council in 1979–80, the 'Four Winds' bus stop 'was capable of withstanding hurricane-force winds, providing shelter from horizontal rain from any direction whilst allowing views of approaching buses'.[37] These functional everyday monuments to the weather have become brutalist architectural icons with a cult following (Figure 6.2).

6.2 'Four winds' bus stop, Lewis, Outer Hebrides. © Alexander Boyd.

For my tour of the bus stops I was in tourist mode, freed from a stint in *Tasglann nan Eileen Siar* (the Hebridean Archives) thanks to a newly available hire car. I'd been lucky to find accommodation, too: the influx of people who had been in Stornoway for the HebCelt music festival were heading home, freeing up Bed and Breakfast rooms and returning their vehicles to the local hire place. My daily walk through town to the archive, where I was looking for records of wind turbines, was pleasant but I was itching to see more of the islands and dip my toes in the sea, so when a (dinky, cute?) Toyota Aygo became available I rented it for the rest of my stay. First I headed southwest, to Harris, to swim in the turquoise water, driving through the hulking central hills and the old clan boundary lines between the two 'islands', which are in fact joined – but by a landscape so rocky and hard to traverse that traditionally it was easier to treat them as islands and travel between them by sea. Then, back to Lewis, to meet with a member of the resistance.

All land is underpinned by geology, but on Lewis and Harris it seems to break free of the usual surface constraints to force a reckoning with the substrate. Stones – the word seems insufficient: huge boulders, whole mountains of rock – dominate the landscape. They are Lewisian gneiss (pronounced 'nice'), which at up to 3 billion years old are some of the oldest rocks on our 4-billion year-old planet. It is so otherworldly – so stripped of the usual ornaments of landscape, trees, and shrubs and hedges and so on – that Stanley Kubrick filmed moonscape scenes for *2001: a space odyssey* here. This openness, this emptiness, is partly geology, but partly human design too. In much more recent planetary history, the indigenous population of the Outer Hebrides have been subject to 'improvements' by outside (mainland) forces. First, cottars and squatters of crofts were forcibly removed in the eighteenth and nineteenth centuries by landowners to enclose the land for more intensive agriculture, or game-keeping. These first disturbances created communities without adequate means to support themselves, who were then offered (or were selected for) 'assisted passage' (to North and South America and Australasia) by landowners, precipitating mass migration with devastating community and cultural effects. The repercussions were still being felt in the twentieth century, when, as historian Iain Robertson argues, war service awakened public opinion, and legislative reforms that allowed application for land to be made against large landowners started a new wave of rural protests.[38]

These uprisings, which occurred across the western Highlands and islands, differed in nature according to where they took place. Lewis and Harris experienced a number of protests from 1919 through to the early 1930s. The populations were relatively high compared to elsewhere, sustained by a kelp industry (the seaweed was burnt to produce soda for potash).[39] Most significantly, by 1919 the entirety of Lewis and Harris were under the ownership of one man: William Lever, Lord Leverhulme, the soap manufacturer. He intended to develop the fisheries, and 'improve the conditions of the crofter population'.[40] This patrician aim to develop and improve was not malign, but – along with Port Sunlight in Merseyside, and an array of land and works in Nigeria and Belgian Congo – it further demonstrated what his biography describes as 'a passion for organising, building, and regulating other people's lives'. In Lewis and Harris, Lever was the 'most significant factor in terms of agitation for land'.[41]

Protesters broke turf dykes to access grazings, raided tenanted farms, marked out crofts, and began to plant and inhabit them. Iain Robertson highlights a 1919 petition from fifty-seven inhabitants of North Tolsta which stated, 'we ourselves and our sons have fought in defence of our King and country and we shall also fight to get the land if steps are not soon taken to see us settled on the land of our ancestors which we consider is ours by right'.[42] Lever was reluctant to prosecute raiders and occupiers, and negotiated smallholding schemes for most of them. By 1923 he had largely given up on his Hebridean plans altogether, and by his death in 1925 had sold large portions of the estate and left the rest in a trust. Lever passed on, but attempts to develop and 'improve' Hebridean land were not over.

It was through these layered geographies of resistance and unrest that I drove in 2022 to meet with Anne Campbell, a member of *Mòinteach gun Mhuileann*/Moorlands Not Turbines group, to discuss a new landscape of protest: the Stornoway General moorland, a few miles from the main town on Lewis and site of a wind farm proposal. The Lewis Wind Power company submitted a planning application in 2003 for a wind farm of 181 turbines to be constructed in the Stornoway General, on land leased from the Stornoway Trust – the community landlord created by deed in 1923 to oversee the land gifted by Lord Leverhulme. *Comhairle nan Eilean Siar*, the local council, publicly supported the scheme. It was a new development for the islands, one that would provide work and investment to help buck the depopulation that had set in through the twentieth century. But a resistance movement formed, that, in its opposition to the Stornoway turbines, identified contemporary energy schemes as the latest manifestation of a long history of oppression. Their critique of 'Big Wind' envisioned an alternative model of wind energy for the Hebrides.

First, the Moorlands Not Turbines group pushed back against the developers' rhetoric of the Lewis interior as an empty wasteland, ripe for development – an old trope used by agricultural reformers, colonial settlers, and fossil fuel developmentalists around the world. The celebrated landscapes of the Outer Hebrides, that are reproduced in tourist literature and through social media, are the machair (grass dunes and plains, rich with plant and animal species); the white-sand beaches and inshore turquoise waters; and the rocky inlets that create an infinitely-expanding fractal coastline, as the mathematician Benoit Mandelbrot theorised in his *The fractal geometry of nature* (1983).[43] Mandelbrot examined how a coastline mapped at a small scale revealed the inlets and sub-bays and sub-peninsulas that mapping at a large scale conveniently smooths into straight lines. The closer you look, and the smaller the unit of measurement, the longer the measurement becomes, taking in all of an island's 'corrugated edges' so that, in fact, a coastline's length is infinite.[44] The Hebridean coastline gives shape to fractal theory, with its endless creeks, inlets, and skerries. Look too hard at the rocky edges, their seaweeds and sea slugs, and the seals, otters, and cetaceans that inhabit them, and you'll miss the moors at the heart of the islands. Tourism directs the gaze outwards, in search of wildness, beauty, and abundant nature. The ever-closer focus Mandelbrot applied to the shore is rarely given to the flat peat bog of the central moors. But this is exactly what Moorland Not Turbines encouraged: a close reading of the moor.

A close reading brings the eye to the ground, where turbines would be placed. Here, a rich mosaic of plant and animal species exists.[45] Sphagnum moss, carnivorous sundew, and orchids create a blanket of cover for insects and small mammals. Predatorial land mammals – such as foxes, weasels, badgers, and stoats – are absent from the islands, allowing birds of prey to thrive. Hen harriers and eagles occupy the skies above the moor where the turbines would turn. The Lewis Wind Farm application included an ornithology report, which noted breeding territories for white-tailed and golden eagles and flightways for short-eared owls, merlin, great skuas, red-throated divers, and whooper swans (among many species).[46] This is a strong refutation of the moor as empty and monotonous. The moor is bejewelled with life and colour.

Those who live by the moor know this and have the words to express it. Anne Campbell produced *Rathad an Isein: The Bird's Road,* in collaboration with Finlay Macleod, Donald Morrison, and Catriona Campbell in response to the wind farm proposal. It is a Lewis moorland and peat bank glossary, a Gaelic record of place which fills the 'empty' moor with the words Hebrideans used to describe it, and their work in it.[47] There is *canach,* cotton grass, and *fianach,* purple moor grass; *bruenloch,* a dangerous sinking bog; and *maoim,* a place on the moor 'where there has been peat movement in the past'. *Àirigh* describes a shieling, shelters made for cattle and their people, and the practice of transhumance whereby cattle were taken to moor lands for summer grazing from May to August. Transhumance was practised in Lewis until the 1950s, with the glossary entry noting that 'summer days on moorland shielings are often recalled as the happiest of peoples' lives'. Folk tales and ghost stories, instructions, warnings, memories, and guidelines are all contained in the glossary, asserting the moor as a place of nature and of people, and a crucible for their culture and history.

The group also drew attention to the existing energy landscape of the peat bog, and its status as 'common grazings', which under Scottish law permits its use for animal grazing and peat cutting by crofters. They photographed the *Garadh Dubh,* an ancient peat embankment running through the wind farm site. Anne described how vulnerable a peat landscape is to disturbance. 'Peat is liquid in nature, so when one part is changed it affects another', she explained. 'For example, if a road is built through an area of peat, the moisture leaches out either side – the peat dries up.' The arrival of wind turbines to the sensitive peat would affect the wider ecology and also interrupt the traditional practice of cutting peat on the moor. Growing awareness of the issue of carbon emissions was making carbon-rich peat cutting more controversial, with social media posts attracting critical comments, for example. The protest group saw it in a different context. Enacting crofter's rights to access and cut peat turfs for fuel is a form of Hebridean resistance and reclamation of identity, a tradition that links them to the protestors who fought Leverhulme, and the ancestors who were evicted from using the land as commons. The practice of peat-cutting asserts a culture that has survived centuries of attempted erasure.

The protestors identified the unequal power dynamics that are present in criticisms of other indigenous cultures, such as whaling, in which the small-scale practitioners keeping culture alive are easier targets than the industrial-scale actors that threaten whole ecosystems. The wind farm would produce low-carbon energy and keep carbon in the ground, but would it help the local population to keep their houses warmer for less? A 2023 survey by the Hebridean housing and energy agency Tighean Innse Gall found that over 80 per cent of households in the Western Isles were in fuel poverty (i.e., spending more than 10 per cent of their household income on heating).[48] Orkney shows that commercial wind farms do little to impact this situation. There, on the islands she describes as 'overflowing with electrons', Laura Watts identifies some of the highest levels of fuel poverty in the country.[49] The moorland protestors challenged the hypocrisy of promising energy abundance but delivering little tangible change to everyday living conditions. Naming the peat in Gaelic (*mòine bhàn*, young peat; *mòine chòsach*, spongy peat; *mòine fhliuch*, soft peats), protecting it and cutting it was, for the protestors, part of the same action. Plenty agreed – the reaction to the wind farm proposals was sizeable. Over 200 crofters lodged objections with the Land Court.[50]

The most striking dimension to the Moorlands Not Turbines movement, particularly in comparison to other anti-wind farm campaigns, is that they fought the large-scale corporate wind farm proposal – but not wind energy in principle. Unlike Country Guardians, who objected to wind energy in the landscape outright, the Lewis protests objected to the manner in which wind was being imposed: through land ostensibly passed to the community from Leverhulme's lordship, but leased to a commercial operator, to turn a profit from the wind resource that would be paid to company shareholders not local people. It is worth noting that a community fund is part of the proposal, into which a projected annual sum of around £900,000 would be deposited – a sizeable amount, but much less than the £5 million a year estimated profit of the community model, let alone the overall profits of the larger commercial model.[51]

While the 181-turbine mega-farm plan was rejected by the Scottish energy minister Jim Mather in 2008, a revised application for 36 turbines – renamed the Stornoway Wind Farm – was granted in 2012. To date, it remains unconstructed.[52] For the wind farm to connect to the national grid (and thus enable the sale of electricity to suppliers), the islands require an underwater interconnector cable to be laid, a decision approved by the electricity industry regulator Ofgem in 2022 – with press reports emphasising the need to unlock the potential of offshore wind energy around the islands.[53] The focus, as elsewhere, has somewhat shifted from onshore wind, with its complications of human inhabitants, to the sea space – though as I'll explore, the idea of the sea as empty, like the land, speaks to particular cultural constructions that allow its exploitation. The planned completion date for the Stornoway Wind Farm, according to their website, is 2030, and at the time of writing, the project – now a joint venture between EDF Renewables UK and ESB, the Irish state energy company – remains approved but not constructed.

In the space afforded by this pause, opponents put an alternative proposal to the local council. Taking cues from successful community-owned turbines that existed in nearby Point and Sandwick, Galson and the Urras, and Barra, they proposed a smaller, community-owned wind farm on part of the proposed site, with all profits going to a community fund. The counter-proposal exerted crofters' rights, alongside those of the landowner, to determine how the land was used. It also challenged the local council on its support for wind energy: if wind energy was such a good idea for Lewis, why let a corporate version take the profits off the island? The counter-move highlighted the power dynamics in play, and the choices available when it comes to building new wind power: alternatives to Big Wind exist.

The chess-board sleight of hand by the protestors was not approved by the local council, but served its purpose to highlight the uncritical deference local governments all too often adopt in the face of corporate 'investment' (read: extraction). In this, they find allies at numerous sites of conflict between corporate energy interests, and indigenous populations, around the world. The ways in which fossil fuel companies have worked against indigenous rights, public health, democratic processes, and environmental protection in places like the oil delta of Nigeria and 'Cancer Alley' in Louisiana is well-documented.[54] Energy scholars show that large-scale wind farms share some of the exploitative approaches to land acquisition and profit extraction that established fossil fuel companies are expert in.

In Mexico's Isthmus of Tehuantepec the rapid expansion of wind 'parks' from two to twenty-nine between 2008 and 2016 has made it the densest concentration of onshore wind parks in the world.[55] Dominic Boyer and Cymene Howe's study of the impacts of wind power in the region highlight the ways in which renewable energy gave new means for the Mexican petrostate to exert power over land and peoples who have already experienced dispossession and disenfranchisement. Rather than offer a new framework for the relationship between state, citizens, and environment, wind power perpetuated the wrongs of colonial expansion and settlement by establishing corporate ownership of shared resources (the wind) and funnelling vast profits out of the region to shareholders (through dividends) and the state (through taxation).

In Ireland, Patrick Bresnihan and Patrick Brodie have researched how big wind farms are inextricable from non-renewable energy systems and tax-evasive capital, and that this is routinely and purposefully obscured from the communities encountering wind devices. The relationship makes Big Wind, and Big Data, 'increasingly formidable in dictating our energy futures'.[56]

Indigenous resistance to wind energy elsewhere connects human and animal histories, with Sámi protests against the Fosen wind farm pinpointing not only damage to ancestral land, but disruption of reindeer migration routes and grazing lands that are fundamental to Sámi culture and identity. That indigenous land is chosen to develop green energy for Norwegian society (which benefits from a sovereign wealth fund created by oil revenues) 'adds insult to injury of communities already struggling [to cope with the effects of] climate change they were not responsible for'.[57]

Resistance to large wind energy proposals on Lewis draws on threads of all of these examples. It highlights the importance of history in understanding the landscapes into which wind energy arrives, and the capacity for energy infrastructure to continue damaging practices or break free from old traditions to establish new, more hopeful, propositions. 'Wildness' is a commodity that attracts developers looking to fill the spaces made by weather, wildlife, and past processes. But, as Kathleen Jamie reminds us, '"wild"' is 'shot over by royalty, flown over by the RAF, or trampled underfoot in the wind-farm gold-rush'.[58] What appears empty rarely is, and by looking more closely at landscapes of protest, we begin to see the fault-lines of identity and power which determine place, its meaning, who claims it, and what we do with it. Dugald Fraser, engineer for the North of Scotland Hydro-Electric Board, spoke to the BBC Home Service in 1953 of bringing power to the glens. 'To me, these pylons striding over the heather in all directions are a symbol. They are carrying on their shoulders a new power, an injection of fresh vitality, a blood transfusion. There is more to it than just a mass of cables and wires and concrete.'[59] Wind turbines and their cables connect air, ground, and grid, but there is indeed more to it. Where they sit and how they operate makes the difference between old systems of top-down power and profit, and the possibilities of new energy dynamics wrought along more just and equitable lines.

7

Offshore

The story of Britain's wind energy has, so far, been grounded in the landscapes of the nation – places which have played a dynamic role in the development of technology, of government policy, of everyday experiences of wind and weather, and of ideas of how and where and in what form we source our energy. In the twenty-first century, the story moves offshore. Britain's first offshore wind installation of two experimental Vestas turbines was built half a mile off the coast of Blyth, in Northumberland in 2000. It was followed by the North Hoyle wind farm of thirty turbines, installed by the energy company National Wind Power Ltd (now RWE npower renewables) in Liverpool Bay off the north Wales coast in 2003, which is still in operation today. By 2023, 3,352 turbines in 50 offshore wind farms supplied the equivalent electricity needs of 50 per cent of the nation's households, from a combined area of seabed equivalent to more than twice the land area of England, Wales, and Northern Ireland.[1] From land-locked beginnings, the conclusive shift sea-wards of the British wind industry opened up new scales of energy production and technology, and re-set perceptions of wind energy.

Development pipeline

Denmark made the first step offshore. The Vindeby wind farm of 11 turbines was built in 1991 and, with capacity of 5 mW, produced enough electricity to power the equivalent of 2,200 homes.[2] Vindeby took the land-based method of anchoring a turbine in a concrete foundation, into shallow coastal water, where it became known as a 'monopile'. It worked. The turbines stayed upright, and, moreover, generated power. Danish success encouraged other nations – Sweden, the Netherlands, the UK – to follow suit. To a greater or lesser extent, all of these countries border the North Sea, and this relatively shallow, small, and windy ocean became a crucible for intensive offshore wind energy development through the 1990s and into the 2000s.

Once Danish developments, and the test site at Blyth, gave the green light to industry that offshore wind could be a contributor to national electricity generation, British offshore wind expanded rapidly. Offshore offered an attractive space for wind energy development. The ocean, after all, was free from the patchwork of landownership and planning constraints that were to be encountered on land. Neighbourly objections, noise complaints, and visual impacts were lessened or absent. At first, offshore wind stayed fairly close to shore and was visible. The view of distant turbines on an oceanic horizon did not seem to provoke the polarised responses that wind turbines in the landscape had. Market research commissioned by National Wind Power found widespread support among residents and visitors to the shoreline from which the North Hoyle wind farm was visible: 62 per cent of residents supported the wind farm and considered a depiction of its visual impact 'acceptable'; the people surveyed who found its visual impact 'pleasing' outnumbered those who found it 'displeasing' by five to one.[3] A strong majority (82 per cent) of those interviewed felt that a higher percentage of the UK's electricity should be generated via renewable sources. With widespread public support, offshore offered space for development at scales that planning constraints onshore could not entertain. Climate change was becoming more visible on the political agenda and the UK government, like other nations signed up to the Kyoto Protocol (agreed in 1997, ratified and brought into effect in 2004), was committed to lowering carbon emissions. In the late-2000s, the 'aspiration' was to produce 20 per cent of national electricity needs from renewable sources, and offshore was seen by government and industry as a space for the kind of scalability that could hit those targets.[4]

At sea, turbines could be – and, incrementally, were – made bigger, and so became more productive. At the time, the 100-kW turbine installed onshore in Orkney in 1951 was the largest of its kind connected to a grid. At the time of writing, the largest turbines connected to a grid are 16 mW machines that form a Chinese wind farm in the Taiwan strait. They each have a rotor diameter of 260 m, and the blades sit atop 152-m towers. To complete a full revolution, the rotors move through 50,000 sq m (or roughly seven football pitches) of airspace. Each turbine produces more than three times the capacity of the Vindeby farm, and 160 times the capacity of the 1951 Orkney turbine. Oceans offered space to substantially grow turbine technology.

Nonetheless, there are environmental constraints to consider. Winds blow stronger and steadier at sea than they do on land, and this increases the further you move from the shore.[5] There is more wind to capture, but the machines must withstand stronger gusts and storms. Deeper waters and distance from land take turbines further away from communities who may object to their presence (or support their arrival), but this increases the cost and difficulty of construction and maintenance. And no matter where they are, turbines need to be connected to the electricity grids they supply.

Connecting land and sea

As we have seen, wind energy has opened up new energy geographies and reframes places as wind-rich rather than wind-swept. Onshore and offshore, these new sites of electricity production have layered over existing, 'legacy', energy systems around which transmission networks were constructed. Laying new cables has been necessary for grid expansion, and this has been costly but necessary at the territorial edges of the mainland. Crossing water adds another barrier, and island energy projects have been particularly constrained by the existing capacities of their connections to the mainland grid. One of the reasons the Lewis Wind Farm project was delayed was due to long negotiations between energy companies, the industry regulator Ofgem, and the Scottish government, over the case for a new interconnector from the Outer Hebrides to the mainland. In 2022 – twenty years since discussions began – Ofgem approved a 1.8 gigawatt subsea cable to run between Arnish and Ullapool.[6] This was a massive increase on the capacity of the originally proposed cable, because in the meantime an 840 mW floating wind farm named *Spiorad Na Mara*/Spirit of the Sea, comprised of sixty-six turbines three miles from shore and run by Canadian firm Northland Power, has been given permission to proceed. It was one of seventeen offshore locations offered to commercial developers for wind farms by the Scottish government's ScotWind project. With more energy due to come 'on stream' from offshore projects, more cables are needed to transmit it.

Interconnectors constrain as well as contain energy flows. In her ethnography of Orkney energy, Laura Watts details the moratorium on energy production imposed on the islanders, who have been too successful at generating electricity from the wind, over the last decade. As we know, Orkney is uniquely wind-rich and can generate more energy than it needs. The excess can be exported

– sold – to the mainland grid. The profitability of the island's renewable energy resources has been recognised and promoted by the local council. Following the uptick in state-funded research and development from the late 1970s onwards, it once again became the preferred site for turbine testing, aided by a cable connection to the mainland installed in 1982.[7] In recent years, the tradition of testing wind energy technology was extended to include wave energy by the establishment of the European Marine Energy Centre, which tests wave devices in cabled berths off Stromness. However, today the connector cable from Orkney to the mainland is a choke point. It could no longer contain the amount of electricity being produced on the islands, which overheated in the connector cable due to the friction between too many electrons.[8] Excess electricity threatened the functioning of the islands' own grid, and wind turbines were ordered to shut down in 2012 by Scottish and Southern Electricity in order to 'keep the lights on' on the islands. This shocked community and private turbine owners, and the local council, and effectively suspended the development of onshore wind energy further.

A new cable, 57 km long, connecting Orkney and Dounreay, was approved by Ofgem in 2023. A press release by SSEN described how the project 'will unlock Orkney's potential'.[9] Also in the works is an offshore project, the West of Orkney Windfarm, which will produce up to 2000 mW through 125 turbines, at a location 30 km west of Orkney, by 2029. Energy companies like to translate capacity to the number of homes supplied with electricity, and this one can boast a headline-grabbing figure of two million.[10] It was granted an option agreement through the same ScotWind leasing round that saw the Hebridean Northland project secure rights to proceed. The seventeen projects will pay in total c. £700 million in option fees to the Scottish government and will occupy over 7000 m² of seabed.[11] While the West of Orkney Windfarm will have its own connector to Caithness, it is clear that the increasing focus on offshore wind energy development has spurred on renewed commitments to island connectivity. Islands have become nodes in an oceanic wind energy network. These large-scale projects leverage large-scale infrastructure deals.

These lines of connection lie between islands and mainlands, and between nations. Britain has six interconnectors (international connectors), linking it with Norway, France, Belgium, and the Netherlands, and the most recent connection (in 2023), Denmark. These cables, which are hundreds of kilometres long and as deep as 600 m below the surface, can currently exchange 7.8 mW between Britain and the continent. As the National Grid frames it, this is enough to supply 15 per cent of national electricity requirement. This is because Britain is now (and has been for some years) a net importer of electricity, with the first quarter of 2024 seeing record high import levels from its five suppliers. The total amount of electricity imported in the first quarter of the year – 11.2 TWh, a 24 per cent increase from the year before – was more than the UK imported from France in the whole of 2020.[12] Changing this state of affairs to make Britain a net exporter of electricity is one of the stated aims of the 2024 Labour government's Great British Energy company, and would signal a shift in national energy security away from reliance on imports.

Interconnectors have strategic dimensions: they can carry electricity between nations, so require cooperation and legislation; and, as with the fibre-optic cables that criss-cross ocean floors and carry most of the world's internet traffic, they are a security risk as a potential sabotage target. (This is nothing new: on the first day of the First World War, the British Navy cut five German seabed cables in a strike on communications.) In November 2022, underwater explosions were registered in the sea east of Bornholm (Denmark), where the Nordstream 1 and 2 pipelines lie. The pipelines are two of twenty-three built by Russia to bring gas to Europe, though use of Nordstream 2 was halted by Germany in 2021 following Russia's invasion of Ukraine. The explosions happened a day before a new Baltic pipeline routing gas from the Norwegian North Sea to Europe – an alternative to Russian gas – opened. Investigations by Denmark and Sweden found the Nordstream explosions to be the result of sabotage but refrained from naming any suspects. Global political instability and conflict has pushed national energy self-sufficiency and security higher up the political agenda. Diversity in energy sources is one means to secure energy supplies that can absorb supply issues, market volatility, and sabotage. Nationally controlled and located energy systems are another.

Enclosing the sea

Offshore wind energy adds new cables to an already well-crossed seabed. In the nineteenth century, at the height of empire, projects to develop telecommunications by wireless and by cable began. Guglielmo Marconi was focussed on wireless communication, transmitting radio waves through the air. Others were exploring telecommunication via cables. John Pender, a Scottish textile merchant, invested in the Atlantic Telegraph Company in 1856. It laid transatlantic cables in 1858–66, and Pender turned his attention to building cable links between Britain and India. On 7 June 1870, the final piece of cable came ashore to Porthcurno, a pristine, white-sand beach edged by golden granite in the far southwest of Cornwall. The first messages between Britain and India were the simple question, 'How are you', and the response, 'all well', and took just five minutes to receive.[13] From this simple exchange, telecommunication grew rapidly. Pender's companies alone laid 73,000 nautical miles of cables.

The reach of Victorian industry down to and across the sea floor made an imaginative impression. Rudyard Kipling wrote a poem, 'The Deep Sea Cables' (1896), that describes

> the descent down to the dark, to the utter dark, where the blind white sea
>   snakes are
> There is no sound, no echo of sound, in the deserts of the deep
> Or the grey level plains of ooze where the shell-burred cables creep.
>
> Here in the womb of the world—here on the tie-ribs of earth
> Words, and the words of men, flicker and flutter and beat—
> Warning, sorrow and gain, salutation and mirth -
> For a Power troubles the Still that has neither voice nor feet.
>
> They have wakened the timeless Things; they have killed their father Time
> Joining hands in the gloom, a league from the last of the sun.
> Hush! Men talk to-day o'er the waste of the ultimate slime,
> And a new Word runs between: whispering, 'Let us be one!'

Kipling's depiction of the cables as blind white snakes, and the sea floor as 'ultimate slime', makes the deep ocean a place of horror. The arrival of human chatter, transmitted by the 'shell-burred cables', disturbs the ooze which has its own voice, humming beneath the surface din. We might read this as the anxiety of modernity, where fast communication unsettles deep time.

Kipling built on a gothic tradition of both monstering the deep, and constructing it as an unknown, into which the networks of Western society arrive. This is reflective of an ocean imaginary which enabled colonisers to lay claim to sea space. In an influential article in 2000, Monica Mulrennan and Colin Scott argued that an understanding of *mare nullius* declared the oceans to be 'vacant of indigenous tenure or authority'. This opened them to European treatment first as an international commons, and then for offshore zones, as subject to the sovereign jurisdiction of states.[14]

European colonial expansion had precipitated a philosophical debate over the freedom of the sea in the early seventeenth century. A Dutch lawyer advising the Dutch East India Company, or *Verenigde Oostindische Compagnie* (VOC), Hugo Grotius, made a case that the ocean could not be occupied or enclosed, and therefore could not be enclosed and owned. Its content could become property, but the ocean itself could not. The title of his essay, *The freedom of the seas; or, the right which belongs to the Dutch to take part in the East Indian trade*, reflected the strategic stakes for naval and imperial powers: keeping the seas allowed European states to do as they pleased in distant seas. A challenge to Grotius came from an Englishman, John Selden, who sought to protect British seafaring interests against the Dutch. Chris Armstrong details the philosophical exchange between the two in his book *A blue new deal: why we need a new politics for the ocean*.[15] Selden's response to Grotius' suggestion that the ocean must always remain in a state of common access was that nothing 'can be said or imagined more absurd'.[16] There were plenty of examples from history and scripture that showed dominion over the ocean was possible. Marine territories could be outlined on a map and easily understood; diminishing fish stocks were evidence that ocean commodities were exhaustible. Ownership was both feasible and worthwhile, Selden argued. It was possible to have a *mare clausum* – an enclosed sea.

Grotius's arguments won the day, and the freedom to roam, and exploit, the oceans shaped the subsequent centuries of colonialism. By the mid-twentieth century, though, the impacts of industrial fishing and the beginnings of offshore oil extraction propelled increasing national claims to the sea and the seabed. Ocean protection – and ocean exploitation – were two forces jointly compelling the process. Long legal discussions and negotiations eventually resulted in the United Nations Convention on the Law of the Sea (UNCLOS; agreed in 1982, and in force from 1994). This set out a series of laws determining who could access the oceans and the ocean floor, which Armstrong characterises as an enclosure of the ocean.[17]

The enclosure expanded 'territorial seas' from three miles from shore to twelve miles. In this zone, nation states have sovereignty and can do as they wish with the water, the seabed, and the airspace above. Crucially for wind energy (and other ventures), UNCLOS also created 'Exclusive Economic Zones' (EEZ) that extend from the 12 nautical mile mark to 200 nautical miles offshore. Nations do not own these areas, but they hold the legal right to use any natural resources contained within them. The UK had already delineated its continental shelf and its right to seabed, subsoil, and natural resource extraction in the 1964 Continental Shelf Act, legislation which allowed the opening up of the North Sea oil and gas fields. UNCLOS applied such an approach unilaterally. As Elizabeth DeLoughrey notes, this 'radical remapping' amounts to the enclosure, and with it control, of 'thirty-eight million square nautical miles of the global sea [or] 35 percent of the world ocean'. A 200-mile Exclusive Economic Zone skirts a territorially small island nation such as the United Kingdom like a resource-rich halo. UK crown dependencies and British Overseas Territories in the north and south Atlantic, Caribbean, Pacific, and Indian oceans mean that the total UK EEZ is 6,805, 586 km sq. It is the largest in the world. I argued earlier that onshore wind redrew the nation from the edges in; the use of the EEZ to develop offshore wind adds an oceanic, porous, valuable, global, energy border.

In the UK the seabed from the tideline to the 12-mile mark is the property of the Crown Estate. The Crown Estate is a collection of marine and land assets and holdings that belong to the reigning monarch. It cannot be sold, and the profits it generates are paid to the government, which returns a percentage to the Royal Household in the form of the Sovereign Grant.[18] It also holds the rights to explore and use the seabed, subsoil, and natural resources of the continental shelf areas out to the 200-mile EEZ limit. Oil, gas, and coal rights are controlled by the state. In 2004, Tony Blair's government awarded the Crown Estate the right to licence the generation of renewable energy on the continental shelf under the Energy Act 2004.[19] This means that the development of offshore wind in the UK has been overseen by the Crown Estate through a series of leasing rounds, a marked difference to onshore wind. It has been an lucrative business: in 2022–23, Offshore Leasing Round Four generated a significant revenue increase for the Crown Estate, which made a record annual profit of £443 million, and was valued at £15.8 billion by March 2023.[20] In 2017, the percentage of the Sovereign Grant was raised from 15 per cent to 25 per cent of Crown Estate profits (ostensibly to cover renovation costs at Buckingham Palace). The Royal Family does very well from wind energy, as does the Treasury.

The 1970s offshore oil boom made the North Sea 'a productive environment of marine capitalism'.[21] Money is being made through offshore wind, too. In an article by Alexandra Campbell on renewable energy in contemporary poetry, I was struck by a quote from the Offshore Valuation Group in 2010. They declared: 'we find ourselves [with offshore renewable energy] in a comparable position to that of the nascent UK oil and gas companies of the 1970s'.[22] While offshore wind energy aims to distinguish – and distance— itself from fossil fuel extraction by emphasising its role to play in generating low-carbon electricity and achieving net zero carbon emissions, in reality the financing and delivery of offshore wind is entwined with fossil capital. The Crown Estate (England Wales and Northern Ireland) and Crown Estate

Scotland's leasing rounds attract proposals from companies aiming to establish wind projects in the sea. Of the recent round of ScotWind projects, BP Alternative Energy Investments and Shell New Energies, renewable arms of the oil multinationals, were among the successful bidders. Oil multinationals are strategically building the renewable energy side of their businesses and investing in offshore wind energy as a way to 'future-proof' their business, access lucrative renewable markets, and offset their ongoing (and still increasing) extraction of fossil fuels.

Eco-wind?

In the 1980s, in an attempt to improve fishing grounds and the environmental record of offshore oil production, the US rolled out the Rigs-to-Reefs pro-gramme. Rather than being completely removed (at considerable cost), decommissioned oil rigs could be left in the ocean to form artificial reefs to support sea life. The platform structures were toppled, partially removed, or towed to a new site, where they were left for corals, seaweeds and fish to colonise. The historian Dolly Jørgenson has written about the Rigs-to-Reefs programme as a key strategy to make the oil industry more 'environmentally friendly', one that worked so well that aquariums across the US recreated rigs-to-reefs in their displays. Vibrant communities of sea-life 'do indeed crawl on and swim through offshore oil structures and artificial reefs', writes Jørgensen. The choice of aquariums to reflect this new marine environment reveals the social, political, and scientific context in which the exhibitions were developed and represents a naturalisation of oil in American cultures and oceans. American oceans, viewed through aquariums, are a 'harmonious meeting place of oil and water'.[23]

Wind energy does not have the same public relations challenge as the oil industry when it comes to its environmental impacts and sustainability efforts, but it would be wrong to think it is free from impacts or controversy. Construction in particular disturbs sea life, with the acoustic impacts of seabed preparation, pile-driving into the seabed, and increased vessel traffic impacting fish and benthic species in particular.[24] The presence of turbine stands can interrupt fish breeding grounds and sea mammal migration routes, and the visual, spatial, and aural presence of turbine rotors above the sea surface can disrupt flight routes of migratory birds (as it does onshore, too). However, there is also overlap between offshore wind sites and marine protected areas, with evidence that, by preventing commercial fishing – particularly trawling, which damages the seabed – offshore wind structures can contribute to ocean conservation.[25] Fishers have been vocal opponents of offshore wind, protesting the reduction of fishing zones by the increasing number of turbines, which pose a navigational risk to boats.

In an echo of the rigs-to-reef programme, the wind industry is more visibly beginning to centre the potential environmental benefits of offshore structures. *Ecowende* is a large wind farm currently under construction 53 km off the Dutch coast near Ijmuiden, due to begin operation in 2026. It is a joint venture by Shell (the oil multinational), Eneco (a Dutch supplier of energy and gas, under state ownership until 2020 and now owned by Mitsubishi and Chubu), and Chubu (Japan's third largest electric utility company), that places its 'nature positive' ambitions at the forefront of its public-facing identity. The *Ecowende* website deviates from the usual aesthetic norm of wind energy companies, which tend to communicate technological proficiency and the scientific sublime through photographs and graphic renderings of machines and plenty of statistics. *Ecowende* instead employs illustrations with watercolour effects that depict wind turbines in the water from the perspective of a gannet flying overhead, for example; or a wind-farm-at-night animated scene with stars twinkling overhead and shoals of fish swimming around the piles below. Think high-quality illustrated children's book rather than shareholder report.

The words match the pictures, with ambitions to make a 'net positive impact' and support a 'flourishing ecosystem' front and centre of the homepage. *Ecowende* commits to a number of strategies, each focused on different species groups. So, for birds, they will use taller wind turbines with higher rotors (thought to reduce bird strike) and place them further apart to create a flight corridor down the centre of the wind farm. They also promise to apply 'location-specific' curtailment for migratory birds, so that when local migration occurs, turbines will temporarily switch off. Other strategies include trialling noise-mitigating pile installation techniques (for the benefit of harbour porpoise, a species know to be adversely affected by noise); and, inspired perhaps by their fossil fuel business arm, by stimulating natural reef formation at the wind farm site. However, 'as this is highly experimental, we cannot yet say much about the size and/or impact of stimulating natural reef formation'.[26]

This ambiguity is both necessary and instructive. Many of the approaches being trialled at *Ecowende* to mitigate impacts on animals and ecosystems are innovative and untested. The wind industry has made much of its contribution to sustainability goals and carbon emission reduction in recent decades but has been less willing to confront the ecological impacts of constructing and operating wind turbines in fragile landscapes, like the peat bogs of Lewis or the seabed. Take bird and bat fatalities from turbine collision, for example. The scientific literature varies wildly, with annual bird and bat fatality rates ranging from about 1–12 and 0.2–53.3 deaths respectively per MW of power generated.[27] Such data nearly always focuses on onshore wind, as at offshore sites the ability to find and count dead bird bodies is almost impossible. To address the ecological impacts of offshore wind, innovation is a pre-requisite, and the ability to work towards best practice across two areas – environment and innovation – is a tantalising mix for a large, ambitious energy conglomerate. *Ecowende* has pitched their 'brand' around being able to improve industry practice. No industry is more adept at offloading the responsibility for climate breakdown than the oil industry, which has actively spread confusion, fought scientific facts, and 'merchandised doubt', as Naomi Oreskes and Eric Conway memorably described it.[28] Now active in the sphere of low-carbon energy and attempting to *address* climate breakdown, we should pay attention to – and challenge where needed – oil companies operating as wind companies who claim to not only limit environmental damage, but improve the lot of species from the seabed to the sky. *Ecowende*'s turbines will, we can say with some certainty, generate about 3 per cent of the current Dutch electricity demand. Whether or not their suite of innovations will work to protect birds, bats, fish, and porpoise, neither we nor they can yet say.

One way that *Ecowende* and other offshore wind farms are backing up their claims to be improving on existing practices, particularly but not only in the area of environmental impact, is through the use of digital surveillance technology. Partly because of the logistical challenges of monitoring machinery at sea, offshore wind has embraced digital technologies as a means to collect data about the functioning, efficiency, and impacts of wind energy infrastructure. This echoes other moves towards digital environmental monitoring, such as Microsoft's plan to build a 'planetary computer' that aggregates global environmental data, made available to individuals and businesses, and the EU's €8 billion project to develop a digital model, or 'digital twin', of the Earth to monitor and predict environmental change.[29] For the wind industry, embracing digital technology has supported a shift away from the precautionary principles previously in play.[30] By committing to data gathering as they go, projects can proceed quickly, capitalising on uncertainty as a learning opportunity. So, in the case of *Ecowende*, we can read the language of their public-facing material to identify data gaps and uncertainties. 'Science suspects that a higher [turbine] tip height will allow birds to move more freely', the website tells us. 'Throughout the project, we will compare the effect of taller wind turbines with the behaviour and the number of collisions of birds in areas where wind turbines are at a normal height.'[31] The language belies the uncertainty: adjectives are tentative, and the tense is future. For those involved, it's a win–win situation: 'Science' gets some data, and the wind project can shout about its innovation and industry-leading practices. The birds? They will have to take their chances.

A group of scholars in the Netherlands are paying critical attention to this shift towards digital governance in energy. They argue that it favours multi-stakeholder collaborations in which private companies are brought in to provide expertise and equipment, with implications for data access and ownership.[32] It also accelerates a move towards automated and data-driven decision making that has obvious implications for the claims of offshore wind to be an employer of the future. Oil rigs run on human labour, and so while governments (particularly in Scotland, home to the majority of the UK's offshore workers) optimistically promise a skills-transfer from a well-paying fossil fuel industry on its way out, to an ascendent offshore renewables industry, the reality is that the skills of one do not map onto the increasingly digitised other.

The academics note that digital tools are often represented as neutral and value-free technological fixes to complex environmental problems, but there are deep questions to ask about the often hidden or opaque politics and finances behind digital technologies, which can have, for example, dual military and environmental uses. One wind farm's observation drone is another belligerent state's spycopter. We have seen the close links between military and energy sectors, in the development of civil nuclear power, the murder of Ken Saro-Wiwa in Nigeria, and Western involvement in conflicts with and between oil states.[33] The links between environmental monitoring, the development of digital technologies, and the pursuit of political and military dominance is also well documented (see the twentieth century's 'race for space', for example).[34] The paper produced by Klopperberg et al., calls for greater transparency and accountability in the use of digital technologies in the wind industry, and attention to be paid to the not-neutral ecological footprint of the tech and the data storage it requires. For the wind industry at large to fulfil their promises of sustainability and 'progressive innovation' (to borrow one more time from *Ecowende*), attention to the social and political dimensions and implications of digitisation is required.

The UK has embraced offshore wind with gusto (Figure 7.1). It offers a chance to skirt some of the complexities that occur when energy infrastructure is developed in full view on land and still draws on (long-challenged) notions

7.1 Beatrice Works suite no. 7 – Assembly offshore, Moray Firth. 2012 edition 20, colour etching, chin collé and hand tinted watercolour, 420 mm x 300 mm. © Sue Jane Taylor.

of the ocean as empty space, ripe for development. This chapter has offered a critical reading of offshore wind, not as a means to detract from its significant achievements and potential, which are remarkable and key to a low-carbon energy future, but to draw attention to the ways in which a renewable energy industry does not in and of itself break free from long-held patterns of dominion, colonisation, and extraction. The UK's offshore wind expansion aims to achieve 50 GW of power production by 2030. The Renewables section of the 2022 British Energy Security Strategy, published by the Johnson government, exclaimed without hesitation that it is 'our history of North Sea oil and gas experience [that] enables us rapidly to deploy our expertise in sub-sea technology and maximise our natural assets'.[35] There is no subtext or close reading needed: offshore wind, to certain interests, is a means to extend the life of the oil and gas industry, rather than break from it. The same document goes on to proclaim that 'we will be the Saudi Arabia of wind power', a phrase I have encountered repeatedly in my research, deployed by Alex Salmond, former First Minister of Scotland with regard to Orkney, and now here, by ex-Prime Minister Boris Johnson. When political visions of wind energy rely on oil metaphors, it is time we applied a close, critical lens to exactly what methods are used, which interests are being met, and what claims are being made by an industry that claims it offers an alternative to fossil-fuelled energy. Remaking offshore wind in the mould of offshore oil and gas weakens the foundations of sustainability that the industry has built itself. If nothing else, reaching for oil metaphors from the past to envisage renewable energy in the future betrays a paucity of imagination and a lack of ambition to think beyond a high-carbon world.

8

Energy imaginaries

The history of wind energy gives us plenty to think with. This final chapter explores some of wind's more speculative possibilities: examples and ideas that challenge or contrast with the established norms and accepted way of doing things. The point of this is not to highlight efficacy – some of these examples have failed or faltered or are impractical. Some of the ideas are less about what we do, and more about how we think. The point is that that they all show a diversity of thought and action in wind energy – a reminder that wind is everywhere, and the ways in which people have used it are rich and varied. They open up new energy imaginaries: ways to (re)think the relationship between energy, technology, place, and people, that differ to the norm, and – perhaps – offer alternatives to the status quo.

Do we need alternatives? Each year wind contributes more to the national energy mix. Put simply, the technology works. Here, both the scale of the challenge of achieving net zero, and the matter of a 'just' transition, come to the fore. If Britain aims to achieve a carbon-free economy and society by 2050 (or sooner) then we need to apply all tools at our disposal, and act at every scale of the social, economic, and political register. Other energy sources will play their role: domestic solar power, heat pumps, building design, and retro-fitting all offer ways to lessen demand and generate heat and electricity at the domestic level. Nuclear and solar power, along with improving battery technologies, offer a future energy diversity at the national scale that can offset the vicissitudes of wind and sun and reduce reliance on gas. Big wind farms work well for both industry and government as they feed large amounts of power to the national grid, and capital to banks, treasury, and shareholders. They are a valuable and necessary component of the UK's net zero plans. But as we have seen, wind energy is – has always been – about more than these two powerful actors. It is also, and very fundamentally, about places, and the people who live in them. We know that 'Big Wind' works far less well for communities inhabiting wind-rich places like Lewis and Orkney, where fuel poverty remains high. We know, too, that policy and established practice can inhibit creative responses and solutions. It is good business, and good politics, to think more carefully and creatively about how wind energy can serve different communities, expand the options for non-fossil fuelled energy provision, and work to undo some of the inequalities that have been exacerbated by past energy production and use.

A literary scholar might look to fiction for new energy imaginaries. Fantasy, science fiction, and the growing genre of climate fiction (cli-fi) take on the challenge of imaging entire worlds and with them, world-views, that differ from our own. A series like N.K. Jemison's *Broken Earth* trilogy imagines a new planetary system, where deep time and geological forces are actively, violently, world-shaping; the struggle to survive on a constantly shifting tectonically alive planet drives her characters (and their evolved powers) to respond in order to survive. A work such as Kim Stanley Robinson's *The ministry for the future* imagines a near-future on our own recognisable planet, where the effects of climate change are more acute and political systems struggle to respond. Compared to the dystopia of much of the genre, this sci/cli-fi novel offers (some) hopeful imaginings of what galvanised social movements and political actors could achieve – as well as some worryingly recognisable scenarios. The wet-bulb heatwave scenario that opens Robinson's book came rushing to mind when reading news of the relentless 2024 heatwave in India, where temperatures in Rajasthan hit 50 °C. Water was too hot to drink, fruit bats fell dead from the trees, and hundreds of people died. Robinson takes climate-related scenarios becoming more familiar and amplifies them, as future climate stress will inevitably do, thinking through for us the possible outcomes. This is part of the ongoing appeal – and terror – of these genres: by imagining new scenarios and new worlds, they help us see our own, anew. A historian, however, tends not to create new worlds but rather look to our own past. There, if you can imagine it, someone will likely have already done it.

Beyond monoculture

The first alternative energy imaginary I'll put forward is one drawn from the examples of community wind turbines, some of which I've already mentioned. Researching these community turbines opened up a new imaginary for me – one that reconfigured what, or who, a wind turbine was for.

In *Tasglann nan Eilean Siar*, the Hebridean archives, lies a long paper trail that details the slow, persistent efforts of the community of Barra and Vatersay to set up a community wind turbine. The two islands (connected by causeway) are the southernmost of the Outer Hebridean archipelago. The community of just over a thousand residents started to meet and discuss the possibility of installing a wind turbine in early 2005, encouraged by an initiative at the time called *Iomairt Aig An Or*, or 'Initiative at the Edge', a partnership programme between the Scottish Executive, Highlands and Islands Enterprise Network, Communities Scotland, Crofters Commissions, Scottish Natural Heritage, the Health Boards and Councils of Highland, Orkney, Shetland, and the Western Isles.[1] Barra and neighbouring Vatersay were designated as an Initiative at the Edge Community from 2004 to 2007, which brought them £30,000 per annum of funding. This money was used to research and initiate the community turbine project. Henk Munneke, from the HIE Community Energy Unit, and the Scottish Community and Households Renewable Energy Unit, spoke to islanders about the Kyoto Protocol and renewable energy targets put in place by governments, and about the renewables obligations in electricity markets. He talked about how a turbine offered communities a way to generate renewable energy and generate income by selling excess power to electricity companies. Island council minutes document this first community meeting about wind energy, and the second, the third, and the many subsequent meetings over the course of the ten years, more or less, that it took for the turbine goal to be realised.

The archive is a testament to community organising. Once the idea of the turbine had been agreed, islanders paid visits to other private and community wind turbines to better understand how they worked. They start talking to academics at universities, who were keen to test new designs and find case studies for student research. A critical step was to establish a company, *Coim-hearsnachd Bharraidh Agus Bhatersaigh* (Barra and Vatersay Community Ltd, hereafter CBAB) which gave them the power to buy land, invest money or lend credit, and borrow and raise money.[2] By 2009, the community had found a turbine supplier (Enercon), if they could raise the money to cover the £998,253 cost. On top of this would be additional costs for grid connection.[3] A company update noted that they were discussing this with SSE, who were 'not overly responsive'. It takes until June the following year for a note confirming that they had accepted the SSE contract for grid connection, at a cost of £87,399. This takes the cost of the project over £1 million.

There is no way the small island community can stump up this kind of money themselves, so the key to the community turbine becomes the availability of finance. The CBAB notes start to betray – in my reading, at least – a note of caution, as the scale of financing begins to hit home. In 2010, someone – we don't know who – writes, 'we need to get some detailed financial projections drawn up for this project'. They go to the Cooperative Bank for a low-cost grant and loan, to minimise commercial borrowing. They don't get it. Here the archive trail goes cold, and I fear the worst for the Barra and Vatersay community turbine project. But then, in 2014, an article in the *Stornoway Gazette* brings good news: the turbine has been installed.[4]

In the end, total costs ran to £2.2 million, and funding was given by Triodos, the UK's leading ethical/sustainable bank, with subsidies from the Scottish government. The paper interviewed Norrie Cruikshank from Triodos, who says that 'most other banks would have run away from a project of this size and complexity … but the community was incredibly motivated'. Local councillor Donald Manford said 'the significance of this achievement cannot be overstated. The single-minded determination to succeed is a tribute to the entire community and our financiers, Triodos Bank.'

Why was the community so committed to this turbine? We know that there was a general intention to contribute to efforts to curb carbon emissions and do right by an environment understood to be in crisis; and by employing local construction companies, the project also brought work to the islands. But the tenacity needed to sustain the community through nearly a decade of organising, fundraising, researching, and planning came first and foremost from the knowledge that the fruits of that labour would be enjoyed by the community itself. The revenue raised by generating electricity on the island would pay for an all-weather sports pitch, support social and respite survives for the elderly, and provide grants for young people to travel to events and courses on the mainland.[5] The knowledge that the benefits would flow back to the community sustained the tenacity and commitment needed to see the project through.

When I traced this story from start to finish, it clarified for me how surely the odds were stacked against any attempts to erect wind turbines that differed from the normal, corporate model. Finance was readily available for large-scale wind farms, but for single turbines, almost impossible to find from the main banks. Wind energy had become a monoculture, which had little room for projects that wanted to work differently from the standard model.

The monocultural approach to agriculture was a key feature of post-enlightenment European scientific agriculture, and colonial rule.[6] It worked from an assumption that raising a single crop could make more productive and profitable use of land by streamlining and intensifying the labour and resources needed to produce timber, or cocoa, or sugarcane. It is the same broad logic that underpinned enclosure: bigger fields could hold more of the same crop, rather than the open-field patchwork of crop rotations that fitted multiple crops into small strips. And it was promoted, and imposed, by colonisers as a superior approach to indigenous methods of raising crops and animals. Indigenous knowledge and techniques, attuned to often highly localised conditions and more resilient to ecological change, were not valued as they were not seen as productive or efficient. As a tool of control over nature with deep class and race dimensions, implementing monoculture also enacted cultural erasure.

Indigenous, post- and de-colonial activists and scholars have made reconnecting with indigenous knowledge of the land central to the reclamation of identity and dignity.[7] Some of the perspectives being gained through this critical rejection of monocultural methods of farming are now informing the movement to recalibrate agriculture around the world, including in Britain, along more environmentally sensitive lines. Regenerative agriculture incorporates nature conservation into agricultural approaches, and aims to improve soil health and, from there, biodiversity, the functioning of the water cycle, and climate resilience. Many different approaches, from permaculture to agroforestry, replace one monocultural approach to agriculture.

I do not intend to get into the pros and cons of regenerative agriculture here. Its interest for me is as an approach pitched intentionally in contrast to monocultural agri-business: how these two ideas, or imaginaries, work from each other. The link to wind comes through the idea of the wind 'farm', as the long-accepted term for large-scale wind energy infrastructure. Sometimes named wind 'parks' elsewhere, in the UK the terminology of the wind farm has become the norm, entrenching the connection between wind technology and place. Meaning is drawn from this language. It makes wind a natural resource and the production of electricity from it a process of cultivation akin to raising crops from the soil. The wind 'farm' goes some way to naturalise the turbine and the power grid in rural landscapes, drawing synergies between energy extraction and agriculture as compatible and comparable.

If the wind farm asserts some affinity with agriculture, then it is with its monocultural form. Wind farms collect multiples of the same machine and place them in orderly rows, somewhat reminiscent of the straight lines of a commercial pine forest (*the* early exemplar of European monoculture). The wind industry, like agri-business, works towards maximising efficiency, productivity, and profitability. Like improved breeds of pigs and sheep in Georgian England, the turbines get ever larger. They are absolute units.[8]

As regenerative agriculture works to diversify what we grow, and how we grow it, I wonder if a regenerative approach to wind energy offers opportunity to imagine more, and more varied, ways to generate electricity from the wind than the corporation-owned wind farm. This is how the Barra and Vatersay turbine works as an energy 'imaginary', in addition to its core function as a successful turbine serving its community. It allows us to consider alternatives to the dominant norm and ask again that question: what, and who, is a wind turbine for? The wind farm works for the collective benefit of providing energy to the national grid, but when we pay dearly for that electricity, in the knowledge of how cheap it can be to produce, we start to question whether it is us it is working for or the structures of finance upon which the whole endeavour turns. The community turbine makes that same collective contribution, generating electricity though inverting the order of supply to the community first and the grid second. The profits that are also part of its generative process route back to the community too. It provides both electrical and financial benefits to the place where the wind is farmed. It is re-generative wind and could be made much easier to support. It shouldn't take ten years of tenacity to raise a community wind turbine.

Beyond extractivism

The 'electric wind' that has been the focus of this book has always been seen as an alternative to other energy fuels, from early experiments through to the present. The logic of that contradistinction has been mutable, finding new emphasis and rationale according to the times. In a period of postwar recovery, wind worked where grid connections did not. After the oil crisis, wind was viewed afresh as a secure and sovereign resource. When it was politic to promote nuclear power, wind joined a non-fossil fuel offering. And now, in an age of climate breakdown, when the mission to decarbonise systems and societies is urgent, wind offers a low-carbon energy source, standing in clean contrast to the dirty destruction of oil, gas, and coal.

We might need wind energy to be clean energy, more than ever before. The reality is that while the point of energy conversion remains alchemically, beguilingly, clean – no smoke, no waste, no residue – the materials and commodity chains that make it possible are less immaculate. Let's take a wind turbine and break it down. The central tower is often steel, a material that retains value and is recyclable. The blades are usually made from glass- or carbon-reinforced fibres in thermoset polymer matrix composites: set resins, such as epoxy or polyurethane.[9] These materials are strong, and light, can withstand high loads and pressures, and do not corrode easily. The resins cover an inner core of typically balsa or foam and can be coated with polyethylene or polyurethane. This mirrors, as it happens, the basic model of a surfboard. Instead of withstanding the impact of waves hitting the shore, a turbine blade is built to withstand the impact of wind on a standing structure. The processes of chemical bonding which give the blades their strength and lightness also make the separation of materials at the end of use a difficult, energy-intensive, and expensive process. Most turbine blades go to landfill. Given that fibreglass and resin alone make up around 75 per cent of a typical wind turbine mass, the waste incurred is a major barrier to making wind turbines a circular product.

Turbines also contain wiring, electronics, transformers, and magnets. Michael Faraday created an electromagnetic generator in 1831. He found that a conductor moved through a magnetic field created electrical current. Older turbines used this basic method, and have electromagnets in the blades, which pass near stationary coils of wire to generate an electrical current. These require a gearbox, and an external power source to provide an initial small electrical charge. High-performance wind turbines today use permanent magnets, which use the magnetic field of strong rare earth elements to generate the electrical current. They require no gearbox, making the overall turbine a simpler, cheaper, and lighter design that needs no external electrical connection and is able to work at low speeds.[10] Permanent magnets make wind turbines efficient and competitive. The rare-earth elements (REEs) they use – mainly neodymium (Nd), praseodymium (Pr), and dysprosium (Dy) – are, despite their name, abundant in the Earth's crust but with the catch that they come in low concentrations in minerals and are hard to separate out. Other REEs, such as lithium and cobalt, are better known, as they are components in batteries and electric vehicles .[11] Production is dominated by China, which in 2023 accounted for more than 77 per cent of the total production of rare-earth elements; other significant producers include Burma/Myanmar (11 per cent) and Australia (almost 9 per cent), Russia, Brazil, India, and the USA.[12] Securing supply chains of these core components has been a strategic concern for nations expanding not just their wind industries, but a whole array of electric products that includes now-everyday objects such as smartphones and LED lights. Rare-earth elements are so valuable today that old mine tailings are being reprocessed to identify and extract every last possible crumb, and former mines in places like the southwest of England, where rare-earth elements are found in small quantities in old tin and copper mines, are being reassessed for productivity.

Most REE mining takes place beyond Europe, and a lot of it in China, around the city of Ghanzou. The environmental impact of rare-earth mines is extensive, and devastating. There are two ways to mine REEs, both of which release toxic chemicals into the environment. The first involves removing topsoil to create a leaching pond, where chemicals are added to the earth to separate the metals. The second involves a similar process, but it is done underground. Both produce toxic waste that can seep into groundwater.[13] Research has found that producing one tonne of rare-earth ore in turn produces 200 cubic metres of acidic waste water.[14] A report by Chen Jie, winner of the 2015 China Environmental Press Awards' Journalist of the Year prize, described the impact of dumping of this untreated wastewater in the Tengger Desert as 'the death of the desert', poisoning the ecosystem and the groundwater for the region.[15] The processes from the REE lifecycle (smelting, separation, processing, and transportation) also produce high carbon emissions, which are rarely factored in to assessments of the turbines (and other products) they end up in. As Julia Adeney Thomas, historian of the Anthropocene, warns, 'there is nothing dematerialised or carbon-free about wind turbines if we look at the total picture'.[16]

An attention to the materiality of a wind turbine opens up a Pandora's box of processes, materials, supply chains, all of which challenge the image of 'clean energy' the wind industry is so adept at presenting. It also reminds us that wind energy is reliant on mines and miners, and the materials they bring up from the Earth's crust, and precedes an afterlife which offers few sustainable routes to circularity. There is a heavy human cost to these processes, with illegal mines operating well beyond health and safety standards, creating health impacts through pollution and directly committing human rights abuses. In the Democratic Republic of Congo, armed criminal organisations and guerrilla factions are at war for power over strategic minerals and the people that mine them.[17] As nations expand their renewable energy infrastructure and embrace electrification, demand intensifies further. Demand for dysprosium and neodymium is estimated to increase seven to twenty-six times over the next twenty-five years as a result of electric vehicle and wind turbines; China's own massive expansion of wind energy may mean that it cannot meet domestic demand, let alone international demand, and there exists currently a gap in annual output and expected growth in demand.

As a historian, I can't answer questions about how to solve future resource questions. But I can pay close attention to these material roots and chains that tie a wind turbine to the ground and think about how this blurs the extent to which wind energy offers a break or a continuation of processes linked to fossil fuel and mineral extraction. This is one further energy 'imaginary' to work with: the imaginary of wind as an extractive, and possibly 'extractivist', process, that punctures a self-congratulatory tendency and forces us to think hard once again about that question: what and who is a wind turbine for?

That wind is extractive is not, in itself, controversial. Many processes are extractive in some sense: by raising crops we extract nutrition and calories and value from soil and sun, for example. Wind energy extracts electricity from the wind. Because that electricity is useful it has value, and because the wind does not deplete through the process, it is renewable. In this respect, wind energy (and other renewables) differ from the 'extractive industries', such as quarrying and mining, which extract valuable materials from the Earth, a finite resource. This distinction is where wind's greater value lies: the ability to provide us with electricity, with neither the reduction of natural resources, nor the production of damaging byproducts.

But as we have just seen, wind energy is not independent from the extractive industry. A focus on the material footprint of a wind turbine expands out from the ground or water in which it sits, via lines of global commodity transportation, to connect with sites of mineral extraction, environmental degradation, and labour exploitation thousands of miles away. Extractive industries have been the focus of critical attention and activism that has reconceptualised them as 'extractivist'. As energy scholar Imre Szeman explains, extractivism is more than just the name for the specific practice of removing raw materials form the Earth's soil. The moment one 'adds the suffix -ism to the noun, extraction is transformed into a system or ideology', that explains the use (and abuse) of natural resources and makes explicit the connection between capitalism and the environment.[18] Thea Riofrancos has characterised extractivism as a kind of 'resource radicalism', a politics that emerged from South America as decades of neoliberalism privatised and exploited natural resources and galvanised left-wing resistance by indigenous, *campesino*, environmental, labour, and feminist groups.[19] These groups refused a capitalism based on exploitation and export of natural resources. Struggles over natural resources were understood to be struggles of territory and sovereignty between powerful political and economic elites on the right (often supported and financed by external interests, through multinational corporations, or US or Chinese investment), and a disenfranchised leftist coalition. It was from this 'critical horizon', Riofrancos argues, that wider discourses of extractivism emerged.[20]

These themes – the use of natural resources, land, indigenous rights – chime closely with the concerns of the Lewis wind farm activists. Though not explicitly framing their protests as against a wider system of extractivism, their concerns mirror those of other groups fighting more visibly damaging industries elsewhere and become part of a bigger critique of capitalism. Take this explanation by Imre Szeman and Jennifer Wenzel: 'when nature appears before us solely as a natural resource, other kinds of relation and value – ecological, spiritual, cultural, aesthetic – are disregarded, becoming unthinkable and sometimes even materially unavailable, when "taking without giving back to the soil" becomes the norm'.[21] It applies very closely to the concerns that Lewis inhabitants have of the disregard by both energy company and local government of the relationship between inhabitants (human and non-human) and moorland, Hebridean history and identity. The close, nuanced, meaningful relationship they have with the place proposed for the wind farm finds no recognition in the vision proposed by the company of it as a site for energy extraction.

Extractivism makes explicit the ways in which specific sites (like mines) and practices (mining, deforestation, land grabbing) operate as part of a bigger system of capitalism, in which economic growth is sustained through heavy environmental costs. Modern capitalism was made possible through fossil fuels, and the processes, power, and capital they unleashed. Wind energy is underpinning the shift away from economies and societies based on fossil fuels, to economies and societies based on an energy mix. If we are to respond to climate change and limit global warming, we need that mix to be dominated by renewable energy, and this is where the idea of extractivism is both hindrance and help. By grouping wind energy in with other extractive industries, it does a disservice to the contribution it is making, and will continue to make, to the crucial shift away from a fossil-fuel-dominated world. By drawing attention to the very real material dimensions of wind energy, hidden beneath the gleaming veneers of white wind turbines, it confronts us with the reality that wind energy relies on 'dirty' industries elsewhere. Until that is foregrounded in plans for net zero and discussion for clean energy futures, the promise of wind energy stands on weak foundations. Extractivism also helps us think harder about how the technology of wind energy functions within and for particular ideologies, so that in a capitalist system the value of wind is dissociated from the places and people that experience it, and is ultimately made abstract, another investment for pension funds alongside oil and gas stocks and shares.

Beneath all these imaginaries of wind energy runs a steady flow of electricity to the grid, a very real movement of particles that is growing year on year, lighting our homes and charging our phones. Many will say that we need to stop worrying about wind and get on with expanding it. History replies that politics, society, environment, and economics have always shaped the forms wind energy takes and whose interests it serves. We can build a world running on renewables in the image of the world that runs on fossil fuels, and perpetuate the inequalities, and injuries, that come with it. Or, we can imagine alternatives. Imre Szeman, the energy scholar who has most informed my thinking around extractivism, proposes that the shift away from fossil fuels and toward a wind-powered future 'opens up the possibility for a political shift from an exploitative, expansionist capitalist system to a system attentive to the subtle needs to the environment and organised around the just sharing of the planet's resources'.[22] This presents opportunity – and challenge. How radical our resources can be is dependent on us, the questions we ask, and the futures we imagine. I learnt recently of a German description for a period when little or no energy can be generated through wind or solar: the *dunkelflaute*, or 'dark doldrums'.[23] It is an evocative term, reinforcing the inseparable relationship between renewable energy systems and the weather they draw value and power from. Maybe I spend too much time in the world of the energy imaginary, but it conjures for me an image of a sailing ship, becalmed, waiting for sea-change. To not attend to the challenges raised by wind energy, to never confront its messy underbelly and accept it as an imperfect system, sends the ship to the dark doldrums, where it will sit, never quite providing the sea-change that clean energy could offer the way we configure our world.

Conclusion

This journey into electric wind ends at somewhere that looks like the beginning. After two centuries of fossil-fuelled modernity, the balance of where we get our electrical power is tipping towards low-carbon, renewable, sources of energy. In 2023, fifty-four countries built new wind power infrastructure. Globally, almost one third of electricity production comes from renewables – wind, solar, hydro-power, tidal, and some biomass.[1] In China, Brazil, the US, and Egypt, and many other countries, wind energy is growing at pace. In Britain new records continue to be broken. On a stormy January day in 2023, wind generated 56 per cent of the nation's electricity, the largest proportion yet, and at the coldest, darkest time of the year.[2] Every day the National Grid reports the proportional sources of the national electricity mix. I check regularly, finding in those days that renewables outpace other sources a reassuring calm that we are on the right track. Often, though, the presence of gas at the top of the production list brings me back down to earth.

The transition away from fossil fuels remains highly contingent. Oil and gas companies, sensing the mood change, add renewable arms to their business at the same time as they drill harder and faster than ever before. Use of wind energy to produce electricity is rising, but so is that of fossil fuels. Nearly two-thirds – 60.7 per cent, to be precise – of global electricity in 2023 was produced by burning fossil fuels. Transport and heating, the other major areas of energy use, are even more dominated by fossil fuels than electricity. Wind energy provides a low-carbon source of electricity, but it has not yet showed us a way to live without hydrocarbons.

While the wind industry, and much of the state and policy planning done around energy, looks relentlessly forward to our 'energy future', we live with a substantial wind energy past. It is a history rich with false starts, paradoxes, and bumps in the road. We have seen how closely connected – dependent, even – on other energy forms wind has been. When James Watt developed his steam engine, he needed a familiar point of comparison to measure its usefulness. He chose the horse, because the engine could do the work of several ponies, and so we still measure engine performance as horsepower. It has been through barrels of oil and tonnes of coal that wind has been valued, emphasising its position as an 'alternative' energy source. Wind's position as an alternative to fossil fuels helps us understand its trajectory both past and future. It complicates the idea of an energy transition, because we know that these take a long time, and don't replace earlier energy forms so much as add new sources. Wind is here, and it works, and it has done for some time. So how do we build towards a world that has abundant energy that brings human and planetary need in sync?

What I argue – and what this book has, I hope, shown – is that we need to start understanding energy as being much more than simply technology. The tech is central to the story – but so are the places it is put, and the people who build, fix, revere, critique, and oppose it. Wind, an animated force of nature, is no passive player in this story. It has tested human ingenuity and created the world and world-views from which wind energy explorations could emerge. The history of wind energy takes us to sites around Britain that have been reconfigured by the presence of the wind. Cultures of survival and use, nuanced knowledge of wind, fed into the more technocratic story of turbine design and development. Folk knowledge, community input, and real-world functionality helped produce data that mattered and turbines that worked. This gets lost in discussions of wind that are only about technological fixes and economic levers.

I followed wind energy to some of its most significant sites in the UK. These took me away from the centres of political power (and central archives), and into regions that have traditionally been overlooked in national politics. The Scottish far north, the deep west of Wales, the coastal southwest: these regions have been described as the 'frayed Atlantic edge' by historian David Gange, and have rich, regionally specific cultures and knowledge traditions inseparable from the landscapes, sea states, and weather conditions which shape them.[3] A history of wind energy maps the nation from these edges in. It offers a counterpoint to the nation mapped through politics, with Westminster, Holyrood, Stormont, and the Senedd at its centres, or through population, with the major cities at its heart. Instead, these are places typically wind-rich, less densely populated, and distant from cities. With these as our starting points we are reminded that environmental conditions, old geologies and newer geographies, and traditions of living with land, sea, and wind shape a nation, its energy past, and future, too. Notions of remoteness and harshness are usually made from a dominant opposite place and perspective. The presence of abundant wind has allowed a sometimes speculative reinterpretation of rural places previously dismissed as unproductive, but a romanticism can also be at work in the celebration of strong winds in islands, highlands, and moorlands. Hugh Piggott, who lives with self-built wind turbines in the offgrid community of Scoraig, northwest Scotland, reminded me of this. He spoke of the darkness, and the winter weather – 'exhausting, with the rain battering on the corrugated iron roof and the wind trying to tear it off'.[4] He described building a wind turbine as therapeutic, that 'instead of being intimidated by the wind you were harnessing it … you could say "yeah, bring it on, the more the better"'. Wind was an aggressive presence, and part of the motivation to build turbines was to 'conquer' it (Hugh's word) and make it useful – to get something out of living with it.

I began researching wind in Orkney, somewhat by accident. I'd gone to research wave power on the islands, but it became clear that that was a relatively recent addition to a many-layered energy story. As I read more, cast my research net out wider, and undertook field work in other places, I came to understand that energy history offered a lens to consider the nation and the ways in which energy, environment, politics, society, and culture interweave. Energy helped me better understand what the nation was and how it worked. In turn, the nation as a geophysical and political entity offered a useful framework for understanding energy. While our environmental challenges are vast and global in nature, a key scale for response, whether through politics or activism, remains national. Energy policy is devised nationally. Rather than diminish the role of the state, this history serves to 'bring the state back into energy history', allowing us to appreciate how state policy responds to global and regional triggers, can drive research and development, and how quickly progress can stutter when governments shift attention elsewhere.[5]

If we are to build our low-carbon energy capacity, consistent low-carbon energy politics is needed. The history of wind energy can seem momentously cumulative. Stutters and starts grew into grids and farms, risks turned to rewards, knowledge, skills, and capacities built over time. A productive industry developed, and wind energy became the sensible economic choice and viable alternative to wean nations off their addictions to fossil fuels. The inconsistencies and false starts are flattened by time. The idea that wind energy was inevitable ignores the decades of state-funded research and development programmes and the major leaps forward that occurred when political ideology centred equality of access to electricity as a dimension of welfare. (A history of Denmark's wind energy is an even stronger endorsement of consistent state support for successful energy industry.) This is worth noting at a time when the short-termism of politics seems ill-suited to the long-term challenges of decarbonisation, and when tech billionaires position themselves as the drivers of innovation.

A temporal flattening narrows what we understand wind energy to be. Its history shows that it has taken different forms and performed different roles according to time, place, and need. Wind energy also exists thanks to the efforts of hippies, visionaries, farmers, and engineers who worked sometimes with, but also often without, state or industry support to make wind energy happen. Their rich and varied visions of what wind could do, and who it could serve, pushed the discourse around wind and renewable energy. People who opposed and disrupted helped to shape wind energy too. Criticism of wind has helped identify its impacts – and its limits. Industry interests do not always intersect with environmental or social interests. There is ample room for more transparent conversations about how and for whom wind works, for centring more equitable practices at its operational heart, for it to fulfil its potential as a true fossil fuel alternative.

Wind turbines have come in different forms and worked at different scales: the history injects some diversity into the singular model of corporate wind energy which is favoured by governments and industry today. It allows us to imagine what more generous visions of wind energy might look like and how they might serve us differently. What if we incentivised more community turbines, for small island communities and for urban communities, like Lawrence Weston in Bristol? There, a grassroots resident-led development trust invited ideas for a community plan. A community-owned turbine was suggested in 2012. Like the Barra and Vatersay turbine, it took years to secure the permissions and funds, but the turbine was completed in May 2023 and sells its output to OVO Energy. It is the UK's biggest onshore turbine and is 100 per cent community owned. It generates enough electricity for the domestic use of Lawrence Weston – about 3,000 homes – and its income will fund a development plan. Energy systems are vast, world-shaping entities, but they also exist and function at very local levels. Communities have always been part of energy history, even if they have not been prominent in its telling, and they seem to me to be a particularly undervalued dimension in industry and state energy planning. The choice does not have to be one or the other. Large-scale state-administered onshore and offshore wind can work with other registers of wind energy, the local, the community, the region.

Energy history shows us to be 'creatures of fossil fuels' but it also shows us to be creatures of the wind.[6] We have sought to understand its character and harness its power. The relationship has been generative, producing not only electricity in ever-increasing quantities, but also new understandings of the world and our place in it. We stand at a climate precipice. At a difficult time during a troubled life, the poet John Clare wrote of how forsaken he felt. He longed for peace and untroubled sleep, the kind from childhood when he slept outdoors, 'the grass below – above the vaulted sky'. We stand, the future stretching uncertainly ahead. The earth below holds the finite riches of fossil fuels, for which we pay a high price twice. We can leave them in place. Look up – to the vaulted sky, where the electric wind swirls endlessly.

Acknowledgements

This book is the result of a long period of research and I have many people to thank. I was a postdoctoral researcher on the Arts and Humanities Research Council 'The Power and the Water: Connecting Pasts and Futures' project when I went to Orkney in search of waves and found winds instead. My colleagues on that project – Peter Coates, Georgina Endfield, Paul Warde, Leona Skelton, Carry van Lieshout, Alexander Portch, and Kayt Button – all got me thinking seriously about infrastructure and power. The History department at the University of Bristol has provided funding for additional research and fieldwork. Special thanks to Amy Edwards, Victoria Bates, Sumita Mukherjee, and Vivian Kong who read some of this in draft form.

My colleagues Sam Williamson (Engineering) and Ed Atkins (Geography) helped me think more expansively about wind energy. So did a workshop at the University of Leicester in 2024 organised by Matt Wilde and Ben Coles on 'the social and material life of Big Wind'. Many thanks to them for including me in the programme. A project with Alison Rust (Earth Science), Mathilde Braddock (Steps in Stone), Sam Le Butt (English Literature), Claire Corkhill (Earth Science), and Isla Gladstone (Bristol Museum) called Wasting Time, funded by the Brigstow Institute, challenged us all to think about how we make sense of the Anthropocene in the city we live in. I had to include William Smith's map in the book. That project grew from a connection made possible by the wonderful Julia Adeney Thomas, honorary Bristolian.

Thank you to the archivists at Orkney Library, *Tasglann nan Eilean Siar*, the National Library of Wales, Liz Bartram and Mildred Cookson of the Mills Archive, and to *Resurgence* magazine for access to their digital archive. Dolly Jørgenson allowed me to share very early rough ideas at an energy workshop at the University of Oulu; Dolly and Finn Arne Jørgenson facilitated a Green Transitions fellowship at the University of Stavanger in 2022. The gift of time and space to think and write came at the perfect moment. August–September in Norway with my fellow fellows, Giulia Champion and Hans Baumann, and the group of PhD students and postgraduates at Stavanger was a dream. Thank you Sebastian Lundsteen, Aster Hoving, Jonas Taudal Baekgaard, Mehdi Torkaman, Mica Jorgensen, and Charlotte Wrigley for showing us the good swimming spots. Thanks to Katie Ritson for suggesting and facilitating an energy quest to Shetland. The swimming we did there ranks as the coldest, most scenic, so far.

Thanks to Robert Suits for the invitation to speak about wind at the University of Edinburgh Fennell Forum on energy, with him and Martin Chick (who also kindly sent me hard-to-find articles on energy economics at various points of this project). Thanks to Ewan Gibbs for wanting to talk energy in Glasgow. Katrina Navickas, Ben Anderson, Linda Ross, and Matthew Kelly ran a workshop on rural modernism that shaped my thinking on energy and landscape. I put together a panel for the American Society for Environmental History Conference in Boston with Linda Ross, Hiroki Shin, and Liz Chatterjee. It went so well we decided to write together – cue a year of Friday zoom calls, in which we talked energy and compared notes on a period of tumultuous politics on both sides of the Atlantic. Those conversations and the article we wrote pushed my thinking on energy into new territory. Last, but not least, thanks to Shannon Kneis and Laura Swift at Manchester University Press for their trust and guidance.

Just as I was getting going with this book project, my family received devastating news: my father, who had had some back pain, was given a terminal cancer diagnosis. I went home to spend time with him and help with care, and he died four months later. His loss has been hard to bear for all of us, and especially my mother. This book is for them both, Walter and Esther.

Notes

Introduction

1 International Energy Agency *Wind energy annual report 2000* (National Renewable Energy Laboratory, May 2001), 172 [accessed 23 April 2023] https://www.nrel.gov/docs/fy01osti/29436.pdf

2 Renewable UK Wind Energy Database, 'wind energy statistics' [accessed 17 January 2024] https://www.renewableuk.com/page/UKWEDhome

3 National Grid, 'Energy explained' [accessed 17 January 2024] https://www.nationalgrid.com/stories/energy-explained/how-much-uks-energy-renewable#:~:text=In%202023%2C%20individual%20renewables%20contributed,4.9%25%20to%20the%20renewable%20mix

4 National Grid Electricity System Operator Limited, *Annual Report and Accounts 2022/23*, 14.

5 Aljazeera news online, 'UK's last coal-fired power plant to close after more than 100 years' (30 September 2024) [accessed 20 January 2025] https://www.aljazeera.com/news/2024/9/30/uks-last-coal-fired-power-plant-to-close-after-more-than-100-years

6 Jillian Ambrose, 'End of an era as Britain's last coal-fired power station shuts down', *Guardian* (30 September 2024) [accessed 20 January 2025] https://www.theguardian.com/business/2024/sep/30/end-of-an-era-as-britains-last-coal-fired-power-plant-shuts-down; Simon Hare, 'Final fuel delivery marks end of the line for coal', *BBC News East Midlands* (1 July 2024) [accessed 20 January 2025] https://www.bbc.co.uk/news/articles/c886qd2g80xo; Rachel Millard, 'UK's reliance on coal-fired power set to end after 140 years', *Financial Times* (4 September 2024) [accessed 20 January 2025] https://www.ft.com/content/5164185d-b0d6-40d1-99b4-59f8039111c2

7 Jean-Baptiste Fressoz, *More and more and more: an all-consuming history of energy* (London: Allen Lane, 2024); Stephen Gross and Andrew Needham, *New energies: a history of energy transitions in Europe and North America* (Pittsburgh, PA: University of Pittsburgh Press, 2023); Sean Kheraj, 'More: energy history and energy futures', Network in Canadian History and Environment blog (10 April 2019) [accessed 23 January 2025] https://niche-canada.org/2019/04/10/more-energy-history-and-energy-futures/

8 Carbon Brief, 'UK Policy Analysis: UK's electricity was cleanest ever in 2024' (2 January 2025) [accessed 23 January 2025] https://www.carbonbrief.org/analysis-uks-electricity-was-cleanest-ever-in-2024/

9 Department for Energy Security and Net Zero, 'National Statistics: Energy trends – imports, exports and transfers of electricity' (December 2024) [accessed 20 January

2025] https://assets.publishing.service.gov.uk/media/6762b2fe3229e84d9bbde776/ET_5.6_DEC_24.xlsx

10 Our World in Data 'Share of electricity production by source, World, 1985–2023 (CC BY licence)' [accessed 20 January 2025] https://ourworldindata.org/electricity-mix

11 Intergovernmental Panel on Climate Change, 'Synthesis report of the IPCC sixth assessment report (AR6)' (March 2023) A.2.1–A.2.2 [accessed 23 January 2025] https://www.ipcc.ch/report/ar6/syr/downloads/report/IPCC_AR6_SYR_SPM.pdf

12 European Union Copernicus Climate Change Service Bulletin, 'Warmest January on record, 12–month average over 1.5 pre-industrial' (9 February 2024) [accessed 20 January 2025] https://climate.copernicus.eu/warmest-january-record-12-month-average-over-15degc-above-preindustrial#:~:text=Samantha%20Burgess%2C%20Deputy%20Director%20of,C%20above%20the%20pre%2Dindustrial

13 IPCC AR6 SYR, B.6.1, Table XX.

14 Andreas Malm, *Fossil capital: the rise of steam power and the roots of global warming* (New York: Verso, 2016), 1, 15.

15 John McNeill, 'Cheap energy and ecological teleconnections of the industrial revolution, 1780–1920', *Environmental History* Forum: the environmental history of energy transitions 24:3 (2019), 492–502.

16 Jim Clifford, 'London's soap industry and the development of global ghost acres in the nineteenth century', *Environment and History* 27:3 (2021), 471–497; Kenneth Pomeranz, *The great divergence: China, Europe, and the making of the modern world economy* (Princeton, NJ: Princeton University Press, 2001).

17 Corinne Fowler, *Green unpleasant land: creative responses to rural England's colonial connections* (Leeds: Peepal Tree Press, 2020); *Our island stories: country walks through colonial Britain* (London: Penguin Allen Lane, 2024).

18 Other nations had significant historical coal industries, notably China and Japan – but their impacts remained relatively contained until the twentieth century. See John McNeill, 'Cheap energy', and Victor Seow, 'Sites of extraction: perspectives from a Japanese coal mine in northeast China", *Environmental History* Forum: the environmental history of energy transitions 24:3 (2019), 463–533; for a study of modern Asian energy regimes, see Victor Seow, *Carbon technocracy: energy regimes in modern East Asia* (Chicago, IL: University of Chicago Press, 2022).

19 Hannah Ritche and Pablo Rosado, 'Global fossil fuel consumption', Our World in Data website (October 2022; revised January 2024) [accessed 20 January 2025] https://ourworldindata.org/fossil-fuels

20 John McNeill's work on global history has been important in the development of the Anthropocene concept. *Something new under the sun: an environmental history of the twentieth century world* (New York: W.W. Norton, 2002) made a case for the twentieth century as environmentally transformative and was published in 2002 – the same year Paul Crutzen landed on the 'Anthropocene' term. In 2016, McNeill and Peter Engelke published *The great acceleration: an environmental history of the Anthropocene* (Cambridge, MA: Harvard University Press, 2016), directly engaging with what had become, by then, an established concept. For an interdisciplinary case for a mid-twentieth century start date, see Jan Zalaciewicz, Colin Waters, Mark Williams, et al., 'When did the Anthropocene begin? A mid-twentieth century boundary level is stratigraphically optimal', *Quaternary International* 383 (2015), 196–203. See also Julia Adeney Thomas, *Altered earth: getting the Anthropocene right* (Cambridge: Cambridge University Press, 2016).

21 Rupert Read, 'Stubborn optimism will pave way to climate disaster', *Byline Times* (25 November 2022) [accessed 1 February 2024] https://bylinetimes.com/2022/11/25/stubborn-optimism-will-pave-the-way-to-climate-disaster/; Rebecca Solnit, 'Biden just betrayed the planet – and his own campaign vows', *Guardian* (14 March 2023) [accessed 1 February 2024] https://www.theguardian.com/commentisfree/2023/mar/14/biden-willow-project-betrayal-campaign-vows-climate-crisis

22 Christina Rossetti, *Sing song: a nursery rhyme book* (London: George Routledge, 1872).

23 Bill Luckin, *Questions of power: electricity and environment in interwar Britain* (Manchester: Manchester University Press, 1990).

24 Katrina Navickas, 'Conflicts of power, landscape and amenity in debates over the British super grid in the 1950s', *Rural History* 30:1 (2019), 87–103.

25 Jane Bennett's *Vibrant matter: a political ecology of things* (Durham, NC: Duke University Press, 2009) and her description of a Texas blackout is an imaginative guide for thinking about grid pathways. Further insight, though a very different approach, into how grids structure energy imaginaries and policies can be found in Elizabeth Chatterjee, 'Asian anthropocene: electricity and fossil developmentalism', *The Journal of Asian Studies* 79:1 (2020), 3–24.

26 Russ Mitchell, 'The energy historian who says rapid decarbonisation is a fantasy', *Los Angeles Times* (5 September 2022).

27 Thomas P. Hughes, *Networks of power: electrification in western society, 1880–1930* (Baltimore, MA: Johns Hopkins University Press, 1983); Diana Montaño, *Electrifying Mexico: technology and the transformation of a modern city* (Austin, TX: University of Texas Press, 2021); Leslie Hannah, *Engineers, managers and politicians: the electricity supply industry in Britain from 1948 to the present* (London: Palgrave MacMillan, 1982); Paul Brassley, Jeremy Burkhardt, and Karen Sayer, *Transforming the countryside: the electrification of rural Britain* (Abingdon: Routledge, 2016); Sorcha O'Brien, *Powering the nation: images of the Shannon scheme and electricity in Ireland* (Newbridge: Irish Academic Press, 2017).

28 Frank Trentmann and Anna Carlsson-Hyslop, 'The evolution of energy demand: politics, daily life and public housing, Britain 1920–70s', *Historical Journal* 61:3, 807–839; Rebecca Wright, 'Mass observation and the emotional energy user', *Canadian Journal of History* 53:3 (2018), 423–449.

29 TEMPEST database [accessed 23 April 2025] https://www.rgs.org/schools/resources-for-schools/tempest-extreme-weather-in-the-uk

30 See Georgina Endfield and Alexander Hall, '"Snow scenes": exploring the role of memory and place in commemorating extreme winters', *Weather Climate and Society* 8:1 (2016), 5–19.

31 Simon Naylor, Neil McDonald, James Bowen, and Georgina Endfield, 'Extreme weather, school logbooks and social vulnerability: the Outer Hebrides, Scotland, in the late nineteenth and early twentieth centuries', *Journal of Historical Geography* 78 (2022), 84–94.

32 Vinita Damodaran, Rohan D'Souza, and Subir Dey, 'Uncertainty and environmental change: Kutch and Sundarbans as environmental histories of climate change', in Lyla Mehta, Nicolai Hans Adam, and Shilpi Srivastava (eds), *The politics of climate change and uncertainity in India* (Abingdon: Routledge, 2022), 27–82; S.D. Smith, 'Storm hazard and slavery: the impact of the 1831 great Caribbean hurricane on St Vincent', *Environment and History* 18:1 (2012): 97–123; Oscar Webber, 'The plantation's role in enhancing hurricane vulnerability in the nineteenth-century British Caribbean', *Alternautas* 5:2 (2018): 29–42; Stuart B. Schwartz, *Sea of storms: a history of hurricanes in the greater Caribbean from Columbus to Katrina* (Princeton, NJ: Princeton University Press, 2015); Greg

Bankoff, *Cultures of disaster: society and natural hazards in the Philippines* (Abingdon: Routledge, 2003).

33 Stephen Pyne, *Fire: a brief history* (Seattle, WA: University of Washington Press, 2019 2nd edn); *Pyrocene. How we created an age of fire and what happens next* (Oakland, CA: University of California Press, 2021); Tom Griffiths, *Forests of ash: an environmental history* (Cambridge: Cambridge University Press, 2001).

34 Mica Jorgensen, 'Wild smoke: managing forest pollution in northern British Columbia since 1950', *Environment and History* 30:2 (2023), 267–290.

35 Martin Mahony and Samuel Randalls, 'Introduction: weather, climate, and the geographical imagination', Mahony and Randalls (eds) *Weather, climate and the geographical imagination: placing atmospheric knowledges* (Pittsburgh, PA: University of Pittsburgh Press, 2020), 3.

36 I am grateful to Giulia Champion for this insight.

37 Olga Tokarczuk, *Drive your plough over the bones of the dead* (London: Fitzcarraldo, 2022 6th edn), 77.

38 Frederik Greve, Karl-Georg Kanz, Michael Zyskowski, et al., 'The influence of foehn winds on the incidence of severe injuries in southern Bavaria - an analysis of the TraumaRegister DGU' *BMC Musculoskeletal Disorders* 21 (2020) https://bmcmusculoskeletdisord.biomedcentral.com/articles/10.1186/s12891-020-03572-z

39 Raymond Chandler, *Red wind: a collection of short stories* (Cleveland, OH: World Publishing Co., 1946).

40 Imre Szeman and Dominic Boyer, 'Introduction', in Szeman and Boyer (eds), *Energy humanities: an anthology* (Baltimore, MA: Johns Hopkins University Press, 2017), 3.

41 Szeman and Boyer, 'Introduction', 7.

Chapter 1

1 City Centre Mural Trail Glasgow website [accessed 23 April 2025] https://www.citycentremuraltrail.co.uk/murals/muralabout/73

2 Seow, *Carbon technocracy*; McNeill, 'Cheap energy'; Rolf Peter Sieferle, *The subterranean forest: energy and the industrial revolution* (Winwick: White Horse Press, 2010), 79.

3 For more discussion on energy densities, see Elizabeth Chatterjee, Marianna Dudley, Linda Ross and Hiroki Shin, 'Low carbon energies for zero carbon futures', *Journal of Historical Geography* (forthcoming).

4 Malm, *Fossil capital*, 17.

5 McNeill, 'Cheap energy', 492.

6 On Barak, *Powering empire: how coal made the Middle East and sparked global carbonization* (Oakland, CA: University of California Press, 2020); Priya Satia, *Empire of guns: the violent making of the industrial revolution* (Redwood City, CA: Stanford University Press, 2018).

7 William Stanley Jevons, *The coal question*, reproduced in Libby Robin, Sverker Sörlin, and Paul Warde, *The future of nature: documents of global change* (New Haven, CT: Yale University Press), 78.

8 Edmund Burke III, 'The big story: human history, energy regimes, and the environment', in Burke III and Kenneth Pomeranz (eds), *The environment and world history* (Berkeley, CA: University of California Press, 2009), 33–53.

9 McNeill and Engelke, *The great acceleration*, 9.

Notes

10 Ian Millar and Paul Warde, 'Energy transitions as environmental events', *Environmental History* 24:3 (2019), 464–471.

11 Greg Bankoff, 'Aeolian empires: the influence of winds and currents on European maritime expansion in the age of sail', *Environment and History* 23:2 (2017) 194; see also Miles Powell, 'Harnessing the great acceleration: connecting local and global history at the port of Singapore', *Environmental History* 27:3 (2022), 407–605.

12 [Accessed 23 April 2025] https://the-past.com/news/huge-early-neolithic-quernstone-unearthed-in-orkney/

13 UNESCO Tentative List 6192, 'Asbads (windmill) of Iran' (2/2/2017) [accessed 23 April 2025] https://whc.unesco.org/en/tentativelists/6192/; Richard L. Hills, *Power from the wind: a history of windmill technology*, (Cambridge: Cambridge University Press, 1994) 12–13; Moslem Mishmastnehi, 'Technological heritage of Persian windmills', *Journal of the British Institute of Persian Studies* (2021) https://doi.org/10.1080/05786967.2021.1960885

14 Hills, *Power from the wind*, 37.

15 Hills, *Power from the wind*, 223.

16 Gross and Needham, *New energies*, 15.

17 Roy Porter, 'Gentlemen and geology: the emergence of a scientific career', *The Historical Journal* 21:4 (1978), 809–836.

18 Nuno Luis Madureira, 'The anxiety of abundance: William Stanley Jevons and coal scarcity in the nineteenth century', *Environment and History* 18:3 (2012), 395–421.

19 Sieferle, *Subterranean forest*, 184–191.

20 Jevons, in Robin et al., *Future of nature*, 78.

21 Paul Warde, 'Commentary', *Future of nature*, 85.

22 Crosbie Smith and M. Norton Wise, *Energy and empire: a biographical study of Lord Kelvin* (Cambridge: Cambridge University Press, 1989), xix.

23 Crosbie Smith, 'Thomson, William, Baron Kelvin', *Oxford Dictionary of National Biography* (2011) https://doi-org.bris.idm.oclc.org/10.1093/ref:odnb/36507.

24 Author unknown, 'Power the story of man's helpers', *Harmsworth Popular Science* (1913), 2517. MA Mildred Cookson Papers.

25 Frederick Albritton Jonsson and Carl Wennerlind, *Scarcity: a history from the origins of capitalism to the climate crisis* (Cambridge, MA: Harvard University Press, 2023), 175.

26 Crosbie and Wise, *Energy and empire*, 301–347.

27 Hughes, *Networks of power*, 39–41.

28 *The Surrey Advertiser* (1 October 1881)

29 Hughes, *Networks of power*, 78.

30 Robert W. Righter, *Wind energy in America: a history* (Norman, OK: University of Oklahoma Press, 1996), 38.

31 Hughes, *Networks of power*, 32.

32 Geoffrey Jones, *Profits and sustainability: a history of green entrepreneurship* (Oxford: Oxford University Press, 2018), 41; Righter, *Wind energy in America*, 42.

33 Righter, *Wind energy in America*, 49.

34 Righter, *Wind energy in America*, 42.

35 Trevor J. Price, 'James Blyth – Britain's first modern wind power pioneer', *Wind Engineering* 29:3 (2005), 191–200, 195.

36 Price, 'James Blyth', 191.

37 Philippe Bruyerre, '1883: An electrical wind turbine in Vienna', *Wind Works* website (22 July 2023) [accessed 23 April 2025] https://wind-works.org/1883-an-electrical-

wind-turbine-in-vienna/, and in *Retrofutur: une autre histoire de machines à vents* (Sainte-Luce-sur-Loire: Bookelis, 2022), 104–105.

38 Matthias Heymann, 'Signs of hubris: the shaping of wind technology styles in Germany, Denmark, and the United States, 1940 – 1990', *Technology and Culture* 39:4 (1998), 649–650; 'Poul la Cour', Poul la Cour Museet website [accessed 19 April 2024] https://www.poullacour.dk/en/the-social-visio/

39 Unless otherwise specified, the sources identified below are held at the Mills Archive (Reading, UK) in the uncatalogued papers of Mildred Cookson. I am grateful to Liz Bartram and Mildred Cookson for making these materials available to me.

40 English Brothers Ltd, 'Electricity and power from the wind' sales brochure (September 1923). MA 231001.

41 Kander, Astrid, Paolo Malanima, and Paul Warde, *Power to the people: energy in Europe over the last five centuries* (Princeton, NJ: Princeton University Press, 2014), 292.

42 Jones, *Profits and sustainability*, 41.

Chapter 2

1 BBC Shipping Forecast, from Monday 4 March 12:00 UTC to Tuesday 5 March 12:00 UTC [accessed 5 March 2024] https://www.bbc.co.uk/weather/coast-and-sea/shipping-forecast

2 Simon Naylor, 'Log books and the law of storms: maritime meteorology and the British admiralty in the nineteenth century', *Isis* 106:4 (2015), 771–797

3 Naylor, 'Log books', 777.

4 JStor Global Plants, 'James Lind 1736–1812' [accessed 5 March 2024] https://plants.jstor.org/stable/10.5555/al.ap.person.bm000033179

5 Ernest Gold, 'Wind in Britain: the dines anemometer and some notable records during the last 40 Years', *Quarterly Journal of the Royal Meteorological Society* 62 (1936), 169, Bib no. 543594, National Meteorological Library, Exeter, UK.

6 Gold, 'Wind in Britain', 169.

7 Gold, 'Wind in Britain', plates XVI, XVIII, and XIX

8 Gold, 'Wind in Britain', 189.

9 Emily Dickinson, poem 1302 *The Complete Poems of Emily Dickinson* (New York, NY: Back Bay Books, 1976).

10 Gold, 'Wind in Britain', 187.

11 Gold, 'Wind in Britain', 186.

12 Brassley et al., *Transforming the countryside*, 1.

13 John Sheail, *Power in trust: the environmental history of the Central Electricity Generating Board* (Oxford: Clarendon Press 1991), 3.

14 Leslie Hannah, *Electricity before nationalisation: a study of the development of the electricity supply industry in Britain to 1948* (London: Macmillan Press, 1979), 43–53.

15 Hannah, *Electricity before nationalisation*, 239.

16 Martin Chick, 'The political economy of nationalisation: the electricity industry', in Robert Millward and John Singleton, *The political economy of nationalisation in Britain, 1920–1950* (Cambridge: Cambridge University Press), 258.

17 Katharine Shillabeer Button, 'The environmental history of the national grid', unpublished thesis (University of Cambridge, 2017), 206–8.

18 TNA HLG 80/63, British Electrical Development Association Incorporated, Committee on Land Utilisation in Rural Areas (Scott Committee): Minutes and Papers. Evidence.

19 TNA CAB 27/617 'Report, Proceedings and Memoranda of Cabinet Committee on Electricity Distribution, 1936–37'.

20 Sheail, 'Power to the people', in Brassley et al., *Transforming the countryside*, 39.

21 See James Greenhalgh, 'Threshold of the state: civil defence, the black out and the home in Second World War Britain', *Twentieth Century British History* 28:2 (2017), 186–208.

22 David Greasely, 'The coal industry: images and realities on the road to nationalisation', in Millward and Singleton, *The political economy of nationalisation in Britain*, 37.

23 Greasely, 'The coal industry', 37; William Ashworth with Mark Pegg, *The history of the British coal industry vol V* (Oxford: Oxford University Press, 1986), 28.

24 Sir William Beveridge, *Social Insurance and Allied Services Report* (London; HMSO, 1942)

25 TNA CAB 117/140, *Report of the Committee on Land utilisation in Rural Areas* (1942), 50.

26 TNA POWE 38/13, 'Nationalisation and Electricity Development in Rural Areas: National Farmers Union' (January 1947).

27 I have written on this in more detail in 'Limits of power: Wind energy, Orkney, and the post-war British state', *Twentieth Century British History* 31:3 (2019), 316–339.

28 House of Commons (6 May 1943) vol. 389 col. 404–5.

29 Johnston, Hydro-Electric Development (Scotland) Bill, House of Commons (24 February 1943) vol. 387 col. 180.

30 Linda Ross, Katrina Navickas, Ben Anderson, and Matthew Kelly, *New lives, new landscapes revisited: rural modernity in Britain* (Oxford: Oxford University Press and the British Academy, 2023).

31 Navickas, 'Conflicts of power', 87–103.

32 Museum of English Rural Life online exhibition 'Landscapes of state industry' [accessed 23 April 2025] https://merl.reading.ac.uk/explore/online-exhibitions/landscape-state-financed-industry/#the_visual_impact_of_power_stations

33 House of Commons (24 February 1943) vol. 387 col. 188.

34 Emma Wood, *The hydro boys: pioneers of renewable energy* (Edinburgh: Luath Press, 2005).

35 Wood, *Hydro boys*, 63.

36 E.W. Golding, *The generation of electricity by wind power* (London: E & FN Spon reprint 1976 [1955]), 70.

37 Righter, *Wind energy in America*, 126–136.

38 Golding, *The generation of electricity by wind power*, 71.

Chapter 3

1 Donna Heddle, 'The Norse element in the Orkney dialect', in Robert McColl Millar (ed.) *Northern lights, northern words. Selected papers from the FRLSU conference, Kirkwall* (Forum for Research on the Languages of Scotland and Ulster, 2009), 48–57.

2 Robert Macfarlane, *Landmarks* (London: Hamish Hamilton, 2015), 227–230.

3 J. Derrick McClure, 'Distinctive semantic fields in the Orkney and Shetlandic dialects, and their use in the local literature', in Millar, *Northern lights*, 65.

4 McClure, 'Distinctive semantic fields', 67.

5 Alexander Fenton, *The Northern Isles: Orkney and Shetland* (Edinburgh: Donald, 1978).

6   Orkney Archive, assorted unattributed photographs: L9829/1, L2549/4, L3868/3, L6198/2, L4431/3. L28703/3, L1743/1.

7   See, Trevor J. Price, 'Edward Golding's influence on wind power', *Wind Engineering* 29:6 (2005), 513–530.

8   NMOA 235838, Edward William Golding and Arthur Stodhart, 'The Selection and Characteristics of Wind-Power Sites. Technical Report C/T 108' (The Electrical Research Association, 1952), 10.

9   NMOA 235840, J.R. Tagg, 'Wind data related to the generation of electricity by wind power technical report C/T 115' (ERA 1957), 14.

10 Golding and Stodhart, 'Selection and Characteristics', 18.

11 Golding, *The generation of electricity by wind power*, 75.

12 NMOA 50471, Edward William Golding, 'Note on the Estimation of the Total Practicable Installed Capacity of Wind Power Plant in any Country', Organisation for European Economic Co-operation Wind Power Working Party Proceedings, 27 March 1952.

13 NMOA 50471, Golding, 'Note', 2.

14 OA CO3/1/14, Minutes of Orkney Council 1950–52.

15 Fiona Graham, 'Power to the People', The Orkney News website (1 December 2021) [accessed 23 April 2025] https://theorkneynews.scot/2021/12/01/power-for-the-people/

16 'New £350000 Power Station Opened', *Orcadian* (17 May 1951).

17 University of Glasgow Archive (UGA) UCS1/104/48, Correspondence between John Brown Ltd and NSHEB.

18 'Second "Electric Windmill"; Eking Out Our Fuel', *Manchester Guardian* (20 March 1952).

19 David Edgerton, *The rise and fall of the British nation: a twentieth-century history* (London: Penguin, 2019), 97.

20 Golding, *The generation of electricity by wind power*, 255.

21 Golding, *The generation of electricity by wind power*, 255–65.

22 'Hurricane damage estimate nears £500,000', *Orkney Herald* (29 January 1952).

23 'Wreckage-strewn countryside', *Orkney Herald* (22 January 1952).

24 'Orkney and the wind', *Orcadian* (24 January 1952).

25 'The angry winds' (syndicated article), *Orkney Herald* (22 January 1952).

26 UGA UCSI/104/48, John Brown and Company papers.

27 NMOA 180857, E.W. Golding and A.H. Stodhart, 'The use of wind power in Denmark: report C/T 112' (ERA 1954).

28 NMOA 50471, OEEC Committee for Productivity and Applied Research, Working Party NO.2 (Wind Power) Memorandum, 1.

29 NMOA 52094, T.G.N. Haldane, 'Problems in large-scale wind-power generation', OEEC Wind Power Technical Papers 1950–1952.

30 Kander, Malanima, and Warde, *Power to the people*, 256.

31 Edgerton, *Rise and fall*, 275; Mattin Biglari, *Nationalising oil and knowledge in Iran: labour, decolonisation and colonial modernity, 1933–1951* (Edinburgh: University of Edinburgh Press, 2024).

32 Pat Thane, *Divided kingdom: a history of Britain 1900 to the present* (Cambridge: Cambridge University Press, 2018), 230–231.

33 Thane, *Divided kingdom*, 220.

34 BBC 'On this day' website, 'Glasgow powers up for the festival' (28 May 1951, reproduced 28 May 2008) [accessed 17 May 2024] http://news.bbc.co.uk/onthisday/hi/dates/stories/may/28/newsid_3005000/3005617.stm

Notes

35 Becky Conekin, *The autobiography of a nation: the 1951 festival of Britain* (Manchester: Manchester University Press, 2003), 140–141.

36 Jonathan Hogg and Kate Brown, 'Introduction: social and cultural history of British nuclear mobilisation since 1945', *Contemporary British History* Special Issue 32:2 (2019).

37 Jonathon Hogg, *British nuclear culture: official and unofficial narratives in the long 20th century* (London, Bloomsbury Academic Press, 2016), 76.

38 Leslie Hannah, *Engineers, managers and politicians. The first fifteen years of nationalised electricity supply in Britain*, 178–81.

39 Hannah, *Engineers*, 181.

40 Hannah, *Engineers*, 243.

41 Alex Lawson 'Hinkley Point C could be delayed to 2031 and cost up to £35b says EDF', *Guardian* (23 January 2024).

Chapter 4

1 NLW CAT Archive Box 25/1–28, Sarah Jenkinson, 'Pioneering', in *Centre for Alternative Technology: Celebrating 25 Years* (2000).

2 The most thorough academic examination of the group to date can be found in Zoe Gardner, 'Landscapes of power: the cultural and historical geographies of renewable energy in Britain since 1870', PhD thesis (2007); an oral history of the group is included in Richard King, *Brittle with relics: a history of Wales, 1962–1997* (London: Faber and Faber, 2022).

3 NLW CAT Archive 6/4, Tim Brown (ed.), *Ten years at the quarry: a short history of the National Centre for Alternative Technology written by members and ex-members of staff* (CAT: Powys, 1985).

4 Walter Schwartz, 'Gerard Morgan-Grenville obituary', *Guardian* (25 March 2009).

5 Gerard Morgan-Grenville, *Built environment* New Faces, New Places 5:3 (1979), 214.

6 Gerard Morgan-Grenville, *Breaking free* (Bideford: Milton Mill Publishing, 2001), 157

7 NLW CAT 6/4, *Ten years at the quarry*, 4.

8 King, *Brittle with relics*, 171

9 NLW CAT 6/4, *Ten years at the quarry*, 39.

10 NLW CAT 6/4, *Ten years at the quarry*, 24–25.

11 NLW CAT 25/1–28, *Centre for Alternative Technology: celebrating 25 Years* (1995), 11.

12 See Vicky Albritton and Frederik Albritton Jonsson, *Green Victorians: the simple life in John Ruskin's Lake District* (Chicago, IL: University of Chicago Press, 2016).

13 NLW CAT 25/1–28, *Centre for Alternative Technology: celebrating 25 years*, 6.

14 Zoe Gardner notes that the *Oxford English Dictionary* attributes the first use of the term to Edward Goldsmith in *The Ecologist* in the same year; Gardner, 'Landscapes of power', 262

15 NLW CAT 25/1–28, *Centre for Alternative Technology: celebrating 25 years*, 7.

16 Emma Schroeder, 'Making earth, making home: technoscientific citizenship and ecological domesticity in the age of limits', Doctoral Thesis (University of Maine, 2021), 5.

17 See Jacob Darwin Hamblin, *Arming mother nature: the birth of catastrophic environmentalism* (Oxford: Oxford University Press, 2013).

18 Elizabeth Chatterjee, 'The poor woman's energy: low-modernist solar technologies and international development, 1878–1966', *Journal of Global History* 18:3 (2023), 439–460; Vandana Shiva, *Staying alive: women, ecology and development* (London: Zed,

1988); Ramachandra Guha, *The unquiet woods: ecological change and peasant resistance in the Himalaya* (Oakland, CA: University of California Press, 2000 [1989]).

19 King, *Brittle with relics*, 177.

20 King, *Brittle with relics*, 177.

21 Gary Snyder, *Four changes* (1970) [accessed 23 April 2025] https://arthurmag.com/2011/01/31/four-changes-by-gary-snyder/

22 Gardner, 'Landscapes of power', 267.

23 Lord Boyd-Orr, 'World population and resources', House of Lords (28 April 1954) vol. 187 col. 134; Lord Merrivale, 'Fuel and power policy' House of Lords (21 January 1959) vol. 213 col. 683.

24 'Energy Policy' House of Commons (16 March 1976) vol. 907 col. 1266.

25 'Nuclear Power', House of Commons (20 December 1976) vol. 923 col. 328.

26 House of Lords (5 November 1975) vol. 899 col. 508.

27 Morgan-Grenville, *Built Environment* 'New Faces New Places', 214–215.

28 For a detailed exploration of science policy 1979–1990, see Jon Agar, *Science Policy Under Thatcher* (London: University College London Press, 2019).

29 P. Ludsager, 'Danish experience of small wind powered generators', in John Twidell (ed.), *Energy for rural and island communities: proceedings of the second international conference, held at Inverness, Scotland, 1–4 September 1981* (Oxford: Pergamon Press, 1981), 107–108.

30 Ludsager, 'Danish experience', 108–109.

31 Interview with Hugh Piggott (14 March 2024).

32 NLW CAT 6/4, *Ten years at the quarry*, 7.

33 NLW CAT 6/4, *Ten years at the quarry*, 6.

34 NLW CAT 6/4, *Ten years at the quarry*, 8.

35 NLW CAT 6/4, *Ten years at the quarry*, 6.

36 Will Steffen, Paul Crutzen, and John McNeill, 'The Anthropocene: are humans now overwhelming the great forces of nature?', 36:8 *Ambio* (2007), 617.

37 Gross and Needham (eds), *New energies*, 90–91.

38 Richard Toye, 'The new commanding height: Labour party policy on North Sea oil and gas, 1964–74', *Contemporary British History* 16:1 (2002), 92.

39 Timothy Mitchell, *Carbon democracy: political power in the age of oil* (London: Verso, 2011), 145–151.

40 Mitchell, *Carbon democracy*, 173.

41 Thomas Turnbull, 'No solution of the immediate crisis': the uncertain political economy of energy conservation in 1970s Britain', *Contemporary European History* 31:4 (2022), 570–592.

42 Harry Roberts, 'Sellafield and British nuclear culture 1945–1992: nuclear imaginaries in the rural periphery' (PhD Thesis, University of Liverpool, 2021).

43 See Frank Zelko, *Make it a green peace! The rise of countercultural environmentalism* (Oxford: Oxford University Press, 2013).

44 NLW CAT 6/5, R.W. Todd, C.J.N. Alty, D.O Hall, J.C McVeigh, P.J. Musgrove, J. Platts, and P.C. Schumacher, *An alternative energy strategy for the United Kingdom* (National Centre for Alternative Technology, 2nd edn 1978).

45 Martin Ryle, 'Preface', in Todd et al., *An alternative energy strategy*.

46 Todd et al., *An alternative energy strategy*, 3.

47 Todd et al., *An alternative energy strategy*, 27.

48 NLW CAT 28/5/1.

49 NLW CAT 28/5/1.

50 Dulas website, [accessed 23 April 2025] https://dulas.org.uk/renewables/solar-energy/.

51 NLW CAT 25/1–28, *Centre for Alternative Technology: celebrating 25 years*, 8.
52 Centre for Alternative Technology website [accessed 23 April 2025] https://cat.org.uk/ what-we-do/

Chapter 5

1 Crispin Aubrey, 'Air of expectation for UK wind power', *Guardian* (9 August 1991).
2 Richard Toye, 'The new commanding height', 93.
3 Seamus Milne, quoted in Turnbull, 'No solution', 573.
4 University of Bristol Special Collections, DM668/6/11 1504261808 Conservative Party manifesto 1974.
5 University of Bristol Special Collections DM668/6/2, 1504264976 Labour Party manifesto, 1974.
6 Giuliano Garavini, 'Thatcher's North Sea: the return of cheap oil and the 'neo-liberalisation' of European energy', *Contemporary European History* 33:1 (2022), 4.
7 Toye, 'The new commanding height', 110.
8 UoB SC DM668/6/11 1501387918 Conservative Party manifesto 1979.
9 UoB SC DM668/6/11 150484776X Conservative Party manifesto 1983.
10 Department for Business, Energy and Industrial Strategy, *UK energy in brief 2021* (National Statistics Authority, 2021) [accessed 3 July 2024] https://assets.publishing.service.gov.uk/ media/618a87f8d3bf7f55f9479789/UK_Energy_in_Brief_2021.pdf
11 Juan Carlos Boué, *The UK North Sea as a global experiment in neoliberal resource extraction. The British model of petroleum governance from 1970–2018* (Platform/PCS, 2018), as cited in Garavini, 'Thatcher's North Sea', 16.
12 Martin Chick, *Electricity and energy policy in Britain, France and the United States since 1945* (Cheltenham: Edward Elgar Publishing, 2009), 115.
13 Chick, *Electricity and energy policy*, 115.
14 George Parker-Jarvis, 'Power of wind and waves', *Observer* (1 December 1991).
15 Aubrey, 'Air of expectation,' *Guardian* (9 August 1991).
16 Aubrey, 'Air of expectation,' *Guardian* (9 August 1991).
17 Paul Brown, 'Winds of change turn Cornish village into seat of alternative power', *Guardian* (28 March 1990).
18 Brown, 'Winds of change', *Guardian* (28 March 1990).
19 Dieter Helm, *Energy, the state and the market: British energy policy since 1979* (Oxford: Oxford University Press, 2003), 130; see also Agar, *Science policy under Thatcher*, 139–161.
20 Chick, *Electricity and energy policy*, 115.
21 John Kemp, 'Thatcher's secret weapon in the miners strikes shuts, ending an era', *Reuters online* 31 March 2015, https://www.reuters.com/article/britain-electricity-oil-kemp-idINL6N0WX3M820150331 cited by Garavini, 'Thatcher's North Sea', 11.
22 The Margaret Thatcher Foundation online archive, Letter from Margaret Thatcher to Armand Hammer, 20 July 1988 [declassified July 2018] [accessed 23 April 2025] https://www.margaretthatcher.org/document/209908
23 Sue Jane Taylor, 'Art and the offshore', in Fiona Polack and Danine Farquharson, *Cold water oil: offshore petroleum cultures* (Abingdon-on-Thames: Routledge, 2021), 158.
24 Derek Spooner, 'The dash for gas in electricity generation in the UK', *Geography* 80:4 (1995), 393–406; Mark Winksel, 'When systems are overthrown: the 'dash for gas' in the British electricity supply industry', *Social Studies of Science* 32:4 (2002), 563–598.

25 Spooner, 'The dash for gas', 400.

26 Paolo Agnolucci, 'The importance and the policy impacts of post-contractual opportunism and competition in the English and Welsh non-fossil fuel obligation', *Energy Policy* 35 (2007), 476.

27 NLW CAT Box 28/5/2.

28 Catherine Mitchell and Peter Connor, 'Renewable energy policy in the UK 1990–2003', *Energy Policy* 32 (2004), 1941–1942.

29 Agar, *Science policy under Thatcher*, 224.

30 Agar, *Science policy under Thatcher*, 228.

31 Agar, *Science policy under Thatcher*, 230.

32 Naomi Oreskes and Eric M. Conway, *Merchants of doubt: how a handful of scientists obscured the truth on issues from tobacco smoke to global warming* (New York, NY: Bloomsbury, 2010), 118.

33 Margaret Thatcher Foundation online archive, Margaret Thatcher, Speech to UN General Assembly (Global Environment) (8 November 1989) [accessed 26 July 2024] https://www.margaretthatcher.org/document/107817

34 Franz-Josef Brüggemeier, Mark Cioc, and Thomas Zeller (eds), *How green were the Nazis? Nature, environment and nation in the Third Reich* (Athens, OH: Ohio University Press, 2005).

35 *The environment white paper: this common inheritance* (Cm 1200) (London: HMSO, 1990), 72–73.

36 Edgerton, *Rise and fall*, 496.

37 Heymann, 'Signs of hubris', 645.

38 Heymann, 'Signs of hubris', 654.

39 Heymann, 'Signs of hubris', 655.

40 California Energy Commission website, '2021 Total System Electric Generation', [accessed 26 July 2024] https://www.energy.ca.gov/data-reports/energy-almanac/california-electricity-data/2021–total-system-electric-generation

41 Eva Oberloskamp, 'Renewable energies in the United Kingdom and the Republic of Germany, 1970s–1990s', in Gross and Needham, *New energies*, 231.

42 National Grid Electricity Operator System Limited, *Annual report and accounts 2020/21*, 10.

Chapter 6

1 For more on Dutch art in this period, see Laura Cummings, *Thunderclap: A memoir of art and life and sudden death* (London: Chatto and Windus, 2023).

2 Dennis O'Driscoll, *Stepping stones: interviews with Seamus Heaney* (London: Faber and Faber, 2008), 24. Paul Warde introduced me to this Heaney quote when we worked together on 'The Power and the Water: Connecting Pasts and Futures' project, and it stayed with me.

3 Sam Wetherell, *Foundations: how the built environment made twentieth-century Britain* (Princeton, NJ: Princeton University Press, 2020), 58.

4 Melanie Tebbutt, 'Rambling and manly identity in Derbyshire's Dark Peak, 1880s–1920s', *The Historical Journal* 49:4 (2006), 1125–1153.

5 See, Marianna Dudley, *An environmental history of the UK defence estate, 1945 – the present* (London: Continuum, 2012).

6 Navickas, 'Conflicts of power'.

Notes

7 Hannah, *Electricity before nationalisation*; Sheail, *Power in trust*; Luckin, *Questions of power*.

8 Sheail, *Power in Trust*, 133–134.

9 In 2019 I participated in an academic conference at the University of Northumbria, 'New Lives, New Landscapes', which explored the concept of 'rural modernism' in depth. An edited volume emerged from that event: Linda Ross, Katrina Navickas, Matthew Kelly, and Ben Anderson (eds) *New lives, new landscapes revisited: rural modernity in Britain* (Oxford: Oxford University Press, 2023).

10 Sheail, *Power in trust*, 137.

11 Cited in Iain Waites, 'The post-war power station and the persistence of an English landscape tradition', in Ross et al., *New lives, new landscapes revisited*, 115.

12 TNA POWE 14/516, Various correspondences, 1951.

13 TNA POWER 14/51, Letter from NFU Caernarvonshire County Branch to Ministry of Fuel and Power, 10 October 1951.

14 TNA POWER 14/51, Correspondence from CA Gresham, Hon Sec. CPRW, to Caernarvonshire County Council, 5 February 1951.

15 It has been surprisingly hard to verify this in the archives. A phantom turbine is even harder to trace than a real one. Confirmation was supplied by the Network for Alternative Technology and Technology Assessment newsletter, *NATTA*, (September/October 1987) for its article on the Mynydd Anelog turbine. NLW CAT 26/8, 'Halting Attempts at Windpower, *NATTA* 49 (1987).

16 Landscape character assessment had been used in landscape professional work since the 1980s. See Emma-Jane Preece, 'Landscape character assessment: a view from the Quantocks', in Peter Coates, David Moon, and Paul Warde (eds) *Local places, global processes: histories of environmental change in Britain and beyond* (Oxford: Windgather Press, 2016), 48.

17 Jeremy Webb, 'Can we learn to love the wind?', *New Scientist* (16 July 1994).

18 NLW North ITV (1234 Prodtape), videocassette recording, 'Wales This Week' (14 May 1993).

19 Pyrs Gruffudd, 'Remaking Wales: nation-building and the geographical imagination, 1925–1950', *Political Geography* 14:3 (1995), 219–239; Tim Cole, 'A picturesque ruin? Landscapes of loss at Tyneham and the Epynt', in Peter Coates, Tim Cole, and Chris Pearson (eds), *Militarized landscapes: from Gettysburg to Salisbury Plain* (London: Continuum, 2010), 95–110; Marianna Dudley, 'Traces of conflict: environment and eviction in British military training areas, 1943–present', *Journal of War and Culture Studies* 6:2 (2013), 112–126.

20 Patrick Devine-Wright, 'Public engagement with large-scale renewable energy technologies: breaking the cycle of NIMBYism', *WIREs Climate Change* 2 (2011), 21.

21 Paul Brown, 'Ingham protest blows out national wind farm plan', *Guardian* (24 September 1996).

22 Brown, 'Ingham protest'.

23 'Whirling words', *The Times* (6 August 1993).

24 Simon Fairlie, 'Dark satanic mills', *The Ecologist* 24:3 (May/June 1994), 85–86.

25 Jamie Merrill, 'Eric Pickles accused of "rejecting wind farms to win votes"', *Independent* (18 October 2018).

26 Polly Toynbee, 'This war on windfarms is the Tories' latest sop to UKIP', *Guardian* (28 October 2014).

27 Robert Watts, 'UKIP celebrates with cheers, souvenirs and a rallying call to black and Asian voters', *Sunday Telegraph* (24 March 2013).

28 Lord Berkely of Knighton, Hansard, 'Energy: Onshore wind farming', House of Lords (15 October 2014) vol. 756 col. 264.

29 BBC News website, 'David Cameron says people are "fed up" with onshore wind farms' (16 December 2014) [accessed 12 July 2025] https://www.bbc.co.uk/news/uk-politics-30504891

30 UK Government Policy Paper, 'Policy Statement on Onshore Wind' (8 July 2024) [accessed 12 July 2025] https://www.gov.uk/government/publications/policy-statement-on-onshore-wind/policy-statement-on-onshore-wind

31 Cara Daggett, 'Petro-masculinity: fossil fuels and authoritarian desire', *Millenium: Journal of International Studies* 47:1 (2018), 25–44. Trish Kahle, *Energy citizenship: coal and democracy in the American century* (New York, NY: Columbia University Press, 2024).

32 Chatterjee, 'Asian anthropocene'.

33 Patrick Devine-Wright and Susana Batel, 'My neighbourhood, my country or my planet? The influence of multiple place attachments and climate change concern on social acceptance of energy infrastructure', *Global Environmental Change* 47 (2017), 110–120.

34 Sylvia Crowe, *The landscape of power* (Oxford: Architectural Press, 1958), 103.

35 The bus stop merch is made by LOOM Graphics, an independent Lewis-based graphic design agency.

36 Daniel Wright, 'Baby brutalism (concrete bus shelters, Lewis, UK)', *The beauty of transport* blog, (2 September 2015) [accessed 23 January 2025] https://thebeautyoftransport.com/2015/09/02/baby-brutalism-concrete-bus-shelters-lewis-uk/

37 'Joy of six: Alan Holling', LOOM website (6 March, year unknown) [accessed 23 January 2025] https://loomgraphics.work/news/joy-of-six-brutalist-bus-stops-isleoflewis

38 Iain Robertson, *Landscapes of protest in the Scottish highlands after 1914: the later Highland land wars* (Farnham: Ashgate, 2016)

39 Robertson, *Landscapes of protest*, 124; Paul Warde, 'Trees, trade and textiles: potash imports and ecological dependency in British industry, c. 1550–1770', *Past and Present* 240 (2018), 47–82.

40 Richard Davenport-Hines, 'Lever, William Hesketh, First Viscount Leverhulme', *Oxford Dictionary of National Biography* (23 October 2004), doi-org.bris.idm.oclc.org/10.1093/ref:odnb/34506

41 Robertson, *Landscapes of protest*, 116.

42 Robertson, *Landscapes of protest*, 118.

43 Brian Russell Roberts and Michelle Ann Stephens (eds), *Archipelagic American studies* (Durham, NC: Duke University Press, 2017), 23.

44 Roberts and Stephens, *Archipelagic American studies*, 23.

45 The Moorland Not Turbines website, formerly at semantise.com but now defunct, presented galleries of wildlife photography as a visual corrective to the notion of the empty moor. I refer to saved images and screenshots collected through my research.

46 Lewis Wind Power, *Stornoway wind farm additional information volume 1* (2020), 8–11. Stornoway Library.

47 Anne Campbell, *Rathad an isein: the bird's road. A Lewis moorland glossary* (Glasgow: FARAM, 2013). The glossary inspired Robert Macfarlane's *Landmarks*.

48 Kirsty MacLeod, Mary Taylor, and Ciara Bolton, *Affordable warmth at home in the Western Isles* (Stornoway: The Energy Advisory Service funded by the British Gas Energy Trust, 2023)

49 Laura Watts, *Energy at the end of the world: an Orkney island saga* (Cambridge, MA: MIT Press, 2019), 53.

50 Global Atlas of Environmental Justice website, 'Proposed wind farm on the Isle of Lewis, Scotland', [accessed 30 July 2024] https://ejatlas.org/conflict/proposed-windfarm-on-the-isle-of-lewis-scotland

51 Global Atlas of Environmental Justice website, 'Proposed wind farm on the Isle of Lewis, Scotland'.

52 Michelle Robson, 'Comhairle hoping wind farm developer "will not walk away"', *Stornoway Gazette* (24 April 2008).

53 Murray Macleod, 'Breaking news: Ofgem gives approval for Western Isles interconnector', *Stornoway Gazette* (15 December 2022).

54 See, for example, Rob Nixon, *Slow violence and the environmentalism of the poor* (Harvard: Harvard University Press, 2013); Barbara Allen, *Uneasy alchemy: citizens and experts in Louisiana's chemical corridor disputes* (Cambridge, MA: MIT Press, 2003).

55 Dominic Boyer and Cymene Howe, *Energopolitics*/Ecologics (Durham, NC: Duke University Press, 2019), xi.

56 Patrick Bresnihan and Patrick Brodie, 'New extractive frontiers in Ireland and the moebius strip of wind/data', *Environment and Planning E: Nature and Space* 4:4 (2021), 1645–1664.

57 Nicholas Coleman, 'Wind turbines, reindeer and green colonialism: a new era of Sámi resistance against Norwegianisaton', LSE Blog (undated) [accessed 30 July 2024] https://blogs.lse.ac.uk/lseupr/2024/03/05/wind-turbines-reindeer-and-green-colonialism-a-new-era-of-sami-resistance-against-norwegianisation/

58 Kathleen Jamie, 'A lone enraptured male', *London Review of Books* 30:5 (6 March 2008).

59 D. Fraser, 'Set squares and concrete', *The Listener* 50:1275 (1953), 218–219; Sheail, 'Power to the people', in Brassley et al., *Transforming the countryside*, 48–49.

Chapter 7

1 Crown Estate *Offshore Wind Report 2023* (2023)

2 Orsted, 'Making green energy affordable White Paper: 1991–2001, The first offshore wind farms', [accessed 29 July 2024] https://orsted.com/en/insights/white-papers/making-green-energy-affordable/1991-to-2001-the-first-offshore-wind-farms

3 Select Committee on Innovation, Universities, Science and Skills, Fifth Report, Written Evidence, Appendix 2: North Hoyle Offshore Wind Farm — Public Attitude Survey (11 June 2008) [accessed 29 July 2024] https://publications.parliament.uk/pa/cm200708/cmselect/cmdius/216/216we95.htm

4 Select Committee on Innovation, Universities, Science and Skills, Fifth Report, (11 June 2008) Written Evidence, Memorandum 49, The British Wind Energy Association [accessed 29 July 2024] https://publications.parliament.uk/pa/cm200708/cmselect/cmdius/216/216we61.htm

5 J. Kaldellis, D. Apostolou, M. Kapsali, and E. Kondili, 'Environmental and social footprint of offshore wind energy. Comparison with onshore counterpart', *Renewable Energy* 92 (2016), 544.

6 Murray Macleod, 'Ofgem gives approval for Western Isles interconnector', *Stornoway Gazette* (15 December 2022); Sandra Dick, 'Storm brews over Isle of Lewis Offshore wind farm', *Herald* (6 July 2023).

7 W.G. Stevenson, 'The work of the North of Scotland Hydro-Electric Board in the field of wind turbine generators', in John Twiddell, Fiona Riddoch, and Bill Grainger (eds), *Energy for rural and island communities III: Proceedings of the third international conference held at Inverness, Scotland, September 1983* (Oxford: Pergamon, 1984), 99.

8 Watts, *Energy at the end of the world*, 27–28.

9 Nadja Skopljak, 'Subsea link to Orkney gets approval, unlocking 'world's greatest resources of renewable electricity', *Offshore Energy* website (18 July 2023) [accessed 14–15 July 2024] https://www.offshore-energy.biz/subsea-link-to-orkney-gets-approval-unlocking-worlds-greatest-resources-of-renewable-electricity/

10 West of Orkney Windfarm website, 'About the project' [accessed 23 January 2025] https://www.westoforkney.com

11 Crown Estate Scotland, 'Scotland Offshore wind leasing delivers major boost to Scotland's net zero aspirations' (17 January 2022) [accessed 16 July 2025] https://www.crownestatescotland.com/news/scotwind-offshore-wind-leasing-delivers-major-boost-to-scotlands-net-zero-aspirations

12 Department for Energy Security and Net Zero, 'Imports, exports and transfers of electricity' Report (27 June 2024).

13 Anita McConnell, 'Sir John Pender', *Oxford Dictionary of National Biography* (23 September 2004).

14 Monica E. Mullrennan and Colin H. Scott, '*Mare Nullius:* indigenous rights in saltwater environments', *Development and Change* 31 (2000), 682 (681–708).

15 Chris Armstrong, *A blue new deal: why we need a new politics for the ocean* (New Haven, CT: Yale, 2022).

16 Armstrong, *A blue new deal*, 36.

17 Armstrong, *A blue new deal*, 49–73.

18 Lorna Scurlock, 'Who owns the seabed and why it matters', *Senedd Research* (22 November 2021) [accessed 23 January 2025] https://research.senedd.wales/research-articles/who-owns-the-seabed-and-why-it-matters/

19 House of Commons Treasury Select Committee, 'Treasury – Eighth Report: The management of the Crown Estate' (22 March 2010) col. 67.

20 Jillian Ambrose and David Batty, 'Windfarms help drive record profit for crown estate', *Guardian* (29 June 2023).

21 Graham McDonald, quoted in Alexandra Campbell, 'Extractive poetics: marine energies in Scottish literature', *Humanities* 8:16 (2019), 2.

22 Campbell, 'Extractive poetics', 9.

23 Dolly Jørgenson, 'Mixing oil and water: naturalizing offshore oil platforms in American aquariums', in Ross Barrett and Daniel Worden (eds), *Oil culture* (Minneapolis, MN: University of Minnesota Press, 2014), 285.

24 Lena Bergström, Lena Kautsky, Torlief Malm, et al., 'Effects of offshore wind farms on marine wildlife – a generalised impact assessment', *Environmental Research Letters* 4:9 (2014), 034012 (12 pages).

25 Juan Carlos Farrias Pardo, Magnus Aune, Christopher Harman, et al., 'A synthesis review of nature positive approaches and coexistence in the offshore wind industry', *ICES Journal of Marine Science* (2023), fsad191 https://doi.org/10.1093/icesjms/fsad191

26 Ecowende website, 'Reef Stimulation' [accessed 20 July 2024] https://ecowende.nl/en/our-innovations/fish-and-benthic-habitats/reef-stimulation/

27 Kaldellis et al., 'Environmental and social footprint of offshore wind energy', 546–547.

28 Oreskes and Conway, *Merchants of doubt*.

29 Both examples are given in Sanneke Kloppenburg, Aarti Gupta, Sake R.L., et al., 'Scrutinising environmental governance in a digital age: New ways of seeing, participating and intervening', *One Earth* 5:3 (2022), 232–241.

30 I am grateful to Helena Solman (Wageningen University) for bringing this research to my attention through her paper at the Big Wind conference (University of Leicester, June 2024), and through subsequent correspondence.

31 Ecowende website [accessed 29 July 2024] https://ecowende.nl/en/our-innovations/birds/taller-wind-turbines/

32 Kloppenburg et al., 'Scrutinising environmental governance', 233.

33 Nixon, *Slow violence;* Mitchell, *Carbon democracy.*

34 Hamblin, *Arming mother nature.*

35 UK Government Policy Paper 'British energy security strategy' (7 April 2022) [accessed 25 July 2024] https://www.gov.uk/government/publications/british-energy-security-strategy/british-energy-security-strategy#renewables

Chapter 8

1 TNES A2016/022 AME BOX 8, IAAO Barra and Vatersay Meeting 23 February 2005.

2 TNES A2016/022 AME BOX 8, Memorandum of Incorporation 7 June 2005.

3 TNES A2016/022 AME BOX 8, CBAB Ltd LDO Update October–November 2009.

4 'Barra turbine could be one of the most productive in Western Europe', *Stornoway Gazette,* (14 January 2014).

5 'Barra turbine', *Stornoway Gazette* (14 January 2014).

6 The best introduction to this rich literature remains James C. Scott's *Seeing like a state: how certain schemes to improve the human condition have failed* (New Haven, CT: Yale University Press, 1999).

7 See Robin Wall Kimmerer, *Braiding sweetgrass: Indigenous wisdom, scientific knowledge, and the teachings of plants* (New York, NY: Penguin, 2020).

8 The Museum of English Rural Life twitter/X account (@TheMERL, 9 April 2018), 'look at this absolute unit.' [accessed 26 July 2024] https://x.com/TheMERL/status/983341970318938112?lang=en-GB

9 Borja Diez-Cañamero and Joan Manuel F. Mendoza, 'Circular economy performance and carbon footprint of wind turbine blade waste management alternatives', *Waste Management* 164:1 (2023), 94.

10 David Piper and Judith Guido, 'Applications of magnets in wind turbines', *Wind Systems Magazine online* (15 March 2021) [accessed 30 July 2024] https://www.windsystemsmag.com/applications-of-magnets-in-wind-turbines/

11 Jaya Nayar, 'Not so 'green' technology: the complicated legacy of rare earth mining', *Harvard International Review* (12 August 2021) [accessed 26 July 2024] https://hir.harvard.edu/not-so-green-technology-the-complicated-legacy-of-rare-earth-mining/

12 Richard Shaw, Gus Gunn, Paul Lusty, et al., 'Raw materials for decarbonisation: the potential for rare earth elements in the UK: Report', British Geological Survey (4 May 2023) [accessed 26 July 2024] https://nora.nerc.ac.uk/id/eprint/534416; Artem Golev, Margaretha Scott, Peter D. Erskine, et al., 'Rare earth supply chains: current status, constraints and opportunities', *Resource Policy* 41 (2014), 52–59.

13 Nayar, 'Not so green'.

14 Liu Hongqiao, 'The dark side of renewable energy', *Earth Journalism.Net* (25 August 2016) [accessed 23 April 2025] https://earthjournalism.net/stories/the-dark-side-of-renewable-energy

15 Chen Jie, 'Death of the Desert', *Dialogue Earth* website, (14 July 2015) [accessed 26 July 2024] https://dialogue.earth/en/pollution/8015-death-of-the-desert/

16 Julia Adeney Thomas, 'Why the Anthropocene is not climate change, and why it matters', *Asia Global Online* (10 January 2019) [accessed 26 July 2025] https://www.asiaglobalonline.hku.hk/anthropocene-climate-change

17 James Rupert, 'In Congo, peace means a halt to "brutal, illegal mining"' *United States Institute of Peace* website (7 March 2024) [accessed 30 July 2024] https://www.usip.org/publications/2024/03/congo-peace-means-halt-brutal-illegal-mining

18 Imre Szeman and Jennifer Wenzel, 'What do we talk about when we talk about extractivism?', *Textual Practice* 35:3 (2021), 516; and Imre Szeman, 'On the politics of extraction', *Cultural Studies* 31:2–3 (2017), 444.

19 Thea Riofrancos, '*Extractivismo* unearthed: a genealogy of a radical discourse', *Cultural Studies* 31:2–3 (2017), 277–306.

20 Riofrancos, '*Extractivismo*', 278.

21 Szeman and Wenzel, 'What do we talk about', 509

22 Szeman, 'On the politics of extraction', 442

23 I am grateful to Marieke Pampus, of the Martin-Luther-Universität, Halle-Wittenberg, for telling me about this term.

Conclusion

1 Hannah Ritchie, Max Roser, and Pablo Rosado, 'Renewable Energy' Our World in Data website (December 2020, revised January 2024) [accessed 28 July 2024] https://ourworldindata.org/renewable-energy

2 Julia Kollewe, 'Wind turbines generate more than half of UK's electricity due to Storm Pia', *Guardian*, (21 December 2023).

3 David Gange, *The frayed Atlantic edge: a historian's journey from Shetland to the Channel* (Glasgow: William Collins, 2019).

4 Interview with Hugh Piggott, 14 March 2024.

5 See Elizabeth Chatterjee, 'Late acceleration: the Indian emergency and the early 1970s energy crisis', *American Historical Review* 129:2 (2024), 429–466.

6 Szeman, 'On the politics of extraction', 441.

Bibliography

Primary sources

Meteorological Office Library and Archive
Mills Archive
National Library of Wales
The National Archives
Orkney Library and Archive
Tasglann nan Eilean Siar (Hebridean Archives)
University of Glasgow Archive
University of Bristol Special Collections

Secondary literature

Adeney Thomas, Julia, *Altered Earth: getting the Anthropocene right* (Cambridge: Cambridge University Press, 2022).

Agar, Jon, *Science policy under Thatcher* (London: University College London Press, 2019).

Agnolucci, Paolo, 'The importance and the policy impacts of post-contractual opportunism and competition in the English and Welsh non-fossil fuel obligation', *Energy Policy* 35 (2007), 475–486.

Albritton, Vicky and Frederik Albritton Jonsson, *Green Victorians: the simple life in John Ruskin's Lake District* (Chicago IL: University of Chicago Press, 2016).

Albritton Jonsson, Frederik and Carl Wennerlind, *Scarcity: a history from the origins of capitalism to the climate crisis* (Cambridge, MA: Harvard University Press, 2023).

Allen, Barbara, *Uneasy alchemy: citizens and experts in Louisiana's chemical corridor disputes* (Cambridge, MA: MIT Press, 2003).

Armstrong, Chris, *A blue new deal: why we need a new politics for the ocean* (New Haven, NJ: Yale, 2022).

Ashworth, William, with Mark Pegg, *The history of the British coal industry vol V* (Oxford: Oxford University Press, 1986).

Bankoff, Greg, *Cultures of disaster: society and natural hazards in the Philippines* (Abingdon: Routledge, 2003).

— 'Aeolian empires: the influence of winds and currents on European maritime expansion in the age of sail', *Environment and History* 23:2 (2017), 163–196.

Barak, On, *Powering empire: how coal made the Middle East and sparked global carbonization* (Oakland, CA: University of California Press, 2020).

Bennett, Jane, *Vibrant matter: a political ecology of things* (Durham, NC: Duke University Press, 2009).·

Bergström, Lena, Lena Kautsky, Torlief Malm, Rutger Rosenberg, Magnus Wahlberg, Natassia Åstrand Capetillo, and Dan Wilhelmsson, 'Effects of offshore wind farms on marine wildlife – a generalised impact assessment', *Environmental Research Letters* 4:9 (2014), 034012 (12 pages).

Beveridge, William, *Social insurance and allied services report* (London: HMSO, 1942).

Biglari, Mattin, *Nationalising oil and knowledge in Iran: labour, decolonisation and colonial modernity, 1933–1951* (Edinburgh: University of Edinburgh Press, 2025).

Boyer, Dominic and Cymene Howe, *Energopolitics/Ecologics* (Durham, NC: Duke University Press, 2019).

Brassley, Paul, Jeremy Burchardt, and Karen Sayer, *Transforming the countryside: the electrification of rural Britain* (Abingdon: Routledge, 2017).

Bresnihan, Patrick and Patrick Brodie, 'New extractive frontiers in Ireland and the moebius strip of wind/data', *Environment and Planning E: Nature and Space* 4:4 (2021), 1645–1664.

Brown, Tim (ed.), *Ten years at the quarry: a short history of the national Centre for Alternative Technology written by members and ex-members of staff* (Powys: Centre for Alternative Technology, 1985).

Brüggemeier, Franz-Josef, Mark Cioc, and Thomas Zeller (eds), *How green were the Nazis? Nature, environment and nation in the Third Reich* (Athens, OH: Ohio University Press, 2005).

Bruyerre, Philippe, *Retrofutur: une autre histoire de machines à vents* (Sainte-Luce-Sur-Loire: Bookelis, 2022).

Burke III, Edmund, 'The big story: human history, energy regimes, and the environment', in Burke III and Kenneth Pomeranz (eds), *The environment and world history* (Berkeley, CA: University of California Press, 2009), 33–53.

Button, Katharine Shillabeer, 'The environmental history of the National Grid', unpublished thesis (University of Cambridge, 2017).

Campbell, Alexandra, 'Extractive poetics: marine energies in Scottish literature', *Humanities* 8:1 (2019), 16 https://doi.org/10.3390/h8010016.

Campbell, Anne, *Rathad an isein: the bird's road. A Lewis moorland glossary* (Glasgow: FARAM, 2013).

Chandler, Raymond, *Red wind: a collection of short stories* (Cleveland, OH: World Publishing Co., 1946).

Chatterjee, Elizabeth, 'Asian Anthropocene: electricity and fossil developmentalism', *The Journal of Asian Studies* 79:1 (2020), 3–24.

— 'The poor woman's energy: low-modernist solar technologies and international development, 1878–1966', *Journal of Global History* 18:3 (2023), 439–460.

— 'Late acceleration: the Indian emergency and the early 1970s energy crisis', *American Historical Review* 129:2 (2024), 429–466.

Chatterjee, Elizabeth, Marianna Dudley, Linda Ross and Hiroki Shin, 'Low carbon energies for zero carbon futures', *Journal of Historical Geography* (forthcoming).

Chick, Martin, 'The political economy of nationalisation: the electricity industry', in Robert Millward and John Singleton, *The political economy of nationalisation in Britain, 1920–1950*, 257–274.

— *Electricity and energy policy in Britain, France and the United States since 1945* (Cheltenham: Edward Elgar Publishing, 2009).

Bibliography

Clifford, Jim, 'London's soap industry and the development of global ghost acres in the nineteenth century', *Environment and History* 27:3 (2021), 471–497.

Cole, Tim, 'A picturesque ruin? Landscapes of loss at Tyneham and the Epynt', in Peter Coates, Tim Cole and Chris Pearson (eds), *Militarized landscapes: from Gettysburg to Salisbury Plain* (London: Continuum, 2010), 95–110.

Conekin, Becky, *The autobiography of a nation: The 1951 festival of Britain* (Manchester: Manchester University Press, 2003).

Crowe, Sylvia, *The landscape of power* (Oxford: Architectural Press, 1958).

Cummings, Laura, *Thunderclap: A memoir of art and life and sudden death* (London, Chatto and Windus, 2023).

Daggett, Cara, 'Petro-masculinity: fossil fuels and authoritarian desire', *Millenium: Journal of International Studies* 47:1 (2018), 25–44.

Damodaran, Vinita, Rohan D'Souza, and Subir Dey, 'Uncertainty and environmental change: Kutch and Sundarbans as environmental histories of climate change', in Lyla Mehta, Nicolai Hans Adam, and Shilpi Srivastava, (eds) *The politics of climate change and uncertainty in India* (Abingdon: Routledge, 2022), 27–82.

Devine-Wright, Patrick, 'Public engagement with large-scale renewable energy technologies: breaking the cycle of NIMBYism', *WIREs Climate Change* 2 (2011), 19–26.

Devine-Wright, Patrick and Susana Batel, 'My neighbourhood, my country or my planet? The influence of multiple place attachments and climate change concern on social acceptance of energy infrastructure', *Global Environmental Change* 47 (2017), 110–120.

Dickenson, Emily, ed. Thomas H. Johnson, *The complete poems of Emily Dickinson* (New York, NY: Back Bay Books, 1976).

Diez-Cañamero, Borja and Joan Manuel F. Mendoza, 'Circular economy performance and carbon footprint of wind turbine blade waste management alternatives', *Waste Management* 164:1 (2023), 94–105.

Dudley, Marianna, *An environmental history of the UK Defence Estate, 1945 – the present* (London: Continuum, 2012). .

— 'Traces of conflict: environment and eviction in British military training areas, 1943–present', *Journal of War and Culture Studies* 6:2 (2013), 112–126.

— 'Limits of power: wind energy, Orkney, and the post-war British state', *Twentieth Century British History* 31:3 (2019), 316–339.

Edgerton, David, *The shock of the old: technology and global history since 1900* (London: Profile Books, 2008).

— *The rise and fall of the British nation: a twentieth-century history* (London: Penguin, 2019).

Endfield, Georgina and Alexander Hall, "Snow scenes': exploring the role of memory and place in commemorating extreme winters', *Weather Climate and Society* 8:1 (2016), 5–19.

Fenton, Alexander, *The Northern Isles: Orkney and Shetland* (Edinburgh: Donald, 1978).

Fowler, Corinne, *Green unpleasant land: creative responses to rural England's colonial connections* (Leeds: Peepal Tree Press, 2020).

— *Our island stories: country walks through colonial Britain* (London: Penguin Allen Lane, 2024).

Fressoz, Jean-Baptiste, *More and more and more: an all-consuming history of energy* (London: Allen Lane, 2024).

Gange, David, *The frayed Atlantic edge: a historian's journey from Shetland to the Channel* (Glasgow: William Collins, 2019).

Garavini, Giuliano, 'Thatcher's North Sea: the return of cheap oil and the 'neo-liberalisation' of European energy', *Contemporary European History* 33:1 (2022), 37–52.

Gardner, Zoe, 'Landscapes of power: the cultural and historical geographies of renewable energy in Britain since 1870' (PhD thesis, University of Nottingham, 2007).

Golding, E.W., *The generation of electricity by wind power* (London: E & FN Spon, reprint 1976 [1955]).

Golev, Artem, Margaretha Scott, Peter D. Erskine, Saleem H. Ali, and Grant R. Ballantyne, 'Rare earth supply chains: current status, constraints and opportunities', *Resource Policy* 41 (2014), 52–59.

Greasely, David, 'The coal industry: images and realities on the road to nationalisation', in Robert Millward and John Singleton, *The political economy of nationalisation in Britain, 1920–1950*, 37–64.

Greenhalgh, James, 'Threshold of the state: civil defence, the black out and the home in Second World War Britain', *Twentieth Century British History* 28:2 (2017), 186–208.

Greve, Frederik, Karl-Georg Kanz, Michael Zyskowski, Francesca von Matthey, Peter Biberthaler, Stefan Muthers, Andreas Matzarakis, Rolf Lefering, and Stegan Huber-Wagner, 'The influence of foehn winds on the incidence of severe injuries in southern Bavaria – an analysis of the TraumaRegister DGU', *BMC Musculoskeletal Disorders* 21:58 (2020), https://doi.org/10.1186/s12891-020-03572-z.

Griffiths, Tom, *Forests of ash: an environmental history* (Cambridge: Cambridge University Press, 2001).

Gross, Stephen and Andrew Needham (eds), *New energies: a history of energy transitions in Europe and North America* (Pittsburgh, PA: University of Pittsburgh Press, 2023).

Gruffudd, Pyrs, 'Remaking Wales: nation-building and the geographical imagination, 1925–1950', *Political Geography* 14:3 (1995), 219–239.

Guha, Ramachandra, *The unquiet woods: ecological change and peasant resistance in the Himalaya* (Oakland, CA: University of California Press, 2000 [1989]).

Hamblin, Jacob Darwin, *Arming mother nature: The birth of catastrophic environmentalism* (Oxford: Oxford University Press, 2013).

Hannah, Leslie *Electricity before nationalisation: a study of the development of the electricity supply industry in Britain to 1948* (London: Macmillan, 1979).

— *Engineers, managers and politicians. The first fifteen years of nationalised electricity supply in Britain* (London: Palgrave Macmillan, 1982).

Heddle, Donna, 'The Norse element in the Orkney dialect', in Robert McColl Millar (ed.) *Northern lights, northern worlds. Selected papers from the FRLSU conference, Kirkwall* (2009), 48–57.

Helm, Dieter, *Energy, the state and the market: British energy policy since 1979* (Oxford: Oxford University Press, 2003).

Heymann, Matthias, 'Signs of hubris: the shaping of wind technology styles in Germany, Denmark, and the United States, 1940–1990', *Technology and Culture* 39:4 (1998), 641–670.

Hills, Richard L., *Power from the wind: a history of windmill technology* (Cambridge: Cambridge University Press, 1994).

Hogg, Jonathan, *British nuclear culture: official and unofficial narratives in the long 20th century* (London, Bloomsbury Academic Press, 2016).

Hogg, Jonathan and Kate Brown, 'Introduction: social and cultural history of British nuclear mobilisation since 1945', *Contemporary British History* Special Issue 32:2 (2019), 161–169.

Hughes, Thomas P., *Networks of power: electrification in western society, 1880 – 1930* (Baltimore, MA: Johns Hopkins University Press, 1993).

Bibliography

Jamie, Kathleen, 'A lone enraptured male', *London Review of Books* 30:5 (6 March 2008).

Jones, Geoffrey, *Profits and sustainability: a history of green entrepreneurship* (Oxford: Oxford University Press, 2018).

Jorgensen, Mica, 'Wild smoke: managing forest pollution in northern British Columbia since 1950', *Environment and History* 30:2 (2023), 267–290.

Jørgenson, Dolly, 'Mixing oil and water: naturalizing offshore oil platforms in American aquariums', in Ross Barrett and Daniel Worden (eds), *Oil culture* (Minneapolis, MN: University of Minnesota Press, 2014), 267–288.

Kahle, Trish, *Energy citizenship: coal and democracy in the American century* (New York, NY: Columbia University Press, 2024).

Kaldellis, J.K., D. Apostolou, M. Kapsali, and E. Kondili, 'Environmental and social footprint of offshore wind energy. Comparison with onshore counterpart', *Renewable Energy* 92 (2016), 543–556.

Kander, Astrid, Paolo Malanima, and Paul Warde, *Power to the people: energy in Europe over the last five centuries* (Princeton, NJ: Princeton University Press, 2014).

Kimmerer, Robin Wall, *Braiding sweetgrass: Indigenous wisdom, scientific knowledge, and the teachings of plants* (New York, NY: Penguin, 2020).

King, Richard, *Brittle with relics: a history of Wales, 1962–1997* (London: Faber and Faber, 2022).

Kloppenburg, Sanneke, Aarti Gupta, Sake R.L. Kruk, Paulan Korenhof, Helena Solman, and Hilde M. Toonen, 'Scrutinising environmental governance in a digital age: New ways of seeing, participating, and intervening', *One Earth* 5:3 (2022), 232–241.

Luckin, Bill, *Questions of power: electricity and environment in interwar Britain* (Manchester: Manchester University Press, 1990).

Ludsager, P., 'Danish experience of small wind powered generators', in John Twidell (ed.) *Energy for rural and island communities: proceedings of the second international conference, held at Inverness, Scotland, 1–4 September 1981* (Oxford: Pergamon Press, 1981), 107–109.

Macfarlane, Robert, *Landmarks* (London: Hamish Hamilton, 2015).

Madureira, Nuno Luis, 'The anxiety of abundance: William Stanley Jevons and coal scarcity in the nineteenth century', *Environment and History* 18:3 (2012), 395–421.

Mahony, Martin and Samuel Randalls (eds) *Weather, climate and the geographical imagination: placing atmospheric knowledges* (Pittsburgh, PA: University of Pittsburgh Press, 2020).

Malm, Andreas, *Fossil capital: the rise of steam power and the roots of global warming* (New York, NY: Verso, 2015).

McClure, J. Derrick, 'Distinctive semantic fields in the Orkney and Shetlandic dialects, and their use in the local literature', in Robert McColl Millar (ed.), *Northern lights, northern words. Selected papers from the FRLSU conference, Kirkwall* (2009), 58–69.

McNeill, J.R. *Something new under the sun: an environmental history of the twentieth century world* (New York: W.W. Norton, 2002).

— 'Cheap energy and ecological teleconnections of the industrial revolution, 1780–1920', *Environmental History* 24:3 (2019), 492–503.

McNeill, J.R., and Peter Engelke, *The great acceleration: an environmental history of the Anthropocene since 1945* (Cambridge, MA: Harvard University Press, 2016).

Millar, Ian and Paul Warde, 'Energy transitions as environmental events', *Environmental History* 24:3 (2019), 464–471.

Millar, Robert McColl (ed.), *Northern lights, northern words. Selected papers from the FRLSU conference, Kirkwall* (Forum for Research on the Languages of Scotland and Ulster, 2009).

Millward, Robert and John Singleton, *The political economy of nationalisation in Britain, 1920–1950* (Cambridge: Cambridge University Press, 1995).

Mishmastnehi, Moslem, 'Technological heritage of Persian windmills', *Journal of the British Institute of Persian Studies* (2021), https://doi.org/10.1080/05786967.2021.1960885.

Mitchell, Catherine and Peter Connor, 'Renewable energy policy in the UK 1990–2003', *Energy Policy* 32 (2004), 1941–1942.

Mitchell, Timothy, *Carbon democracy: political power in the age of oil* (London: Verso, 2011).

Montaño, Diana, *Electrifying Mexico: technology and the transformation of a modern city* (Austin, TX: University of Texas Press, 2021).

Morgan-Grenville, Gerard, *Built environment* New Faces, New Places 5:3 (1979), 214–216.

— *Breaking free* (Bridport: Milton Mill, 2001).

Mullrennan, Monica E. and Colin H. Scott, '*Mare Nullius:* indigenous rights in saltwater environments', *Development and Change* 31 (2000), 681–708.

Navickas, Katrina, 'Conflicts of power, landscape and amenity debates over the British super grid in the 1950s', *Rural History* 30:1 (2019), 87–103.

Naylor, Simon, 'Log books and the law of storms: maritime meteorology and the British admiralty in the nineteenth century', *Isis* 106:4 (2015), 771–797.

Naylor, Simon, Neil McDonald, James Bowen, and Georgina Endfield, 'Extreme weather, school logbooks and social vulnerability: the Outer Hebrides, Scotland, in the late nineteenth and early twentieth centuries', *Journal of Historical Geography* 78 (2022), 84–94.

Nixon, Rob, *Slow violence and the environmentalism of the poor* (Cambridge, MA: Harvard University Press, 2011).

O'Brien, Sorcha, *Powering the nation: images of the Shannon scheme and electricity in Ireland* (Newbridge: Irish Academic Press, 2017).

O'Driscoll, Dennis, *Stepping stones: interviews with Seamus Heaney* (London: Faber and Faber, 2008).

Oberloskamp, Eva, 'Renewable energies in the United Kingdom and the Republic of Germany, 1970s–1990s', in Stephen Gross and Andrew Needham (eds), *New energies: a history of energy transitions in Europe and North America* (Pittsburgh, PA: University of Pittsburgh Press, 2023), 220–246.

Oreskes, Naomi and Eric M. Conway, *Merchants of doubt: How a handful of scientists obscured the truth on issues from tobacco smoke to global warming* (New York, NY: Bloomsbury, 2010).

Pardo, Juan Carlos Farrias, Magnus Aune, Christopher Harman, Mats Walday, and Solrun Figenschau Skjellum, 'A synthesis review of nature positive approaches and coexistence in the offshore wind industry', *ICES Journal of Marine Science* (2023), fsad191 https://doi.org/10.1093/icesjms/fsad191

Pomeranz, Kenneth, *The great divergence: China, Europe, and the making of the modern world economy* (Princeton: Princeton University Press, 2001).

Powell, Miles, 'Harnessing the great acceleration: connecting local and global history at the port of Singapore', *Environmental History* 27:3 (2022), 407–605

Porter, Roy, 'Gentlemen and geology: the emergence of a scientific career', *The Historical Journal* 21:4 (1978), 809–836.

Preece, Emma-Jane, 'Landscape character assessment: a view from the Quantocks', in Peter Coates, David Moon, and Paul Warde (eds), *Local places, global processes: histories of environmental change in Britain and beyond* (Oxford: Windgather Press, 2016), 47–52.

Price, Trevor J., 'Edward Golding's influence on wind power,' *Wind Engineering* 29:6 (2005), 513–530.

— 'James Blyth – Britain's first modern wind power pioneer', *Wind Engineering* 29:3 (2005), 191–200.

Pyne, Stephen, *Fire: a brief history* (Seattle, WA: University of Washington Press, 2019 2nd edn).

— *Pyrocene. How we created an age of fire and what happens next* (Oakland, CA: University of California Press, 2021).

Righter, Robert W., *Wind energy in America* (Norman, OK: University of Oklahoma Press, 1996).

Riofrancos, Thea, '*Extractivismo* unearthed: a genealogy of a radical discourse', *Cultural Studies* 31:2–3 (2017), 277–306.

Roberts, Brian Russell and Michelle Ann Stephens (eds), *Archipelagic American studies* (Durham, NC: Duke University Press, 2017).

Roberts, Harry, 'Sellafield and British nuclear culture 1945–1992: nuclear imaginaries in the rural periphery' (PhD Thesis, University of Liverpool, 2021).

Robertson, Iain, *Landscapes of protest in the Scottish highlands after 1914: the later Highland land wars* (Farnham: Ashgate, 2016).

Robin, Libby, Sverker Sörlin, and Paul Warde, *The future of nature: documents of global change* (New Haven, CT: Yale University Press, 2013).

Ross, Linda, Katrina Navickas, Matthew Kelly, and Ben Anderson (eds) *New lives, new landscapes revisited: rural modernity in Britain* (Oxford: Oxford University Press, 2023).

Rossetti, Christina, *Sing song: a nursery rhyme book* (London: George Routledge, 1872).

Satia, Priya, *Empire of guns: the violent making of the industrial revolution* (Redwood City, CA: Stanford University Press, 2018).

Scott, James C., *Seeing like a state: how certain schemes to improve the human condition have failed* (New Haven, CT: Yale University Press, 1999).

Schroeder, Emma, 'Making Earth, making home: technoscientific citizenship and ecological domesticity in the age of limits', Doctoral Thesis (University of Maine, 2021).

Schwartz, Stuart B., *Sea of storms: A history of hurricanes in the Greater Caribbean from Columbus to Katrina* (Princeton, NJ: Princeton University Press, 2015).

Seow, Victor, 'Sites of extraction: perspectives from a Japanese coal mine in northeast China', *Environmental History* 24 (2019), 463–533.

— *Carbon technocracy: energy regimes in modern east Asia* (Chicago: University of Chicago Press, 2021).

Sheail, John, *Power in trust: the environmental history of the Central Electricity Generating Board* (Oxford: Clarendon Press, 1991).

— 'Power to the people: power stations and the national grid', in Paul Brassley et al., *Transforming the Countryside*, 38–50.

Shiva, Vandana, *Staying alive: women, ecology and development* (London: Zed, 1988).

Sieferle, Rolf Peter, *The subterranean forest: energy and the industrial revolution* (Winwick: White Horse Press, 2010).

Smith, Crosbie and M. Norton Wise, *Energy and empire: a biographical study of Lord Kelvin* (Cambridge: Cambridge University Press, 1989).

Smith, S.D., 'Storm hazard and slavery: the impact of the 1831 great Caribbean hurricane on St Vincent', *Environment and History* 18:1 (2012): 97–123.

Spooner, Derek, 'The dash for gas in electricity generation in the UK', *Geography* 80:4 (1995), 393–406.

Steffen, Will, Paul Crutzen, and John McNeill, 'The Anthropocene: are humans now overwhelming the great forces of nature?' *Ambio* 36:8 (2007), 614–621.

Stevenson, W.G., 'The work of the North of Scotland Hydro-Electric Board in the field of wind turbine generators', in John Twiddell, Fiona Riddoch, and Bill Grainger (eds), *Energy for rural and island communities III: Proceedings of the third international conference held at Inverness, Scotland, September 1983* (Oxford: Pergamon, 1984), 99–106.

Szeman, Imre, 'On the politics of extraction', *Cultural Studies* 31:2–3 (2017), 440–447.

Szeman, Imre and Dominic Boyer (eds), *Energy humanities: an anthology* (Baltimore, MA: Johns Hopkins University Press, 2017).

Szeman, Imre and Jennifer Wenzel, 'What do we talk about when we talk about extractivism?', *Textual Practice* 35:3 (2021), 505–523.

Taylor, Sue Jane, 'Art and the offshore', in Fiona Polack and Danine Farquharson, *Cold water oil: offshore petroleum cultures* (Abingdon-on-Thames: Routledge, 2021), 156–175.

Tebbutt, Melanie, 'Rambling and manly identity in Derbyshire's Dark Peak, 1880s–1920s,' *The Historical Journal* 49:4 (2006), 1125–1153.

Thane, Pat, *Divided kingdom: a history of Britain 1900 to the present* (Cambridge: Cambridge University Press, 2018), 230–231.

Todd, R.W., C.J.N. Alty, D.O Hall, J.C. McVeigh, P.J. Musgrove, J. Platts, and P.C. Schumacher, *An alternative energy strategy for the United Kingdom* (National Centre for Alternative Technology, 1978 2nd edn).

Tokarczuk, Olga, *Drive your plough over the bones of the dead* (London: Fitzcarraldo, 2022 6th edn).

Toye, Richard, 'The new commanding height: Labour party policy on North Sea oil and gas, 1964–74', *Contemporary British History* 16:1 (2002), 89–118.

Trentmann, Frank and Anna Carlsson-Hyslop, 'The evolution of energy demand: politics, daily life and public housing, Britain 1920–70s', *Historical Journal* 61:3 (2018), 807–839.

Turnbull, Thomas, '"No solution of the immediate crisis": the uncertain political economy of energy conservation in 1970s Britain', *Contemporary European History* 31:4 (2022), 570–592.

Twidell, John (ed.), *Energy for rural and island communities: proceedings of the second international conference, held at Inverness, Scotland, 1–4 September 1981* (Oxford: Pergamon Press, 1981).

Waites, Iain 'The post-war power station and the persistence of an English landscape tradition' in Linda Ross et al., *New lives, new landscapes revisited: rural modernity in Britain*, 115–137.

Warde, Paul, 'Trees, trade and textiles: potash imports and ecological dependency in British industry, c. 1550–1770', *Past and Present* 240 (2018), 47–82.

Watts, Laura, *Energy at the end of the world: an Orkney island saga* (Cambridge, MA: MIT Press, 2019).

Webber, Oscar, 'The plantation's role in enhancing hurricane vulnerability in the nineteenth-century British Caribbean', *Alternautas* 5:2 (2018), 29–42.

Wetherell, Sam, *Foundations: how the built environment made twentieth-century Britain* (Princeton: Princeton University Press, 2020).

Williams, Raymond, *The country and the city* (London: Vintage, 2016; 1973 1st edn).

Winksel, Mark, 'When systems are overthrown: the 'dash for gas' in the British electricity supply industry', *Social Studies of Science* 32:4 (2002), 563–598.

Wood, Emma, *The hydro boys: pioneers of renewable energy* (Edinburgh: Luath Press, 2005)

Wright, Rebecca, 'Mass observation and the emotional energy user', *Canadian Journal of History* 53:3 (2018), 423–449.

Zalaciewicz, Jan, Colin Waters, Mark Williams, Anthony Barnosky, Alejandro Cearreta, Paul Crutzen, Erle Ellis, Michael Ellis, Ian Fairchild, Jacques Grinevald, Peter Haff,

Bibliography

Irka Hajdas, Reinhold Leinfelder, John McNeill, Eric Odada, Clément Poirier, Daniel Richter, Will Steffen, Colin Summerhayes, James Syvitski, and Naomi Oreskes, 'When did the Anthropocene begin? A mid-twentieth century boundary level is stratigraphically optimal', *Quaternary International* 383 (2015), 196–203.

Zelko, Frank, *Make it a green peace! The rise of countercultural environmentalism* (Oxford: Oxford University Press, 2013).

Index

Index